# POLITICAL IDEAS OF THE ENGLISH CIVIL WARS 1641–1649

DOCUMENTS IN POLITICAL IDEAS

General editor: *Bernard Crick*

POLITICAL IDEAS OF THE ENGLISH CIVIL WARS 1641–1649
*Andrew Sharp*
BRITISH SOCIALISM SOCIALIST THOUGHT FROM THE 1880S TO 1960S *Anthony Wright*

Forthcoming:
THE POLITICAL PHILOSOPHY OF EDMUND BURKE
*Iain Hampsher-Monk*
BRITISH CONSERVATISM
*Frank O'Gorman*

# POLITICAL IDEAS OF THE ENGLISH CIVIL WARS 1641–1649

A collection of representative texts with a commentary

*Andrew Sharp*

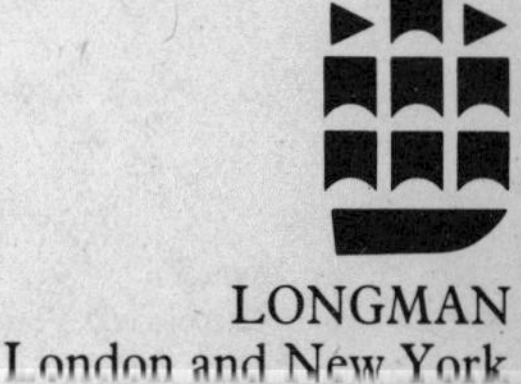

LONGMAN
London and New York

LONGMAN GROUP LIMITED
Longman House, Burnt Mill, Harlow
Essex CM20 2JE, England
*Associated companies throughout the world*

*Published in the United States of America
by Longman Inc., New York*



First published 1983

BRITISH LIBRARY CATALOGUING IN PUBLICATION DATA

Sharp, Andrew
Political ideas of the English Civil Wars
1641–1649. – (Documents in political ideas)
1. Ideology 2. Great Britain – History –
Civil War, 1642–1649 3. Great Britain–
Politics and government – 17th century
I. Title II. Series
320.941 JN531

ISBN 0-582-29554-8

LIBRARY OF CONGRESS CATALOGING IN PUBLICATION DATA

Main entry under title:

Political ideas of the English civil wars, 1641–1649.

(Documents in political ideas)
1. Political science – Great Britain – History – Sources. 2. Great Britain – Politics and government – 1642–1649 – Sources. I. Sharp, Andrew, 1940–
II. Series.
JA84.G7P67 1983 320'.0942 82-17266
ISBN 0-582-29554-8

Set in 10/11 pt Linotron 202 Plantin
Printed in Hong Kong by Hing Yip Printing Co.

CONTENTS

To my father and mother

# EDITOR'S PREFACE

Students of political ideas will be familiar with the debate among their teachers about texts and contexts, whether the study of political ideas primarily concerns the meaning of a text or an understanding of the main ideas of an epoch. Both should be done but not confused; and texts need setting in their context. But it is easier for the student to find and to read the texts of political philosophers than to be able to lay his hands upon the range of materials that would catch the flavour of the thinking of an age or a movement, both about what should be done and about how best to use common concepts that create different perceptions of political problems and activity.

So this series aims to present carefully chosen anthologies of the political ideas of thinkers, publicists, statesmen, actors in political events, extracts from State papers and common literature of the time, in order to supplement and complement, not to replace, study of the texts of political philosophers. They should be equally useful to students of politics and of history.

Each volume will have an authoritative and original introductory essay by the editor of the volume. Occasionally instead of an era, movement or problem, an individual writer will figure, writers of a kind who are difficult to understand (like Edmund Burke) simply by the reading of any single text.

*B. R. C.*

# AUTHOR'S PREFACE

The readings published in this book have been taken from the huge quantity of political debate published in England from 1641 to 1649 during what is arguably the worst political crisis through which the English have lived. My wish has been to allow those who lived during those times of war and revolution to speak for themselves across the gulf of time to men and women of the late twentieth century. My method has been to select individual examples of a wide range of representative argument, to modernise the seventeenth-century English of each gobbet, and to preface each one (or related few) with some brief remarks mostly about what twentieth-century scholars have had to say about their authors, the argument they contain and the context of debate. I have also indicated where that modern work may be found. I have not, however, been able to forbear further intrusion into the dialogue between past and present. I have provided an introductory essay in which I try to outline the main forms of argument visible at the time and to trace their utilisation and transformation under the extreme challenge of a political crisis which ended in the collapse of the old regime, symbolised in the trial and execution of Charles I and formalised in the abolition of kingship itself.

An Italian writer preceding me in a similar but less ambitious exercise – he collected specimens of radical argument only – has spoken grimly of the 'tyranny of space' restricting his choices of documents and his chances of commenting on them (Gabrielli 1959). I make the same observation and apologise for the consequences of its truth. Where I have left out more than one sentence from an original source I indicate this by using *four* dots; where I have left out less, *three* dots are used. I have shown the sources which I mention in the Introduction and in the Headnotes to each document by putting the author's name and date of publication in round brackets – in the way that Professor Gabrielli's work is referred to above. At the end of the book the reader will find, as part of a Guide to Further Reading, a section called Bibliography and References. That section names more fully each source that I refer to, and also provides a selection of further works that the reader might like to consult. But space has not allowed me to specify to which precise parts of the sources I refer. The Guide to Further Reading itself is designed to help a student who is interested in the period and its problems. It is not at all exhaustive, but it will provide a good start. Finally, lack of space has dictated that I cannot give the honorifics that are their due to the modern writers whose works I have relied on, nor even indicate that they have other than surnames. The pleasing custom to the contrary has had to bow to necessity.

I cannot realistically blame other matters of presentation on lack of space. My aim has been to remove as much as possible of the archaic patina that comes between the modern non-specialist reader and the seventeenth-century sources. I have tried not to edit anything of substance out of the sources, but occasionally I have had recourse to altering the authors' grammatical constructions for the sake of the modern reader whose syntactical breath will not usually be as good as theirs. At those few points, and also where I have felt obliged to add explanations or translations, I have used [square] brackets. This use of square brackets will not be confused with my use of them in the Introduction and Headnotes to provide numerical cross-references to documents contained in this collection. The punctuation and spelling of the documents have been modernised for easier reading, though some may think I have not gone far enough in that I persist with the seventeenth-century habit of italicising quotations from the Christian Scriptures, and I am rather freer in capitalising the names of offices and institutions than a modern reader might feel necessary. For the sake of the reader who wishes to return to the original sources, I have, where appropriate, given the 'Wing number' of the source. The reference is to D. G. Wing's *Short title catalogue* which lists books published in English between 1641 and 1700, and the number will help the student to locate the libraries in which the sources are held and to obtain microfilm copies of them (see sections A and B of the Guide to Further Reading, pp. 238–40). Where I name the source, its author, its date of publication and the pages from which I have taken material, I have often again used square brackets. This is because some books and pamphlets have no page numbers or are mispaged, have no date of publication or name an author equivocally or not at all. The square brackets in these instances enclose guesses and corrections. Other mysteries regarding references to books (eg. *DNB*, *OPH*) can be solved by looking up the abbreviation in the Bibliography and References.

However, the editorial detail need not detain the ordinary reader. My hope has been to entertain as well as instruct; and the presentation is designed to be as self-explanatory as possible. I have aimed to provide as wide a coverage of the thinking of the variously-situated political actors as is consistent with allowing each to have enough space to present a tolerably full argument or complete assertion. The novelty of the collection lies just in this, because earlier collections of writings of the period have tended very much to concentrate on the radical end of the spectrum and to ignore much parliamentarian, royalist and centrist thought (section B, Guide to Further Reading). These less radical writings are not only interesting in themselves – and a brute fact of the times – but they provide a context for and give resonance to the reformist and revolutionary ideas which are more familiar to the casual student. But the proof of that pudding will be in the eating. Nevertheless, I must admit that I have not concentrated as much as I might on characterising the precise political persuasion of each writer and have rested content with indicating it only in so far as I thought it necessary for the student's comprehension. This is partly because the volatility of partisanship during those years precludes the possibility of giving any tolerably *brief* character of a person's politics, but mostly because the history of ideas ought to be more than a dreary catalogue of practical prescriptions for action and an assessment of the success or failure of those prescriptions and of those who made them. I want to present the political thought of the time as political thinking ought to be presented – as an activity, which, while it is not independent of other activities (like making war, constructing alliances, putting together programmes with political appeal or even winning arguments) is nevertheless subject to its own constraints and possibilities. Partly it is a matter of people thinking and arguing in ways which have been commonly accepted in the past; partly it is a matter of them responding to their contemporaries' recent and living moves in public debate. It is a process as 'real', if you like, as the economic, constitutional, social and political processes of a society. And it has a history of its own. In reading such a history one can learn much about the economic, constitutional and social and political history of a period (and I have tried to provide examples of much argument germane to these concerns). But I have tried to concentrate on the structures of argument and the rhetorical devices in which the debaters had to deal if they were to be understood by, and if they were to move, their fellows. The point is that in many respects the concerns of civil war are not ours, and that in many ways they argued differently from us.

Some may detect a certain effeteness in such an enterprise and argue that I should have concentrated on providing general historians of England with more grist to their mill, or else that I should have picked what is relevant to our own problems and commitments today. It may well be that, a hemisphere away from my fellow scholars, I cannot quite share their concern with their old world or their new. However that may be, my view is that the arguments deserve reading so that they may be understood (as much as possible: Mulligan *et al.* 1979) for what they were, and that we already have enough of them being treated as minor functions of political activity or as evidence for the nature of the society which produced them. We can learn from them; and there is a sociology of knowledge: but first we have to know what the arguments were.

I cannot close without thanking those many people who helped me in producing this modest work. The *cognoscenti* will already recognise my debt to John Pocock, my old teacher at Canterbury. He and Peter Laslett introduced me to the subject. Judith Richards and Colin Davis read parts of the manuscript at an early stage with a savage sympathy I did not take enough notice of. However, Bernard Crick, the general editor of this series, did make me alter some few pieces. That he had delivered to him not quite what he first had in mind did not diminish the industry and kindness with which he treated both me and the book. Maurice Goldsmith, Gordon Schochet, Glen Black, John Graham, Tony Smith and Tom Sharp gave me much material, moral and intellectual support when I worked on the book in Oxford, Cambridge and London during leave in 1978–79. When I was in Oxford, Joan Thirsk let me give an earlier version of the Introduction to her research seminar there, at which time she and others tried to correct some of my more egregious errors. My colleagues Patrick Lacey and Kenneth Larsen helped me with my Latin and Greek. The staffs of the Bodleian, the Anderson Room at the Cambridge University Library and at the British Library were unfailingly helpful to me as they are to others; and I owe special thanks to the staff of the Interloan Section of the Auckland University Library who found themselves dealing with many unfamiliar, complicated and urgent requests. The Auckland University Council granted me leave and provided research grants over the years. Without that help this book would not have been possible. Nor would it have been so easy had it not been for Robert Chapman, Professor of Political Studies at Auckland, who subtly but firmly organised it so that I could complete the manuscript in the midst of my teaching duties. Heather Devere and, most especially, Marjorie Gould, bore the brunt of the typing with efficient good humour. For reasons no writer and few readers will need rehearsing, my greatest debt is to my wife Jane.

*Andrew Sharp*
Auckland

## ACKNOWLEDGEMENTS

We are indebted to the Royal Historical Society for permission to reproduce extracts from *The Clarke Papers*, Vol I, 1891 edited by C. H. Firth.

# INTRODUCTION

## 'CONFUSIONS AND REVOLUTIONS'

In August 1642 the kingdom of England and Wales began to make war against itself. The numbers involved in the military encounters were not great – on 2 July 1644 there were just under 40,000 soldiers at Marston Moor, the largest pitched battle – but the disruption of normal life was considerable. As contemporary lament had it, the shock was awesome: father fought against son, brother against brother; wives and daughters became widows and orphans. And not only were families, the fundamental loci of affection and allegiance, torn apart; the land itself was 'desolated' and trade 'disrupted'. The war, entered into unwillingly by all but a few, was accompanied by continual pleas for peace. Nevertheless, the first round of hostilities ended in 1646 only because the King, Charles I, no longer had the military capacity to continue fighting against the armies raised by his two Houses of Parliament and by his northern subjects, the Scots. Nor was a political settlement possible, given the conflicting interests of the King, the Parliament, the Parliament's 'New Model Army', the Scots and the city of London – and given the complex array of differences among parties operating within and between those great corporate interests. A second war was therefore fought in 1648. This time the Scots fought with their King – professing detestation of the antimonarchism and the religious sectarianism and Erastianism of their old, but foreign, allies – and Parliament found its more conservative supporters to be wavering, lukewarm and prone to desert its ranks. In the event the New Model, constituted by Parliament in 1645 as a reaction to its military weakness of the early war years, was victorious. It had threatened *coup d'état* from 1647; on 6 December 1648 it finally purged the Parliament, and it was the 'Rump' – as the purged Parliament was henceforth maliciously named – that gave constitutional form to the practical revolution that had occurred.

In fact the Rump always acted hesitantly and with a marked lack of enthusiasm, only goaded to action by the threats and blandishments of military leaders like Oliver Cromwell and his son-in-law, Henry Ireton. Nevertheless, it did make a revolution in the winter of 1648–49, and one that has continued to grip the English – and Marxian – imagination to a great variety of effects ever since. The Rumpers declared that the 'original' of all political power lay, 'under God', with 'the people' [11.5]; they tried and executed 'Charles Stuart' for treason [3.7]; and they abolished the office of Kingship and the House of Lords, thus anulling all hereditary claims to political office. Finally, in March 1649, they proclaimed a new regime, a 'Commonwealth . . . without King and Lords'. As the social fabric seemed to have been rent by the events of war, so the constitution of authority seemed to have been destroyed in a hideous burst of innovation.

At least this was the way conservatives viewed it; and the conservative view was the predominant one, certainly among the political nation. Modern historians emphasise that it was in the absence of any other politically viable alternative that the remaining directive minority of the English political élite stumbled upon a republican form of government by early 1649 – an establishment very few had intended. Had Charles been willing to compromise his attachment to an episcopal Anglican Church, unified, and intolerant of other views as to doctrine and discipline; had he been trusted enough for his assurances regarding the liberties, properties and parliamentary privileges of the people to be believed, he would probably have survived, and so would a 'moderated' Kingship, 'under law', and along the lines of reforms he had assented to in 1641. It could not be. He would not compromise and he could not be trusted. Accordingly the Rump faced the problem of all future interregnum regimes: unable to claim a title to rule by ancient law, it nevertheless had to attempt to make this strongest of all claims to political legitimacy; but its failure to do so was as certain as anything is in politics, and it had to make alternative claims, according to other political formulae [11.6]. From 1649 to 1660, until the restoration of Kingship, the ruling groups experimented: first with the continued rule of the Rump, then, in 1653, with 'Barebone's' Parliament – the 'Parliament of the Saints'. From 1654 to 1658, there were two forms of protectoral regime under Oliver Cromwell and his son, Richard; and a final 'year of anarchy' saw rule by the Rump, by alliances of Army officers, and by a restored pre-purge 'Long Parliament'. The interregnum regimes had enemies to the left and to the right (not that they used these terms – an explosion of political consciousness does not easily lend itself to description in terms of stable spectra): populist democrats, classical republicans, millenial enthusiasts and austere ideologues of rule by 'the Saints' posed as much a threat to them as old cavaliers and new royalists – the last a continually growing group, alarmed by the fact and implications of the King's death, and hankering, amid instability, for a durable political order. It is little wonder that in the end the 'ancient constitution' was restored in 1660. The King and the old authorities were reinstated; the process of Anglican Church settlement was put under way; the ruling tradition of conservative legalism was reaffirmed. The interregnum years were an appropriately anticlimactic sequel to a constitutional revolution made so hesitantly and amid such great lack of consensus.

This book collects some documents illustrative of that dissensus as it was expressed from 1641 to 1649 in the debates that accompanied – and partly constituted – what Anthony Ascham was, in 1648, to see as years of 'confusions and revolutions'. What Ascham was saying was that although they wanted an authority which could restore and sustain civil peace, Englishmen – like all men everywhere – lived in a political world of sheer contingency, one in which no government could ever truthfully claim a clear and unambiguous title to obedience, in which each man must inevitably, at recurring junctures, be called upon to decide for himself where his obligations lay, in which there was no choice but to cling to a political order – unjust, temporary and endangered as it might be – as a refuge from a chaos that threatened both life and spiritual equanimity. In 'confusions', he held, things fall apart and no one knows to whom allegiance is due; in 'revolutions' the political world turns in directions envisaged by the programmes of no one; unplanned changes threaten the inherited fabric of things, and it is the danger of blood-drenched anarchy and not the opportunities for remaking the world that seem most manifest. Ascham's was not a sanguine view – in common with most of his respectable contemporaries, and unlike some of us in our less stoical moments – he held no hope at all to lie in revolution. He was to expand his thoughts of 1648 into a defence of the new Commonwealth in 1649; and the new version has rightly been taken by a modern commentator to represent the 'pessimistic' mode of justification of an emerging regime which could, after all, be hailed by such as John Milton in his famous *Tenure of Kings and magistrates* (1649) as a popular regime of the Christian elect (Zagorin 1954). Yet whatever else may be said about his thinking, it certainly figures by comparison with what had gone before.

He had seen the King and Parliament divide, each claiming to fight for pretty much the same thing: the laws, liberties, properties, privileges, and Protestant religion of all Englishmen. He had seen Parliament invite the Scots in to further their ends [3.22], and then the Scots and the English fall out over whether or not there should be a Presbyterian Church settlement on the Scots model of firm clerical rule, independent of State – 'Erastian' – control. He had seen the emergence, in the working-class southern suburbs of London and in the ranks of the New Model, of 'sectaries' and 'levellers', who, by 1645, were claiming that neither King nor Parliament nor Scots nor the ruling London oligarchy had given or would give them their 'birthright' in civil and religious matters. He had seen the New Model turn on its creator with demands for religious and civic renewal. He had seen Parliament itself divided between 'presbyterian' and 'independent' as older questions of church doctrine and discipline compounded with those regarding a 'final settlement' with Charles to yield an acid capable of eating out old alliances and rendering the new highly unstable.

It would be a highly apolitical citizen who had not seen all this, for each action in the public drama was described, analysed, justified and attacked in full public gaze. In November 1641, the Commons, obviously dividing into royalist and parliamentarian camps, had narrowly agreed to the *Grand Remonstrance*, complaining to the King of his many (over 120 they counted) illegal actions since the beginning of his reign in 1625. More significantly, they had published their remonstrance at large, to the people. The lid was off. Censorship was already ineffective because of the interest of many of the parliamentarians in allowing debate on church doctrine and discipline to proliferate. Those political conflicts that up until then had largely been fought out at the King's court, in country houses and in the Courts at Westminster and the localities – and fought out among the directive minority – were now made public. George Thomason, a London bookseller, collected over 12,000 'tracts' (i.e. books, pamphlets and broadsheets) between 1641 and 1649 (after a slow beginning in 1640) – and this represents perhaps only four-fifths of what poured from the presses. This was the period, too, which saw the origin of regular newspaper journalism. Ascham and his contemporaries were witness to the unparalleled spectacle of an early modern society discussing its political and social arrangements in the greatest imaginable depth.

The basis of the right to political authority was often the central issue at stake. It was not an issue they discussed from choice, as a political philosopher might, but it was taken with a deadly seriousness – as well it might be in conditions where they thought their immortal souls as well as their lives and livelihoods were at stake – a seriousness that can too easily be overlooked by the historian concerned only to describe the political manoeuvrings of the time or to relate what was said either to those manoeuvres or with the great settled social interests which existed and were threatened in the upheavals of war. Not everyone felt as threatened by the changes as Ascham. Some indeed welcomed them and would have wished the world 'turned upside down' so that the poor and dispossessed might have justice (Hill 1972). Nevertheless, Ascham was not far from the central perception shared by his contemporaries. He had seen that as the great central institutions of English political life fell apart in conflict, so had the reigning formula of government dissolved into its separate and conflicting elements. He had seen a society, fairly well united in 1642 in a shared understanding of who had authority and why, demonstrating to itself that the old seeming-certainties were in fact no more than a series of ramshackle fictions, incapable of operating as formulae for authority and obedience when urgently called upon to do so in conditions of political conflict. The received wisdom regarding authority had foundered, as a Marxist might now say, on its own contradictions. Radicals exploited the contradictions; an Ascham could only regret them. In the end the old formulae were to be reassembled, but not before an explosion whose tremors are still felt today.

I intend to let the debaters speak for themselves about what concerned them, but not before I have tried to reconstruct the ideological matrix from which they operated, and which, like any customarily accepted collection of unsystematic beliefs, proved so fruitful of opposing ideas when questioned. I hope this will help the reader understand more readily why the debaters said what they did, and help dissipate that reasonable impatience which tends to assail one when faced with people who speak only of what concerns themselves and in ways to which they, and not we, are thoroughly accustomed. My attempt, then, is one of historical reconstruction; but it is one made in the service of a belief that they can still speak to us on many important matters regarding that cluster of concerns that usually go under the name of problems of political obligation.

## THE IDEOLOGICAL MATRIX

### *Legal constitutionalism*

The English of 1640 inherited a view of politics and society which was to be severely tested over the following twenty years but which nevertheless emerged, substantially the same, at the Restoration. It was (and it still exists) a view at once conservative and legalistic, the characteristic of which was to bring all disputed activities to the bar of law and custom, secure in the belief that these would provide just and acceptable solutions to all the exigencies of collective life, whether they concerned the smallest details of domestic and local living or the greatest issues concerning government and obedience at a national level. It is a way of thinking which assumes that there is no problem as to the value and obligatory force of the system of law and custom as a whole, and which takes for granted that the welfare of all is the consequence of its proper working.

Such a way of thinking was the central ideological point of departure in the seventeenth century; and it was one that most articulate Englishmen – certainly those of the ruling élite – never departed from with any feeling of comfort. 'Innovation' and 'innovators' were the enemy and the solution to all difficulties was thought to lie in adherence to the law of the land or perhaps in a 'restoration' of it if it were thought to have been 'innovated upon' in any way. They conceived of the law as a systematic whole, like a body in which the parts mutually depended on each other. If the function of any part were threatened or disrupted, the whole was in danger. This was their 'ancient constitution'. It had been handed down to them by their ancestors, and recorded in all its detailed provisions in the judicial decisions of the Common Law Courts, including the 'High Court' of Parliament. These decisions were no more than the recording of the common custom of the land, a custom that had existed before the record – 'time out of mind' as the phrase went – each part long tried and tested and thus uniquely tailored to fit English circumstances and provide for any emergent exigency. Statutes were conceived of not so much as having a life of their own as created by legislative activity but rather as 'confirmations' of already existing customs. The greatest of all, Magna Carta itself, was thought merely to have confirmed the already existing custom of England; and civil war thinkers are to to be found asserting that it had itself been since confirmed thirty-three times (McIlwain 1940; Gough 1955; Pocock 1957).

The great statutes were at once evidence of the importance of the belief that law should be 'known and declared', and repositories of the most important of the particular liberties and rights that the English enjoyed. The nineteenth chapter of Magna Carta for instance, spoke of the necessity for 'due process' in legal trials: each man must be tried by a jury of his peers, might not give evidence against himself 'upon interrogatories', must be promptly tried on a known charge and so on. And there were many other important rights, and rules of procedure laid down in statute. But it was not just the substance of the law – custom and statute – which was important. According to this mode of legalistic thinking, no identifiable man or institution was the creator of the constitution. Rather, the general and diffused usage — and thus consent – of generations had insensibly formed and sustained it. This meant that it embodied, as it were, its own justification for existing as a set of duties laid upon each and every Englishman: because it was the creature of consent it was likely to work in practice as an expression of the interests of all; and as an expression of the nation's will it could command the respect due to that which the generations of Englishmen had committed themselves. Even more it meant that there was no man or institution with authority 'over' it. This is why Sir Edward Coke – the most illustrious of all the common-law commentators and one endlessly quoted by civil war debaters – had been able to claim that 'Magna Carta is such a fellow he will have no sovereign'. *This is why the Roman law tag that the King was *legibus solutus* ('free from the laws') was regarded with such suspicion in the pre-war years of the Stuarts. Since no particular man or institution had created the law there was no one that was not bound by its requirements or could change it at will. The law set out limits to the powers it granted magistrates. The King, Lords, Commons and Courts at Westminster were as subject to it as the Justices of the Peace, Sheriffs, Lord-Lieutenants and so on in the shires and boroughs. And if law was to be made (and it was clearly recognised by the early part of the century that law *was* made as well as discovered) there were both irrevocable power-diffusing procedures for introducing change and severe restrictions on what could be

* Though perhaps this is not what he *really* said, (Russell (1979)).

changed. The procedures required that new laws could not be made without the joint consent of Kings, Lords and Commons in Parliament assembled; and new laws could not be made which would breach the 'fundamental laws' – like the provisions regarding legal trials in Magna Carta, the rules prohibiting free quarter during times of peace, or the provisions for diffused legislative power themselves. The law might give the King his 'prerogative' powers as 'supreme magistrate' and it might give the two Houses inalienable 'liberties and privileges' annexed to those who shared the high function of legislation with him: but these prerogatives, liberties and privileges were bounded and limited by that same law. Powers there were, but none were unlimited.

The law also laid down the 'rights, privileges, liberties and properties' of the subject. Both the rulers and the ruled, it was said, had a 'propriety' in what they held by law. And the law as a whole was theirs too. It was inherited by all Englishmen and not granted them by any superior magistrate. The only way in which alienation of particular legal rights could be accomplished – besides such punishments as outlawry for breach of the laws – was with the consent of those whose rights they were. Thus no tax, indeed no variation in the subjects' obligations, could be introduced without the consent of England being registered in the formal workings of King-in-Parliament as they issued in statute. And thus (to give examples relating to magistracy) the King's powers of calling, proroguing and dissolving Parliaments could not be abridged without statutory action; nor could his prerogatives be added to except in the same way as the Elizabethan Act of Supremacy (1559) had granted the headship of the Anglican Church to English monarchs. Governors had their powers and subjects their rights, all of them set in the matrix of law. To do justice, to give 'to each his own', was precisely to give them what was theirs by law. 'The Lords', Cromwell was to be heard reminding their enemies in 1648, 'have as good a right to their powers as I have to the coat upon my back.' It was a common form of argument. The law ruled all, and it exhausted the requirements of justice.

Consequently, Stuart political debate was highly jurisprudential. As every beginning student of early Stuart history will be drearily aware, the leading form of political debate during the first forty years of the century was legal. There were great cases on the rights and privileges of Parliament; there were cases on the rules governing representation; there were cases of impeachment against the King's great servants brought by the Commons to the bar of the

Lords; above all there were the celebrated cases brought by private individuals in attempts to challenge Charles I's powers to force loans from his subjects and to levy Ship Money and thus tax his subjects without their consent in Parliament. Policy disagreements and conflicts of interest were fought out in the Courts. The bar was the forum, and legal rules and procedures provided the language and structure of debate. Claims were expressed as ones to antecedent rights. The *Petition of Right*, drawn up by Parliament in 1628 for presentation to an estranged King, claimed for Parliament and subjects no more than that which was already due to them by 'laws and statutes of the realm'.

The Parliamentmen (Members of the Lords and Commons) of 1640 started out from this point. They remembered Calvin's Case, the impeachment of Buckingham, the *Petition of Right* and the great Ship Money Case. Before there was any royalist party they proceeded to voice their claims, expressing their disgust with the King's servants and policies in the old ways. They objected to the canons made by the Synod of the church earlier that year; by mid-1641 they had impeached and executed the earl of Strafford and begun proceedings against the archbishop of Canterbury, William Laud; soon they were to complete the statutory abolition of the prerogative Courts and were to impeach thirteen of the bishops. The canons, it was claimed, had not been made according to the proper procedures of legislation and they spoke of the King's prerogative so as to suggest he was above the law; Strafford and Laud had tried to subvert the 'fundamental laws'; the bishops (besides opposing the purification of the church) had been instruments in kingly encroachments on the law and had, moreover – much against the ancient customs and privileges of Parliament – claimed that their presence in the Lords was necessary if any statutes were to be passed.

Though the legalism of the civil war politicians was to be subject to stresses it could not well withstand over the next six years, William Prynne, in his *Brief memento to the present unparliamentary juncto* of 1648, was still able to quote no fewer than 100 declarations of Parliament and the New Model – and declarations as late as June 1648 – to the effect that the 'cause' for which they had taken up arms and still fought was precisely the old one for the preservation of the rights, liberties and properties of the people, the privileges of Parliament and the just prerogatives of the King. He might further have noted that the tracts of one of his great radical enemies, John Lilburne, the 'leveller', while they demonstrated a clear antipathy to the law as it expressed the rights of the magistrate, are still full of innumerable references to Magna Carta, Coke's commentaries on the common law, and the 'legal fundamental liberties' of the people [10.2]. By 1648 the two old enemies were at least one in opposing the 'usurpations' of Cromwell and the army 'grandees': all that the revolutionaries had done was against the law. This was true enough – the revolutionaries did have no lawful title to act – but Cromwell and the 'independents' who made the revolution were none the less concerned to give their actions a proper face: when the regicides came to execute Charles Stuart, they did so only after a trial at law. Judges were appointed by the Rump; a charge was drawn up, and the forms of legal procedure were observed as closely as possible by the High Court of Justice. The Rump's official defence of 1649 dwells on the legality of their acts and their wish to conserve the substance of law except in so far as it authorised King and Lords [11.6].

### *The idea of subordination*

Stuart Englishmen – scarcely less than Elizabethan – pictured society as a hierarchy: first the King; then the *nobiles majores*, (the families of dukes, marquesses, earls, viscounts and barons); then the *nobiles minores* (first the families of baronets – the hereditarily knightly families – then of the four orders of knights, then those of esquires and lastly of gentlemen). The two archbishops and twenty-odd bishops of the Anglican Church took their place in this hierarchy of honour: archbishops after dukes and bishops after viscounts. These noble families were the families who disposed of the wealth of the society, who bore the title at least of 'Mr' and 'Mrs' – i.e. 'master' and 'mistress' – and who took precedence in the ceremonial life of the State and in the localities. As for the rest of the society (perhaps 95 per cent of a total population of 5½ million in England and Wales), its members were defined by occupation: merchants, traders, seamen, artisans, apprentices, cottagers (rural labourers), rogues and vagabonds (Laslett 1965). The College of Arms dealt only with the affairs of the upper reaches, dispensing coats of arms to those who were wealthy enough, and recording – often with pious fraud – the antiquity of the great families. The College was as much the instrument of the parliamentarians as the royalists. Parliament took care to preserve its records during the wars and to reform it. And heraldry was a common hobby. It accorded with the view that hierarchies of subordination on earth imitated the cosmic hierarchy. God was the master of the universe and beneath him were ranged all creatures – intellectual, animal and inanimate. In the heavens a hierarchy of subordination did His will: Archangels, Angels, Cherubims, Seraphims and Powers. On earth there were Emperors, Kings, Princes and all the ranks of nobility. Beneath them were the common people, distinguished far less carefully and formally. Each rank had its own virtues and its own duties, chief among which was that of obedience to superiors.

Each household was in turn a 'little commonwealth' in which the father, like the biblical patriarch, ruled his wife, children and servants. Masters ruled apprentices; schoolmasters their pupils; and so on. Animals were made subordinate to man; and inanimate things too, according to the account of creation in *Genesis*, were given to mankind for their use and benefit. This was the 'great chain of being', a harmony of corresponding realities at all levels of superordination and subordination. It was natural, i.e. a creation of God's law and not of man's; it was rational (to be subordinate *meant* to obey); and it was commanded directly by God in many places in the Bible [e.g. 1.1.2, 2.2, 4.3]. No man was free. He was born to subordination. Men were not equal. There were distinctions between the ranks, the sexes and ages, and the distinctions were as real in their laying of obligations on people as concrete social life can make them.

Indeed there was no conflict perceived between the divinely ordained order and the detailed prescriptions of positive law. The positive laws were the creation of human prudence guided by divine providence through time, giving detailed expression to the general rule of subordination (Pocock 1966). Nor did the workings of time threaten the idea of order or its expression in positive law: families and individuals might rise and fall as 'fortune' or 'providence' dictated, but the frame in which they did so remained as a permanent measure of their failures and successes (Sharp 1974). Two commandments from the second table of the Decalogue seemed to sum up a man's duties to other men: the fifth, 'Honour thy father and thy mother', was construed as a command to obey those magistrates whom the law provided [1.1.1–1.1.3]; the eighth, 'Thou shalt not steal', meant that nothing that was a man's by positive law should be taken from him [11.1]. The duty of subordination was one owed to God; the substance of particular duties was specified in man's law.

### *Providence and prophecy*

Obedience to God's law in Scripture and to man's law recorded in statute and custom were thought, by and large, to guarantee the continued and peaceful existence of a stable, hierarchical society. But individuals and families rose and fell, men were born and died, there were conflicts among people and states, and – as always – the sinful often seemed to prosper. It was at such points that the English had recourse to the idea of God's detailed providence of the things of life. His finger was to be discerned moving all; His mysterious will might judge, to punish or reward, on earth as well as in heaven; men could not judge His ways. Human lives provided the *dramatis personae* in what Cromwell's old tutor, Thomas Beard, called, in the title of his famous book, *The theatre of God's judgements*. This unstructured providentialism was typical of the Calvinism of the times: God moved as He would, men must follow. The trope was commonplace and used as often in a mood of conservative acceptance of things as it was as a way of accepting uncomfortable changes and conflicts [11.1–11.3].

But the English also inherited a more structured providentialism. The Bible was not simply a storehouse of God's commands and *exempla* for mankind; and besides proclaiming and demonstrating His power, it was in addition a book of prophetic history. It was the record of His dealings with His 'peculiar nation', Israel, and of the words of prophets concerning the future of God's dealing with mankind. Christ would come to redeem mankind and His people would then be saved. But Antichrist and his host would remain, to frustrate the setting up of that New Jerusalem which would herald the Second Coming of Christ and the Last Judgement. From the time of the Reformation and especially after the restoration of Protestantism under Elizabeth, Englishmen had tended to see themselves as God's new Israel, a 'peculiar people' set aside by Him to oppose and destroy Babylon, the city of Antichrist – in a word, Rome. The story went that the first Protestants had been English, Wycliffe and Huss among them; Protestant martyrs had sacrificed their lives rather than embrace Queen Mary's catholicism; the foreign policy of the Catholic powers, especially Spain, was clearly aimed at the destruction of God's nation; Catholic and Jesuit plots to overthrow the State had never ceased. John Foxe's *Booke of martyrs* (1563) which recorded much of this was chained to the pulpit with the Bible in the parish churches; and memories of the Spanish Armada, and the Jacobean popish plots lingered in memory (Haller 1963). Millenarian expectation – fixed on the idea that Christ would return after (or for) 1,000 years in a time of turmoil and trouble – and the anxious scrutiny of events in an endeavour to discern God's will for man in them were perhaps as characteristic of establishment Anglicanism as of the more enthusiastic puritans of the seventeenth century. God's people, united under a 'Godly prince', must oppose Antichrist and prepare for the last days. Charles I and Laud seem to have believed in the coming of the millennium as much as their opponents – though these were, by the time of the calling of the Long Parliament, much less inclined to identify Laudian episcopacy with the church of the Saints (Lamont 1969). Still, the structured providentialism of millenarian expectation provided a way in which change and disorder could be domesticated, uncomfortable as they might be. They were a consequence of God's foreordained dispensations; one could live with them; one could even welcome them.

## THE DISSOLUTION OF THE MATRIX

### *Royalists and parliamentarians, 1642–45*

When the English directive minority stressed the virtues of law and order, and when they applied the rules of law and the overriding demands of order to their political problems, they were practising a deontological style of political thinking. 'Deontology' is the science of duty (*deon* in Greek means duty), and their prime concern was to discover the duties to which each man, ruler and subject alike, was bound. These duties were paramount; they were owed to God who would enforce them; and their force could not be weakened by extrinsic considerations. 'Machiavellian' calculations of private interest were frowned upon as the expression of an arbitrary self-will which would not be bound by authority (Raab 1964). Such men – and they still exist (Shklar 1964; Held 1975) – hardly felt themselves free to frame ends of political action which might then be pursued by various means decided upon in the light of practical possibility. They felt themselves to be like judges whose duty it was to see that justice was done – i.e. that the law be obeyed – though the heavens might fall. It was not so much that they did not see that politics is a human activity, the rules of which are constructed by men and which might be varied and changed as circumstances suggested – though they did not see it easily – it was more that, given their view of customary arrangements as embodying a divinely established order as it emerged through time, they found it hard to imagine that the laws which governed them *might* be better. Thus they considered that the duties they had by law were as sacrosanct as their rights to change it; and it was, moreover, evident to them that duties oblige each man unproblematically, whereas the right to change the law could be exercised only in an – often unlikely – agreement with others. Some people, church reformers, practised what might perhaps be thought of as a telelogical style of thinking – one concerned to attain concrete political goals by means of 'policy' – but even so, they tended to make their claims in a language which suggested that they wished to return to old forms of church discipline and doctrine now lost. It was a *re*formation they aimed at, and one that would enable them to live out what they took to be already their duty laid out in the Pauline rules for church government (Haller 1938).

This is not to say that the English at the start of the civil wars did not conceive that there were not ends to which their rule-governed dutiful activity was directed. They considered, however, that the attainment of those ends – the glorification of God, personal salvation, peace and plenty in the State – was guaranteed in dutiful action according to law and Scripture.

These ends were not guaranteed at all. By late 1641 the populace had been thoroughly roused by parliamentary agitation against the Laudian English church. The bishops, the church hierarchy, the royal court – Queen Henrietta Maria was a Catholic – even royalists at large, came to be depicted as papists, the Babylonish and antichristian host who would oppose the reformation of the church in the last days before the rule of the 'Saints' and the return of Christ. The Parliament itself was divided as to the direction which church reformation should take. Indeed, it was never to reach agreement. The Westminster Assembly at Sion House was to present it with a Presbyterian formula for settlement, but it was too clericist for many who wanted a State-controlled 'Erastian' church, and it imposed too great a uniformity for the congregational beliefs of those who would be 'independent' of too centralised a control, whether by State or clergy. In 1641 then, the religious organisation of the State was at issue, and the King's supremacy was challenged in the light of religious duties now seen as separate in substance from legal ones. Parliament, sensing the dangers of disorder in this, might well have joined with the King in quieting the issue, but in November news of a rebellion in subject Ireland had arrived at Westminster. The popish rebellion must be crushed; an expeditionary army must be mounted; but who would control the army? At this point the constitutional issues on which the war between King and Parliament was fought emerged with horrid, insoluble, clarity. During

1641 the King had made a number of concessions, embodied in statute, which satisfied most and which in fact were to survive the Restoration settlement. He had abolished his 'prerogative Courts', he had agreed that Parliaments should be called at least triennially, and he had declared that non-parliamentary taxation was illegal. But could the King be trusted not to undo these reforms if he had an army at his disposal? He had called no Parliament from 1629 to 1640; he had called his 'Short Parliament' of 1640 only for taxation to supply wars against a Protestant Scotland opposed to Laudian episcopacy; he had made his concessions of 1641 gracelessly and unconvincingly. Parliament, thus fearing and distrusting the King, sought to claim command of the Militia – the ancient military force of the kingdom arrayed from the counties – for itself. Its claim to do so was far from an unambiguously good one in law. The King's counsellors – perfectly in accord with the ruling, legalist paradigm – saw the issue as 'the fittest subject for a King's quarrel' (Schwoerer 1971); and so in 1642, royalist and parliamentarian drifted into war, both sides claiming to act to preserve the law and both claiming to be acting legally. Who had legal power to control the military force of the kingdom?

The matrix now separated into its component parts; each part was in turn dissected and laid open to inspection, so that only nostalgic conservatives like William Prynne of 1648 [3.6] could conceive of its being reconstituted to its former organic integrity.

The problem set for the art of propaganda was to demonstrate that one's own side and not the other was acting legally (Sirluck 1959). In the opposing pamphlets legal commentator was confronted with legal commentator, gloss with gloss, statute with statute, customary practice with customary practice. Parliament forever insisted it fought not against the King, to whom each man was obliged by Oath of Allegiance, but against his 'evil counsellors'; royalists insisted, backed by the King, that treason was being committed – harm was being 'compassed on the King's body'. There was also much discussion as to whose right it was to declare authoritatively just what the law was – an obvious necessity in conditions where it was on the one hand believed that recourse to law would show a man his duties, and where on the other hand it was evident that such recourse could not give a clear direction to 'conscience'. It was at this juncture that both parliamentarians and royalists searched for a 'supreme power', 'sovereign' or 'final arbiter'. Much has been written on the development during this period of the idea of legal sovereignty, a power which some writers placed in the King, others in the two Houses, others in the Commons alone, or in 'the people' (docs and headnotes Parts 4, 6, 7, 8). What these debates indicate in general though, is the extreme unwillingness of the participants to contemplate unauthorised action – action not enjoined on them or permitted by a power superior to themselves. If law bound a man, if a man – or woman, or servant, or child – had duties, those duties were laid upon them by a law not of their own making; arbitrary wilfulness was as much a sin in the magistrate as in the subject; only law-abiding acts were free from the taint of self-will. Impelled by considerations such as these, royalists and parliamentarians inevitably if clumsily pitched upon ideas of final arbitration (judgement) as to what the law in fact was, and even on the idea of absolute legislative sovereignty: inevitably because they had no difficulty in picturing a paradigmatic judge and lawgiver – God, the author and sustainer of creation, who instructed His rational creatures to obey on pain of damnation; inevitably also because they palpably needed an instructor from whom to learn their duties; clumsily because they did not like to think of any man or men with an arbitrary right to command.

It was from such a state of principled confusion that they hacked out their differing versions of the nature and limits of supreme power. Most used positive law and Scripture as the sources of rules from which they extracted their doctrines, though it is perhaps symptomatic of the failure of the native tradition that many turned to such foreigners as Mario Salamonio, Jean Bodin and Juan Mariana to strengthen their cases. English thought was not isolated from the Continent (Salmon 1959), and already there was a rich rhetoric designed to condemn borrowings from Jesuits, monarchomachs – French 'king-killers' – and Scottish sectaries. How could such men, asked David Owen in *Puritano-Jesuitismus* (printed under differing titles in 1610, 1642, 1643 and 1663) teach Englishmen their duties? But wherever the English found their sources, their quest for sovereignty was mounted as much in the service of elucidating duties as of competition for power. Thomas Hobbes it is true, deduced the necessity of sovereign power from teleological considerations of the necessity for self-preservation and tried to show that false claims to sovereignty were merely power-plays; but his attempt to argue this way is no less indicative of a cast of mind happier at contemplating externally imposed duties than the pursuit of concrete wants or detailed visions of an ideal future. The authoritarianism of both royalist and parliamentarian goes very deep:

Prynne and Henry Parker could no more condone disobedience to Parliament than bishops Maxwell or Bramhall could to a King. One of the intellectual events of the period most fascinating to witness is Philip Hunton's wrestling with the idea that there might be no legal authority at all in England [8.6].

The doctrine of sovereignty in institutions, while it could do a great deal of harm to the idea of a customary constitution – in Sir Robert Filmer's view custom was simply those national habits which happened to have been allowed or commanded by the sovereign (Pocock 1957) – nevertheless at least conserved the basic authoritarianism of the age. It did not deny what most believed at the outset of the wars; that authority inhered in the offices which 'magistrates', i.e. rulers, occupied. It was neither the character of the officer as witnessed by his actions nor his capacity to offer reasoned elaborations of his decisions that was the source of his power. It was the mere fact that he occupied his office as of right. And so it was in the answers given to questions regarding personal rights to authority that, in the end, the very nature of authority itself came to be questioned. Orthodoxy had it that superior powers must be obeyed whatever they commanded and however questionable even, their right to command [4.1–4.3]. But what if one wished to question the right to command obedience, as parliamentarians wished to question the King's? Scholastic tradition – from Aristotle through Aquinas and the jurisconsults of the Renaissance – had it that a *tyrannus in titulo* need not be obeyed. The usurper – one who exercised an authority not rightfully his – was a 'tyrant in title'. Both royalists and parliamentarians scoured the records of the English past to find evidence of the historic rights the institution they defended had exercised; they did so in search of 'encroachments' on power, episodes in which either institution had grasped powers not its own. A conqueror, like William the Norman, parliamentarians suggested, need not be obeyed, and all kingly claims based on his were an encroachment on Anglo-Saxon liberties. Conquest could not yield a title . . . The other kind of tyranny was *tyrannus in exercito*: the maleficent exercise of powers which were nevertheless rightly held and exercised in accordance with law. At this point the legalism of the parliamentarians fell away and give birth to a new formula for the right to authority and the duty of subjection. Herbert Palmer and Jeremiah Burroughes, for instance [5.2.1; 5.2.2], began to argue that obedience is owed only to he who rules not only lawfully but well. Authority, in their thought, begins to emerge as depending on the right actions of the magistrate and on his ability to articulate and justify the ends to which his rule is a means. A deontological politics begins to give way to a teleological mode.

Thus it is that it was more in their development of theories as to the grounds of resistance rather than in their talk of sovereignty that the parliamentarians provided the basis for radical politics: if the right to authority and the duty of obedience are to be based on the right action of the magistrate, then it is hard to deny the populace at large the liberty of assessing the magistrate's performance. As Parliament claimed to judge the King, so men more radical would come to judge not only the King but Parliament itself.

## *Radicals, 1645–49*

Intellectual movements are more complex than military ones; and the process I have suggested to have occurred was far messier on the ground than any brief campaign history can suggest. For one thing, the royalist–parliamentarian debate of 1642 to 1645, and the 'independent'–conservative debate of 1646 to 1651, remained and were to continue in a markedly casuistical style (Wallace 1968). Casuistry is the science of instructing a pre-obliged conscience where its duties lie, and it does so by bringing the great complexity of current facts to order at the bar of agreed rules. This method of argument could have survived only where the criticisms of the matrix were not entirely assimilated – or believed – and where the issues were still thought to be reducible to those about facts of illegal action. Certainly, as the Army leadership and their 'independent' allies grew more estranged from the majority in a 'presbyterian' Parliament who would by 1647 gladly have settled for the reforms of 1641, criticisms of their treatment of King and Parliament could very easily be couched in legalistic terms; even so, Cromwell and Ireton may still be observed hankering after the old ways in 1647 and 1648, and so may the revolution-making Rump in 1649 [11.1; 11.6]. For another thing, the emergent 'leveller' radicalism, if mothered in the womb of libertarian – even antinomian heresy (Morton 1970) – was fathered in the public arena of competing authorities and duties alleged by royalist and parliamentarian. However much a John Lilburne's or a Richard Overton's interest in reform placed them against the traditional directive minority of their society, they did not consider themselves free from obligations. Some of their sectarian followers might have embraced the antinomian belief that the grace of God's entering a man freed him from all law, but the leveller leaders did not. Lilburne argued from law consistently, though until 1648 the scope of the reforms he desired kept him from his ultimate point of rest in a quasi-royalist opposition to the new 'grandees'. Even the much more radical Overton, author of a theory of the rights of man, based his theory on a notion not of Christian liberty, but on one which emphasised the creature's duty of obedience to its creator [10.3].

Nevertheless, leveller radicalism, libertarian sectarianism in the city, the populism of the Army, the lightly figured providentialism of a Cromwell, and the millenarianism of the politically articulate in the period after the first war do represent a clear departure from the legalism of royalist and parliamentarian. The law was no longer thought to exhaust the content of duty, and the magistrate was no longer thought to have the right to command simply by virtue of his office.

The leveller leaders were immensely talented practical propagandists; eclectics, they took what they wanted from where they found it. Parliamentarians had insisted that the 'ancient constitution' had been encroached upon by conquest; royalists had replied that in fact all parliamentary powers and popular rights had, as a matter of historical fact, derived from the will of Kings (headnotes and docs Part 7). Their long researches into the medieval past had been made in search of the original constitution of authority now encroached upon. The levellers picked the eyes of both sets of assertions. Contemporary positive law was no more than the will of a tyrant; the Lords were his 'creatures'; so were corrupt corporations; oligarchs in the City and in Parliament now sought to emulate Kings and perpetrate the tyranny. Monopolies and tithes were the policies of tyrants. Where parliamentarians spoke of the antique existence of their freedoms and privileges 'time out of mind' [8.5], the levellers spoke of Parliament encroaching on Anglo-Saxon freedoms. And where such as Parker, unable to specify the detail of 'ancient constitution', had spoken of the rational necessity of imagined acts of consent that must have constituted and bounded political authority [8.6], the levellers were happy to insist that a new constitution might well *now* be set up by an Agreement of the People (headnotes to [10.4]).

Neither parliamentarians nor royalists had entirely confined themselves to argument from law and its history – argument the thoroughly normative purpose of which was to demonstrate the proper content of the law and its origin (perhaps since 'degenerated' from) in the will of some authorised actor. Aristotelians in search of a 'first cause', they had also turned to Scripture to show how it was that the original author had in turn been authorised by a higher power. But more importantly perhaps, from the point of view of the development of radical political thinking, they had at times produced rationalist and telelogical doctrines in which the emphasis fell not on the authoritative origins of power but of its ends and purposes. Royalists and parliamentarians had in fact at times spoken of the ends and purposes of political activity as justifying legally ambiguous action, but they had always taken care to assert that the 'trust' the institution they defended had for the 'common weal' or 'popular safety' was a legal one, theirs by custom and 'known and declared law'. It was one the ultimate force of which – to breach some laws – would be felt only in 'emergency', in cases of 'necessity'. The levellers for their part were happy to be entirely rationalist. Freed by their anti-Normanism from respecting the law as a source of duty, they claimed that power was entrusted to magistrates for the good of the people, and that if magistrates did not fulfil their trust, the people might 'reassume' their power and reconstitute authority anew. The rule *salus populi suprema lex est* to which they, like Parker, appealed, is, in form, a law. Indeed, it presented itself as the 'supreme law'. Like any valid law it imposes a duty; but not one of obedience. It rather makes it incumbent on the magistrate to pursue an ever-receding policy outcome: the 'safety' or 'health' of 'the people' (as its Latin might be Englished). And who better to know what the safety and health of the people consists in than the people themselves? Who better to judge the magistrate as he seeks what can never be finally attained?

Though Lilburne had started out as a millenarian, the leveller leadership had no very clear vision of the concrete collective ends of human association. In their Agreements of the People, designed to be ratified by the people as written constitutions, they aimed at a 'minimal State'. The powers of government would be held on trust and would be restricted so that it could not infringe the people's rights. Each man's Christian beliefs were his own – here leveller schooling in the theory and practice of a disparate and often warring sectarianism, externally threatened by both Anglican and Presbyterian demands for enforced uniformity, bears its fruit. Each man's property and liberty was absolutely guaranteed to him – and here their experience of 'arbitrary government' at the hands of all successive regimes is evident. Even the more remarkable demand from the lower reaches of the loose federation of the 'party', the demand that women should share in the franchise and be allowed to preach the word (Gentles 1978), was no more than one for a framework of settled law within which each man – and now woman – should be able to choose his or her life's activity. The levellers have thus been seen as 'possessive individualists', philosophers of the *petit bourgeoisie*, and the harbingers of the bourgeois revolution (Macpherson 1962). However that may figure in relation to the details of their doctrine – at times they seem too equalitarian (headnotes and [11.1]), at times too inequalitarian (Laslett 1964) to make the view convincing – their programme was less one aimed at tranforming the lives of individuals to conform with a vision of the ends of political life than one of readjusting the duties and of extending the rights of people to allow them an extended area of Christian and civil liberty.

Such liberty, at once Christian and civil, was the constant demand of the Army declarations of 1647, and it was to be presented in various colours of emphasis from then on until the Restoration. Parliament, their emergent argument went (Kishlansky 1979b), corrupt, and 'backsliding' from its engagements to the contrary, was now denying the 'birthrights' of Englishmen for which it had claimed to fight in 1642. This theme was the anvil on which the officers and soldiers forged a new kind of political thought as the spring and summer of 1647 wore on. While they continually claimed Parliament's original authorisation as a ground for their actions, they made two much more revolutionary claims: that the 'cause' for which they fought in itself justified their fighting, and that they, 'private men', could nevertheless claim the right to act politically because it was they who had born the 'heat of the day', sacrificing their lives and estates in the process. They argued in such a way as to suggest that ends, not duties, justify political action; and that virtuous action, not duty, generates rights. Army ideology had it that the magistrate could claim authority only in so far as his acts were right; authority was the rightful possession of those who acted rightly; rights and duties were not permanently settled but the correlatives of conscientious action to a good end. The bland rule-utilitarianism of their royalist and parliamentarian mentors (the easy assumption that the legal distribution of authority would always attain the ends of life) had given way to an act-utilitarianism which could, in principle, reject any settled rule at all.

To speak of 'the Army' as having a single view is of course to simplify matters: the officer-leadership of 1647 started out intent only on a settlement between themselves, the Parliament and the

King, though they finished the year advocating a toned-down leveller type of Agreement of the People; but their more radical fellows among the officers and rank and file gradually came to wish the abolition of King and Lords and a greatly extended franchise for the election of a 'Representative of the People' which would be a 'supreme power' but which would be limited by the terms of a written constitution. In brief, the ends they had in view were various and unclear. Such a context of disagreement and continual change of stance bred a marked reliance on the 'testimony of events' written by the finger of God as indicating what the future should be; and it encouraged reliance on the more structured providentialism of millenial expectation. Men were the instruments of God's will, and political activity was to be judged according to how it conformed with His plan.

Many conclusions were consistent with recourse to providence and prophetic history. In Cromwell and Ireton it led to a cautious empiricism in decision-reaching followed, however, by a courage and thoroughness in execution of decisions that was a consequence of an utter conviction of acting as the Lord's instruments [11.1; 11.2]. In the sectarian virtuoso, Lawrence Clarkson – and later in John Milton and in the political formula for the Parliament of the Saints in 1653 – it could lead to the conclusion that 'men fearing God and of approved integrity' should rule, and that only 'the elect' really mattered in politics at all. The unregenerate were indeed the antichristian enemy [10.5]. (An oligarchy of 'Saints' was as much a production of the 'puritan' consciousness as the insistence that all powers should be obeyed – and of the contrary ideals of liberty of conscience and obedience only to 'true magistracy'.)

The explicit millenarianism of such as William Sedgewick could, by 1648 [10.7], lead to a populist–militarist vision of the rule of the poor and outcast – a vision which would have horrified earlier radical millenarians like Jeremiah Burroughes, who, it is true, urged Parliament to a holy war against the forces of evil in 1642 [5.6] (Walzer 1965), but thought that while the people were the 'voice of many waters' of the *Revelation* vision of the fall of Babylon, nevertheless thought the great men were the 'lightening' which would join with the lesser to strike at the citadels of wickedness (Christianson 1978).

What stands as common among these various interpretations of the workings of God in the world though, is the common insistence that God provides victory, that God disposes the *de facto* array of the warring interests that clash, and that God now acts, not so much as a scourge for the wicked – the normal interpretation of why there should be wars and tyranny – but at the head of His victorious Saints. Gerrard Winstanley, the digger, was one of the few who were interested in what we would call politics who would not appeal to the sword of an avenging army. The ends of life are God's; they may be seen revealed in prophecy and the testimony of events; the 'new Israelites' – the poor and oppressed – must now separate themselves from the world of human subordination and domination to wait while the Spirit moves to destroy and transform the 'violent and bitter people'. The poor must dig the common land and live in expectation. No faith is to be placed in the sword. Still, in common with other radical millenarians, Winstanley acted out a politics aimed at an end and not a politics of duty. And while he would advocate only careful extra-legal action even though he condemned the whole of the old law as rooted in conquest and the providence of evil, others would declare all-out war on the old order. So far as they were concerned, it had nothing to recommend it at all, and the old duties had entirely ceased to oblige.

### *The pursuit of interests: an epilogue*

As the matrix was dissected into its conflicting elements the subjects' duties became far from clear, and attempts were made to fix them by means of oaths, covenants and declarations; but these too were conflicting, contradictory and impossible of performance. The force of events – 'necessity' it was often called – rendered laws and oaths and all the duties based on them powerless. During the wars some made attempts to argue that the *de facto* distribution of forces coincided with the jurisdic shape of the old constitution of duties. Parliamentarians spoke of the 'interests' of Parliamentmen as being precisely consonant with their acting dutifully, and Charles Herle could not resist remarking that 'every day's experience teaches us that interests are a better State security than oaths' [8.7]. Normal royalist propaganda claimed that the King could have no interest other than his kingdom's good; and in his *Answer to the nineteen propositions* of 1642, Charles himself spoke of the constitution mixing the power of monarch, aristocracy and democracy in such a way as that, none prevailing, the interests of all would be secured [3.4]. And Ireton in 1647 provided a remarkable account of how it was that the great 'permanent interests' of the nation were already settled in 'ancient constitution' [11.1]. But in general, the prohibition on Machiavellian considerations of interests remained in force. The disaster of war, it was often alleged, was to be laid at the doors of those 'factions' or 'parties' – note that 'faction' = 'fraction' and 'party' = 'part' – who pursued their private interest at the expense of the interest of the whole: this was the trouble with courtiers; this was the trouble with the few who had led Parliament against their King. The ruling assumption was that only lawful action could attain the interests of the kingdom, not to mention the fulfilment of God's ordinance.

Nevertheless the language of interests had a foothold, and a future was to lie with those who saw that the 'interests' of the kingdom did not in fact coincide with the just claims of the protagonists in the wars. Thomas Povey argued for moderation on these grounds in 1643; and royalist defeatists like Marchamont Nedham were to argue from 1647 onwards that the 'public interest' demanded that all the great 'interests' – the Army, Parliament, 'independents', 'presbyterians', the Scots, and the royalists – should modify their just claims to bring about the greater end of settlement ([9.1] and headnotes). Ascham's defeatist republicanism is remarkable only in that he could no longer see what just claims might consist in. The problem, by 1648, could be seen as one of reconstructing a frame of duty in which interest and duty would be combined anew.

This new line of thought teased out the assumption, implicit in normal thought, that the ancient constitution protected the interests of all; and the tendency was to a Machiavellian and prudential politics, the bias of which was towards criticism of the old jurisdic structure and to the construction of a republic out of the concrete, secular interests of the nation. Nedham himself was to turn republican; but the tendency is best displayed in James Harrington's *Oceana* of 1656, the book that was to inspire the revolutionary generations in France and America during the next century. Harrington taught that men's duties now lay in constant civic activity dedicated to the end of the maintenance and expansion of a great landed republic. The duties of citizens – much more arduous than they had ever been considered to be under the 'ancient prudence' of the now-exploded constitution of authority – coincided with their interest in the cultivation of land and commerce. One reads Harrington in the realisation that Rennaisance political thinking had at last arrived in England; the classical virtue of worldly prudence had been introduced into the canon of public virtues. The contrast between Harringtonian and civil war thinking is marked: for Harrington, prudence consists in knowing how to meet the demands of ideals by manipulating the quite unmysterious, secular, social forces which the prudent operator confronts. Harrington's political actor no longer inhabits the world of the old matrix in which prudence realises God's plan, the general outlines of which are clear and consist in peaceful submission to superiors; nor does he inhabit the world of a Cromwell in 1647 as the matrix dissolved, one in which a man is unsure of the end and distrustful of the means [11.1]; nor, finally does he (*pace* Pocock 1977) await the coming of the millennium, expecting, and fighting for the rule of the Godly. Harrington's thinking, which he himself placed quite consciously in opposition to both the radicalisms and conservatisms of the civil war years, proclaims his transcendence of their mistakes in tones less confident only than those of Hobbes, who, in his great *Leviathan* (1651) had dismissed them as philosophical errors. In a Harringtonian world, the ends of politics should guide political activity; laws and duties are merely a means to those ends. The old mistakes must be put aside.

Yet the mistakes live on. I will finish here where Harrington began, on the title page of *Oceana*, quoting Horace. The poet has Tantalus, unable to satisfy his hunger or his thirst, turning on the spectator and demanding, *quid rides? mutato nomine, de te fabula narratur*: why do you laugh? Change the names and the story is about you.

*Part one*
# THE PEOPLE ARE INSTRUCTED IN THEIR DUTIES

## 1.1 THREE CATECHISMS

From John Henry Blunt (ed.), *The annotated Book of Common Prayer* (1893), 467–68; *The humble advice of the Assembly of Divines* (1647) 34–7: Wing W 1437; John Ball, *A short catechism* (19th edn, 1642), 33–4: Wing B 563.

Catechisms were designed to teach the principles of Christianity to the public at large. They expounded the Apostles' Creed, the Ten Commandments and the Lord's Prayer. All Englishmen were required to learn the Anglican Catechism by rote before they could take communion. Their superiors in the church and in the family (parents and masters) were obliged by a canon law of 1604 to see they performed this task. The Anglican catechumen was asked what he learned from the 'two tables' of the Commandments. He was to reply first what was meant by the First Table (the first four Commandments in *Exodus* xx) which taught him his duties to God; and then he was to answer the questions appropriate to the Second Table: 'What is thy duty to thy neighbour?' The Presbyterian Larger Catechism and John Ball's Catechism attempted to elicit more specific answers to questions as to the meanings of each separate Commandment. The Larger Catechism was the product of the Westminster Assembly, completed in 1648, and only marginally successfully imposed on the population during the interregnum. The version here represents its form in late 1647 when it was presented by the Assembly to Parliament for approval. It differs very little from the final form (Torrance 1959). John Ball's Catechism was first published in the 1620s and was to reach a 56th impression by 1678 – a remarkable example of a common genre of private enterprise catechism-production by a puritan divine who died in 1640. The rote learning required was typical of the authoritarian society of the seventeenth century (Laslett 1965), and what the people were required to learn speaks for itself. Whatever other theological differences stood between Anglican, Presbyterian and independent puritan and were expressed in their catechisms, they speak with one voice in regard to the importance of obedience and social hierachy. Schochet (1969, 1975) writes interestingly of the texts and the context.

### 1.1.1 *The Anglican Catechism*

'What dost thou learn by these commandments?' .... 'My duty towards my neighbour is to love him as myself, and to do to all men as I would they should do unto me; to love, honour, and succour my father and mother; to honour and obey the King and all that are put in authority under him; to submit myself to all my governors, teachers, spiritual pastors, and masters; to order myself lowly and reverently to all my betters; to hurt nobody by word nor deed; to be true and just in all my dealings; to bear no malice nor hatred in my heart; to keep my hands from picking and stealing, and my tongue from evil-speaking, lying, and slandering; to keep my body in temperance, soberness, and chastity; not to covert nor desire other men's goods, but to learn and labour truly to get mine own living, and to do my duty in that state of life unto which it shall please God to call me'.

### 1.1.2 *The Larger Catechism*

*Ques.* Which is the fifth commandment?
*Ans.* 'Honour thy father and thy mother', etc.
*Ques.* Who are meant by 'father' and 'mother' in the fifth Commandment?
*Ans.* By 'father' and 'mother' in the fifth commandment are meant not only natural parents but all superiors in age and gifts, and especially such as by God's ordinance are over us in places of authority, whether in family, church, or commonwealth.
*Ques.* Why are the superiors styled 'father' and 'mother'?
*Ans.* Superiors are styled 'father' and 'mother' both to teach them in all duties towards their inferiors like natural parents, to express love and tenderness to them according to their several relations, and to work inferiors to a greater willingness and cheerfulness in performing their duties to their superiors as to their parents.
*Ques.* What is the general scope of the fifth commandment?
*Ans.* The general scope of the fifth commandment is the performance of those duties which we mutually owe in our several relations: as inferiors, superiors, equals.
*Ques.* What is the honour inferiors owe to their superiors?
*Ans.* The honour which inferiors owe to their superiors is all due

reverence in heart, word, and behaviour; prayer and thanksgiving for them; imitation of their virtues and graces; willing obedience to their lawful commands and counsels; fidelity to [and] defence and maintenance of their persons and authority according to their several ranks and the nature of their places; bearing with their infirmities, and covering them in love; that so they may be an honour to them and to their government.

*Ques.* What are the sins of inferiors against their superiors?

*Ans.* The sins of inferiors against their superiors are all neglect of duties required toward them; envying at, contempt of, and rebellion against their persons and places and to their lawful counsels, commands and corrections; cursing, mocking, and all such refractory and scandalous carriage as proves a shame and dishonour to them and their government.

*Ques.* What is required of superiors toward their inferiors?

*Ans.* It is required of superiors, according to that power they receive from God and that relation wherein they stand [to others], to love, pray for and bless their inferiors; to instruct, counsel and admonish them; countenancing, commending and rewarding such as do well, discountenancing, reproving and chastising such as do ill; protecting and providing for them all things necessary for soul and body; and by grave, wise, holy, and exemplary carriage to procure glory to God, honour to themselves, and so preserve that authority which God hath put upon them.

*Ques.* What are the sins of superiors?

*Ans.* The sins of superiors are, besides the neglect of the duties required of them, an inordinate seeking of themselves (their own glory, ease, profit or pleasure); commanding things unlawful or not in the power of the inferiors to perform; counselling, encouraging, or favouring them in that which is evil; dissuading, discouraging or discountenancing them in that which is good; correcting them unduly; carelessly exposing them to wrong, temptation and danger; provoking them to wrath; or in any way dishonouring themselves or lessening their authority by an unjust, indiscrete, rigorous or remiss behaviour.

*Ques.* What are the duties of equals?

*Ans.* The duties of equals are to regard the dignity and worth of each other in giving honour to go one before another, and to rejoice in each other's gifts and advancements as in their own.

*Ques.* What are the sins of equals?

*Ans.* The sins of equals are, besides the neglect of the duties required, the undervaluing of the worth, envying the gifts, grieving at the advancement or prosperity of another, and usurping preeminence one over another.

### 1.1.3 *John Ball's Catechism*

*Ques.* What is the fifth commandment?
*Ans.* 'Honour thy father and thy mother', etc.
*Ques.* Who are to be understood by 'father' and 'mother'?
*Ans.* Not only parents but also all superiors in office, age and gifts.
*Ques.* What is it to honour?
*Ans.* To acknowledge the excellency that is in men by virtue of their place, and to carry ourselves accordingly towards them.
*Ques.* Are only the duties of inferiors here intended?
*Ans.* No, but of superiors and equals also.
*Ques.* What then is the main duty of the commandment?
*Ans.* That we are carefully to observe that order which God hath appointed amongst men, and do the duties which we owe unto them in respect of their places and degrees.
*Ques.* What is the duty of inferiors?
*Ans.* They must be subject, reverent and thankful to their superiors, bearing with their wants and recovering them in love.
*Ques.* What is the duty of superiors?
*Ans.* To carry themselves gravely, meekly, and after a seemly manner towards their inferiors.
*Ques.* What is the duty of equals?
*Ans.* To regard the dignity and worth of each other, modestly to bear themselves one toward the other, and in giving honour, to go one before the other.

*Part two*
# THE DANGERS OF DISORDER

## 2.1 DISORDER PREDICTED

From Griffith Williams, *A discovery of the mysteries, or the plots and faction of a prevalent faction in this present Parliament* (Oxford, 1643), 55–7: Wing W 2665.

It is more common to find statements of the dangers of disorder than of the virtues of order during the civil war period. The claims of order (recorded in Greenleaf 1966a and Daly 1979b) tended to be taken for granted. Williams (1589?–1672) was a ferociously high church and hard-line royalist from the beginning. He became a royal chaplain in 1636 and was bishop of Ossory in Ireland by 1640. He was at the King's side at the first pitched battle, at Edgehill, and was author of several pamphlets which supported the King but embarrassed his more moderate advisers. In this extract he discerns the levelling tendencies of the King's opponents. It will be noticed how – in common with many other royalists – he conflates the aims of the parliamentary leadership with those of their most radical sectarian supporters.

Though among the works of God, every flower cannot be a lily, every beast cannot be a lion, every bird cannot be an eagle, and every planet cannot be Phoebus, yet in the school of these men, this is the doctrine of their to be new erected church: that with God *there is no respect of persons*, and neither *circumcision availeth any thing, nor uncircumcision*; but whether they be *bond* or *free*, masters or servants, *Jew*, or *Gentile, Barbarian, Scythian*, a country clown, or a court gallant, rich or poor, it is all one with God. These titles of honour (Kings, lords, knights and gentlemen) are no entities of God's making, but the creatures of man's invention, to puff him up with pride and not to bring him unto God. And therefore though for the bringing of their great good work to pass they are yet contented to make the Earl of Essex their general and Warwick their admiral, and so Pym and Hampden great officers of state, yet, when the work is done, their plot perfected and their government established, then you shall find, that as now, they will eradicate episcopacy and make all our clergy equal, as if all had equally but one talent and no man worthier than another; so then there should be neither King, lord, knight nor gentlemen, but a parity of degrees among all these holy brethren. And to give us a taste of what they mean: as the Lords' concurrence with them enabled them to devour the King's power, so they have since, with great justice, prevailed with the House of Commons to swallow up the Lords' power and have most fairly invaded their privilege (when they questioned particular members for words spoken in that House) and then the whole House (when they brought up and countenanced a mutinous and seditious petition, which demanded the names of those Lords that consented not with the House of Commons in those things which that House had twice denied)...

Because Christ saith *Call no man father on earth, for one is your Father which is in heaven*, the child must not call him that begat him and nurseth him his father, nor kneel unto him to ask him blessing, nor perform many other such duties which the Lord requireth and the Church instructeth her children to do to this very day. And this foolish doctrine of calling no man 'father', no man 'master' or 'lord' and the like, in their sense (because they understand not the divine meaning of our Saviour's word) hath been the cause of such undutifulness and untowardness, such contempts of superiors and such rebellions to authority as is beyond expression, when as by their disloyalty, being thus bred in them from their cradle, they first despise their father, then their teachers, then their King, and then God himself.

## 2.2 THE SIN OF DISORDER SPECIFIED

From William Prynne, *A plea for the Lords* (1648), 67–9: Wing P 4032.

Prynne (1600–69) had been viewed by Archbishop Laud as a puritan nonconformist dangerous enough to warrant his ears being 'cropped' twice before the civil wars. A staggeringly prolific writer of pamphlets and books, Prynne then became a leading parliamentary apologist, not only for a reformed church and the right of resistance but for parliamentary sovereignty. By 1648, however, he had well and truly emerged as a champion of the 'ancient constitution', defending in particular the rights of the King, Lords and State-controlled Presbyterian Church against the encroachments of the Commons and the attacks of extra-parliamentary radicals. Here he gives chapter and verse against the sin of disorder at the end of a book defending the House of Lords. That Lamont called his excellent biography of Prynne *Marginal Prynne* (1963) is no mistake: Pryne could no more resist quoting authorities than he could cease from writing. An MP from 1646, he was a victim of Pride's Purge but, as might be expected, continued to write as a constitutionalist–royalist.

Oh consider therefore what I have written to undeceive your judgements; and reform your practice. Consider that dominion, principality, regality, magistracy and nobility are founded in the very law of nature, and God's own institution. He subjected not only *all beasts and living creatures to the sovereign lordship of man, to whom he gave dominion over them* (*Genesis* i. 28) by virtue whereof men enjoy far greater privileges than beasts, but likewise one man unto another as *children to their parents, wives to their husbands, servants to their masters, subjects to their kings, princes and magistrates, soldiers to their captains, mariners to their shipmasters, scholars to their tutors, people to their ministers** – which order, if denied or disturbed, will bring absolute and speedy confusion in all families, corporations, states, kingdoms, armies, garrisons, schools, churches, and dissolve all human societies, which subsist by order and subordination only to one another. And seeing monarchy, royalty, principality, nobility (yea, titles of honour and nobility, as kings, princes, dukes, lords, etc.) are as ancient almost as the world itself, universally received and approved among all nations whatsoever under heaven, and honoured with special privileges, as not only all eminent authors and experience manifest, but [also] these ensuing scripture texts: *Genesis* xii. 15; xiv. 1–10; xvii. 6, 16; xx. 2; xxi. 22, 23; xxv. 16; xxvi. 1, 8, 26; xxxvi. 15–18, 29–43; xxxix. 1, 2; xli. 40–47, xlvii. 23, 26; *Exodus* i. 8; *Numbers* xx. 14, etc.; xxi. 1, 18, 21, 33; xxii. 7, 10, 14, 15, 40; xxiii. 17; vii. 2, 3, 10; xvi. 2; xxvii. 2; xxxii. 2; *Deuteronomy* xvii. 14–16; *Joshua* i. 16–18; v. 1; viii. 9–12; *Judges* ix. 6, 18; *1 Samuel* viii. 5, 6; *2 Samuel* xi. 2; *1 Kings* iv. 34; x. 15, 28, 29; xx. 16; xxiii. 22; *Job* iii. 14; xxxvi. 7; *Psalms* ii. 2, 10, . . . lxxii. 10; cii. 15; cxxxvi. 17, 18; cxxxviii. 4; *Proverbs* viii. 15, 16; xxx. 31; *Ecclesiastes* x. 16, 17; . . . *1 Samuel* v. 11; xxix. 2, 6, 7; *Daniel* iv. 36; v. 9, 10, 23; vi. 27; *Matthew* viii. 9; *Mark* vi. 21; x. 42; *1 Corinthians* viii. 5; *Romans* [xiii]. 1–4; *1 Timothy* ii. 1–2; *Titus* iii. 1–2; *1 Peter* ii. 13–15; *Acts* ix. 27,

* Here Prynne fills his margin with a note shorter by far than many he provided: *Genesis* iii. 16; *Exodus* xx. 12; *Ephesians* v. 22–30; vi. 1–10; *Romans* xiii. 1–3; *Titus* iii. 1; *Colossians* iii. 20, 22; *1 Peter* i. 13, 14, 18, iii. 15; *Hebrews* xiii. 17; *Joshua* i. 16–18; *Matthew* viii. 9.

which I wish our Sectaries, Levellers and Lilburnists to consider and study (with the others forecited). It will be a mere desperate folly and madness in any man to prove antipodes to this institution of God, nature, nations; to run quite contrary to all men and to level the head, neck and shoulders to the feet; the tallest cedars to the lowest shrubs; the roof of every building to the foundation stones; the sun, moon, stars, heavens to the very earth and centre, and even men themselves to the meanest beasts. I shall therefore conclude with St Paul's serious admonition, which these refractory persons have quite forgotten (*Romans* xiii. 1–2) *Let every soul be subject to the higher powers. For there is no power but of God: the powers that be are ordained of God. Whosoever therefore resisteth* (much more oppugneth, abolisheth) *the power, resisteth* (oppugneth, abolisheth) *THE ORDINANCE OF GOD: and they that resist. . . . shall receive to themselves DAMNATION* [Prynne's emphasis and additions retained] . . . (which St Paul likewise seconds almost in the self-same words which you may do well to peruse and study, *1 Peter* ii.13).

*Part three*

# THE LAW AND THE PEOPLE'S SAFETY: ROYALIST AND PARLIAMENTARIAN, 1641–1649

## 3.1 JOHN PYM ON THE SUFFICIENCY OF LAW

From *The speech or declaration of John Pym* (1641), 2–5: Wing P 4293.

A parliamentary leader in opposition to Charles I since 1628, Pym (1584–1643) was to guide the Long Parliament to war against him (Hexter 1941). Here, in a speech of May 1641 against Charles's most hated of 'evil counsellors', Thomas Wentworth, 1st Earl of Strafford, he demonstrates the parliamentarians' trust in 'the law', thoroughly confounding in typical fashion the positive laws of the realm with the standard by which he thought they ought to be measured. He was to be often quoted with approval during the 'paper war': by his supporters – as standing for the properties, liberties and privileges of people and Parliament – and as often by royalists, as evidence of how far the parliamentarians had receded by 1642 from their hypocritically legalistic pre-war position. Sirluck (1959) provides the context.

That which is given me in charge is to show the quality of the offence, how heinous it is in nature, how mischievous in the effect of it: which will best appear if it be examined by that law to which he himself appealed, that universal, that supreme law, *salus populi*. This is the element of all laws out of which they are all derived, the end of all laws to which they are designed, and in which they are perfected. . . . The law is that which puts a difference betwixt good and evil, betwixt just and unjust. If you take away the law all things will fall into confusion; every man will become a law to himself, which in the depraved condition of human nature must lead to many great enormities. Lust will become a law, and envy will become a law; covetousness and ambition will become laws. . . . The law is the safeguard of all private interest. Your honours, your lives, your liberties and estates are all in the keeping of the law. Without this, every man hath a like right to anything.

## 3.2 PARLIAMENT'S AIMS IN PEACE AND WAR (1641, 1643, 1646)

From *A protestation to be taken for the defence of the protestant religion* (1641), extracted from *OPH*, II, cols. 776–7; *A solemn league and covenant for the reformation and defence of religion* (1643), extracted from John Rushworth, *Collections*, (1721–22, V, 478); *A declaration of the Commons* (April 1646) extracted from *A collection of all the publicke orders and declarations* (1646), 879: Wing E 1279.

Samuel Rawson Gardiner, the great historian of this period, called the *Protestation of 3 May 1641*, 'the Tennis Court Oath of the Puritan Revolution'; the *Solemn League and Covenant* of November 1643 bound the two nations of Scotland and England in war against the royalists; the *Declaration of April 1646* reiterated the old legalist commitments of Parliament. All three were to be quoted by angry royalist – and later 'presbyterian' – conservatives, as they saw Parliament gradually abandon its carefully if vaguely stated role of defender of the ancient constitution. There never was to be agreement reached among Parliament's supporters or opponents as to what the proper church settlement should be: 'temple-work' proved abortive; but everyone knew that in carrying out their revolution the 'independents' had both broken their oaths and receded from the 'known and declared law'; and not many were happy with this. They were happiest when working under colour of legality.

### *3.2.1 The Protestation (May 1641)*

I, A. B. do, in the presence of Almighty God, promise, vow, and protest to maintain and defend, as far as lawfully I may, with my life, power, and estate, the true reformed protestant religion expressed in the doctrine of the Church of England, against all popery and popish innovations and according to the duty of my allegiance to his majesty's royal person, honour and estate; as also the power and privilege of Parliament, the lawful rights and liberties of the subjects, and every person that maketh this protestation in whatsoever he shall do in the lawful pursuance of the same . . . As far as lawfully I may, I will oppose, and, by good ways and means, endeavour to bring to condign punishment, all such as shall by force, practice, counsel, plots, conspiracies or otherwise, do anything to the contrary in this present Protestation contained. And further I shall, in all just and honourable ways, endeavour to preserve the unity and peace betwixt the three kingdoms of England, Scotland and Ireland: and neither for hope, fear, or other respect, shall relinquish this promise, vow and protestation.

### *3.2.2 The solemn league and covenant (September 1643)*

We... having before our eyes the glory of God.... [are] determined to enter into a mutual and solemn league and covenant, wherein we all subscribe; and each one of us for himself, with our hands lifted up to the most high God, do swear:

I. That we shall sincerely, really, and constantly, through the grace of God, endeavour in our several places and callings the preservation of the reformed religion in the Church of Scotland, in doctrine, worship, and discipline, against our common enemies; the reformation of religion in the kingdoms of England and Ireland in doctrine, worship, discipline and government, according to the word of God, and the example of the best reformed churches; and we shall endeavour to bring the churches of God in the three kingdoms to the nearest conjunction and uniformity in religion, confession of faith, form of church government, directory for worship, and catechising, that we and our posterity after us may, as brethren, live in faith and love, and the Lord may delight to dwell in the midst of us....

III. We shall with the same sincerity, reality and constancy, in our several vocations, endeavour with our estates and lives, mutually to preserve the rights and privileges of the Parliaments, and the liberties of the kingdoms, and to preserve and defend the King's majesty's person and authority, in the preservation and defence of the true religion and liberties of the kingdoms, that the world may bear witness with our consciences of our loyalty, and that we have no thoughts or intentions to diminish his majesty's just power and greatness.

### *3.2.3 A declaration of the Commons (April 1646)*

We are so far from altering the fundamental constitution and government of this kingdom by King, Lords and Commons, that we have only desired, that with the consent of the King, such powers may be settled in the two Houses without which we can have no assurance but that the like or greater mischiefs than these which God hath hitherto delivered us from may break out again and engage us in a second and more destructive war.

## 3.3 'THIS LAW IS AS OLD AS THE KINGDOM'

From *The declaration or remonstrance of the Lords and Commons in*

*Parliament* (19 May 1642), extracted from *An exact collection of all the remonstrances* (1643), 197–8, 206–8: Wing E 1533.

This declaration of 19 May 1642 represents Parliament's mature pre-war response to the royalist claim that they were acting illegally in wanting to appoint the King's counsellors, in disposing of the Militia, and in legislating by ordinance without the King. It is one of many declarations of the 'paper war' period, in which, unable to argue from the strict letter of the law, Parliament nevertheless claimed the right to act alone in conditions of 'necessity' to preserve the law, not against the King himself but from his 'evil counsellors'. Modern commentators (Allen 1938; Hexter 1941; Gough 1955) dilate on the incoherence of the position. Parliament's substantive and obviously novel claims against the King were soon to be elaborated in the *Nineteen Propositions* of 1 June: they would effectively choose his civilian and military officers, educate his children, and join him in church reform and the appointment of those peers who would vote in Parliament. Charles's response to the *Nineteen Propositions* is the subject of [3.4] below.

That which we desired was that in regard of the immanent danger of the kingdom, the Militia, for the security of his majesty and his people, might be put under the command of such noble and faithful persons as they had all cause to confide in. And such was the necessity of this preservation that we declared that if his majesty should refuse to join with us therein, the two Houses of Parliament, being the Supreme Court and highest Council of the kingdom, were enabled by their own authority to provide for the repulsing of such immanent and evident danger – not by any new law of their own making (as hath been untruly suggested to his majesty) but by the most fundamental law of the kingdom, even that which is fundamental and essential to the constitution and subsistence of it . . .

His majesty hath more reason to find fault with those wicked counsellors who have so often bereaved him of his honour and his people of the fruit of many gracious speeches which he made to them – such as those in the end of the last Parliament: that on the word of a King, as he was a gentleman, he would redress the grievances of the people as well out of Parliament as in it. Were the searching of studies and chambers (yea the pockets) of some both of the Nobility and Commons the very next day, the commitment of Master Bellasis, Sir John Hotham and Master Crew, the continued oppressions by Ship Money, Coat and Conduct Money . . . and other ensuing violations of the laws and liberties of the kingdom (all which were the effects of evil counsel, and abundantly declared in our [*Grand Remonstrance*]...) the actions of love and justice suitable to words such as those?...

The King is pleased to disavow having any...evil counsel or counsellors as are mentioned in our declaration[s], and we hold it our duty to avow there are such – or else we must say that all the ill things done of late in his majesty's name have been done by himself, wherein we should neither follow the direction of the law nor the affection of our own hearts – which is as much as may be to clear his majesty from all imputations of misgovernment, and to lay the fault upon his ministers...The false accusing of the six MPs...the denial of the Militia, the sharp messages to both Houses contrary to the customs of former Parliaments, the long and remote absence of his majesty from Parliament, the heavy and wrongful taxes upon both Houses, the cherishing and countenancing a discontented party in the kingdom against them: these certainly are the fruit of very ill counsel, apt to put the kingdom into a combustion, to hinder the supplies of Ireland and to countenance the proceedings and pretensions of the rebels there. And the authors of these evil counsels we conceive must be known to his majesty; and we hope our labouring with his majesty to have these discovered and brought to a just censure will not so much wound his honour in the opinion of his good subjects as his labouring to preserve and conceal them. And whereas his majesty saith he could wish that his own immediate actions which he avows on his own honour might not be so roughly censured under that common style of 'evil counsellors', we could also wish that we had not cause to make that style so common. But how often and undutifully soever these wicked counsellors fix their dishonour upon the King by making his majesty the author of those evil actions which are the effects of their own evil counsels, we, his majesty's loyal and dutiful subjects, can use no other style, according to that maxim in law: the King can do no wrong, but if any ill be committed in matter of State, the Council, if in matter of justice, the Judges, must pay for it....

Let all the world judge whether we have not reason to insist upon it, that the strength of the kingdom, [the Militia], should rather be ordered according to the direction and advice of the Great Council of the land, equally entrusted by the King and the kingdom, than that the safety of King, Parliament and kingdom should be left to the devotion of a few unknown counsellors, many of them not entrusted at all by the King in any public way, not at all confided in by the kingdom....

The votes at which his majesty takes exception are these:

I. That the King's absence, so far remote from the Parliament, is not only an obstruction but may be a destruction to the affairs of Ireland.

II. That when the Lords and Commons shall declare what the law of the land is, to have that not only questioned and controverted but contradicted, and a command that it should not be obeyed, is a high breach of the privilege of Parliament.

III. That those persons that advised his majesty to absent himself . . . are enemies to the peace of the kingdom . . . That the kingdom hath been of late and still is in so eminent a danger from both enemies abroad and a popish and discontented party at home, that there is an urgent necessity of putting his majesty's subjects into a posture of defence for the safeguard both of his majesty and his people. That the Lords and Commons, fully apprehending that danger . . . have in several petitions addressed themselves unto his majesty for the ordering and disposal of the Militia of the kingdom in such a way as was agreed upon by the wisdom of both Houses to be most effectual and proper for the present exigencies of the kingdom, yet could not obtain it, but his majesty did several times refuse to give his royal assent thereunto. That in that case of extreme danger and his majesty's refusal, the ordinance of Parliament agreed upon by both Houses for the Militia doth oblige the people, and ought to be obeyed by the fundamental laws of the kingdom.

By all which it doth appear that there is no colour of this tax, that we go about to introduce a new law, much less to exercise an arbitrary power, but indeed to prevent it. For this law is as old as the kingdom: that the kingdom must have a means to preserve itself, which, that it may be done without confusion, this the nation hath entrusted certain hands with a power to provide in an orderly and regular way for the good and safety of the whole. [This] power, by the constitution of the kingdom, is in his majesty and his Parliament together; yet since the prince, being but one person, is more subject to accidents of nature and chance whereby the commonwealth may be deprived of the fruit of that trust which was in part reposed in him, in cases of such necessity – that the kingdom may not be enforced presently to return to its first principles and every man left to *do what is right in his own eyes* without either rule or guide – the wisdom of this State hath entrusted the Houses of Parliament with a power to supply what shall be wanting on the part of the prince, as is evident by the constant custom and practice thereof in cases of nonage, natural disability, and captivity. And the like reason doth and must hold for the exercise of the same power in such cases where the royal trust cannot be or is not discharged, and [where] the kingdom runs an evident and immanent danger thereby: which danger, having been declared by the Lords and Commons in Parliament, there needs not the authority of any person or court to affirm. Nor is it in the power of any person or court to revoke that judgement.

## 3.4 THE KING STANDS BY THE LAW

From *His majesties answer to the XIX propositions* (1642), 2–3, 12, 17–22: Wing C 2122.

Charles I (1600–49) put his name to this piece of royalist propaganda, which, elicited as a passing response to the *Nineteen Propositions*, was to become the most-discussed single statement made during the civil wars. It was really written by others though: probably Lucius Cary (2nd Viscount Falkland) and Sir John Colepepper, two of his advisers. It is entirely typical of the royalist propaganda of the 'paper war' in its stress on the illegality of Parliament's actions, the novelty of its claims, and the determination of the King to preserve the law. (Wormald 1951). However, it proved an ideological disaster. It not only repopularised the classical prescription of Polybius (*c.* 204–122 BC) for mixed government and thus made the path easier for the growth of a classical republican ideology during the interregnum (Fink 1945; Pocock 1975), but it suggested to parliamentarian propagandists that the three 'estates' of King, Lords and Commons were equal sharers in 'supremacy', and that the Lords and Commons had legal power to 'restrain tyranny'. The royalists had to busy themselves showing that the King was 'head' of the three 'estates', and that the bishops – who had been left out of the *Answer* – were indeed the 'first estate' (Weston 1960, 1965, 1970). The ideas in the *Answer* were to have a long future (e.g. Weston 1965; Vile 1967; Dickinson 1976).

They have thought for to remove a troublesome rub in their way – the law. To this end, that they might undermine the foundations of it, a new power hath been assumed to interpret and declare laws without us by way of extemporary votes, without any case judicially before either House (which is in effect the same thing as to make laws without us), orders and ordinances made only by both Houses (tending to pure arbitrary power) were pressed upon the people as laws, and their obedience required to them. . . . Their next step was to erect an upstart authority without us (in whom, and only whom, the laws of this realm have placed that power) to command the Militia. . . . They have likewise broached new doctrine: that we are obliged to pass all laws that shall be offered to us by both Houses . . . It highly concerns both you in duty, and the commonwealth in consequences . . . that neither one estate transact what is proper for two, nor two what is proper for three, and consequently that (contrary to our declared will) our forts may not be seized, our arms may not be removed, our monies may not be stopped, our legal directions may not be countermandered by you, nor we desired to countermand them ourself, nor such entrances made upon a real war against us upon pretence of an imaginary war against you, and a chimera of necessity. . . .

[The demands in the propositions] are too much in the style, not only of equals, but of conquerors . . . (as is, there being differences and suits between two persons, whereof one would have from the other the several parcels of his ancient land and he should propose to [the other] by way of accommodation that he would quit to him all those in question, with the rest of his estate, as the most necessary and effectual means to remove all those suits and differences). But we call God to witness that, as for our subjects' sake these rights are vested in us, so for their sakes as well as our own we are resolved not to quit them nor to subvert . . . the ancient, equal, happy, well-poised and never-enough-commended constitution of this kingdom, nor to make ourself of a King of England a Duke of Venice, and this of a kingdom a republic.

There being three kinds of government amongst men – absolute monarchy, aristocracy and democracy – and all these having their conveniences and inconveniences, the experience and wisdom of your ancestors hath so moulded this out of a mixture of these as to give this kingdom (as far as human prudence can provide) the conveniences of all three without the inconveniences of any one, as long as the balance hangs even between the three estates and they run jointly on in their proper channel, begetting verdure and fertility in the meadows on both sides, and the overflowing of either on either side raise no deluge or inundation. The ill of absolute monarchy is tyranny; the ill of aristocracy is faction and division; the ills of democracy are tumults, violence and licentiousness. The good of monarchy is the uniting a nation under one head to resist invasion from abroad and insurrection at home; the good of aristocracy is the conjunction of counsel in the ablest persons of a state for the public benefit; the good of democracy is liberty, and the courage and industry which liberty begets.

In this kingdom the laws are jointly made by a King, by a House of Peers, and by a House of Commons chosen by the people – all having free votes and particular privileges. The government according to these laws is trusted to the King. Power of treaties of war and peace; of making peers; of choosing officers and councillors for state, judges for law, commanders for forts and castles; giving commissions for raising men to make war abroad or to prevent or provide against invasions or insurrections at home; benefit of confiscations; power of pardoning – and some more of the like kind – are placed in the King. And this kind of regulated monarchy, having this power to preserve that authority without which it would be disabled to preserve the laws in their force and the subjects in their liberties and proprieties, is intended to draw to him such a respect and relation from the great ones as may hinder the ills of division and faction, and such a fear and reverence from the people as may hinder tumults, violence and licentiousness. Again – that the prince may not make use of this high and perpetual power to the hurt of those for whose good he hath it – . . . the House of Commons (an excellent conserver of liberty, but never intended for any share in government or the choosing of them that should govern) is solely entrusted with the first propositions concerning the levies of monies (which is the sinews as well of peace as war) and the impeaching of those, who for their own ends . . . have violated that law which he is bound . . . to protect, and to the protection of which they were bound to advise him . . . And the Lords, being trusted with a judicatory power, are an excellent screen and bank between the prince and the people, to assist each against any encroachments of the other, and by just judgements to preserve the law which ought to be the rule of every one of the three . . .

Since therefore, the power legally placed in both Houses is more than sufficient to prevent and restrain the power of tyranny, and without the power which is now asked from us we shall not be able to discharge that trust which is the end of monarchy; since this would be a total subversion of the fundamental laws and that excellent constitution which hath made this nation so many years both famous and happy to a great degree of envy; since to the power of punishing – which is already in your hands according to law – . . . the power of preferring be added, we shall have nothing left to us but to look on; since the encroaching of one of these estates upon the power is unhappy in the effects both to them and all the rest; since this power of at most a joint government in us with our councillors . . . will return us to the worst kind of minority, and make us despicable . . . and beget endless factions and dissensions . . . both in the chosen, and the Houses that choose, and the people who choose the chosers; since so new a power will undoubtedly intoxicate persons who were not born to it, and beget not only dissensions among them as equals, but in them contempt of us as become an equal to them, and insolence and injustice towards our people – as now so much their inferiors – which will be the more grievous unto them, as suffering from those who were so lately of a nearer degree to themselves...; since all great changes are extremely inconvenient and almost infallibly beget yet greater changes, which beget greater inconveniences; since as great a one in the church must follow this of the kingdom; since the second estate would in all probability follow the fate of the first... till all power being vested in the House of Commons, and their number making them incapable of transacting affairs of state with the necessary secrecy and expedition – those being entrusted to a close committee – at last the common people (who in the meantime must be flattered, and to whom licence must be given in all their wild humours, however contrary soever to established law or their own real good) discover this *arcanum imperii* [secret of State]; that all this was done by them but not for them, grow weary of journey-work and set up for themselves, and call parity and independence liberty, devour that estate which had devoured all the rest, destroy all rights and proprieties, all distinctions of families and merit; and [since] by this means this splendid and excellently distinguished form of government [will] end in a dark, equal chaos of confusion, and the long line of our ancestors in a Jack Cade or a Wat Tyler: For all these reasons, to all these demands our answer is *nolomus leges Angliae mutari*. [We do not wish to change the laws of England.]

## 3.5 THE LAWS CONSTITUTE THE SAFETY OF THE PEOPLE: A PARLIAMENTARIAN'S VIEWS

From Robert Austin, *Allegiance not impeached* (1644), 8–12: Wing A 4253.

Austin was an obscure Cambridge doctor of divinity and clergyman who wrote only one tract besides *Allegiance not impeached*. The *DNB* (*Dictionary of National Biography*) can only say he flourished about 1644. In this extract he tries to show, in typical moderate parliamentarian fashion, that commitment to *salus populi* is precisely commitment to the totality of the laws of England. It was part of a case that allegiance was owed not to the King's 'natural' but to his 'politic' person – not to the man but the office – and that 'defensive resistance' to the King's 'personal' commands was justified by the positive laws when he acted illegally in such a way as to threaten the existence of those laws. The last thing he wants to contemplate is any natural right of 'natural', i.e. real, people to resist. More will be seen of this attitude in Part 5 below.

The chief political principle in nature is *salus populi suprema lex*, that is, the safety of the commonwealth is the chiefest law. And from this flow two more: (1) The whole commonwealth is more to be esteemed than one member, and (2) there must be a power always in the commonwealth to save itself from ruin. And these three follow one upon the other... Now because the strength of our cause depends much upon these principles, give me leave to dwell a little upon each of them, and to explain them and prove them....

'The safety of the people is the chiefest law', where ... by 'people', we are to understand the persons of men, together with the order of government under which they live. So says Aquinas in his *Summa* (q. 3 sects 1, 2), 'a people is a multitude of men comprehended under some kind of order'. S. Augustine – out of Cicero – defines a people thus: 'A people is a multitude of men knit together by consent of law and participation of utility.' (*Civitate Dei*, book 2 chap. 21, and book 19 chap. 21) [It is] as if he should have said, a people is a multitude of men gathered together and conjoined in the fellowship and participation of the same laws and liberties to their mutual benefit and emolument. Whence Aquinas infers, 'that to the nature and essence of a people it is required that their living together be ordered by just laws'.

So that in a people there are two things ... to be considered. First the *materiale*, and secondly the *formale*, as the logicians speak; or, to speak in terms of the law, there is a natural and political capacity in the people. The natural capacity are the men themselves as they are God's creatures; the political are their laws and liberties which are men's constitutions. And thus *populus*, the people, doth signify the whole commonwealth, consisting both of governors and those that are governed. All, thus joined together by consent of just laws and constitutions, are called *populus*, a people.

And thus at first the word 'people' was used amongst the Romans till the Roman Senate, for their greater reverence and authority, severed themselves from the people, taking to themselves the name of Senate, whence grew that common saying ... 'the Senate and the people of Rome have commanded this'. (As we used to say 'the King, and the Lords and Commons have enacted this'.) .... Now if thus we take the word 'people' when we say 'the safety of the people is the chiefest law', by it we must understand the safety of the whole commonwealth ... both of governors and of governed;

and not only in their persons, but chiefly in their laws and privileges wherein the very essence of a people doth . . . more especially consist. By the 'safety of the people' must be understood the safety of the whole commonwealth, and that not only in its natural but chiefly in its politic capacity.

But if we distinguish . . . the King from the people, as head from members (for though they may not be divided they may be distinguished), then because head and body must be homogeneous (that is of the same kind and nature) hence it will follow that as the head hath its natural and politic capacity by itself, so the people must have theirs by themselves also. And so the body [must] answer to the head in each of these capacities accordingly and by good agreement make up one body politic or commonwealth. As for example, first: as in the King there is a natural capacity, which is his person, and a politic (which is his Crown and dignity and such other flowers of the Crown as belong unto it), so in the people there shall be considerable both their natural capacity (which are their persons) and also their politic respect or capacity . . . (which are their liberties and privileges or such rights as belong to them). Secondly: as the King in his natural capacity is ever accompanied with the politic . . . and the politic capacity is as it were appropriated to the natural, so shall it be also here. The natural capacity of the people shall be ever accompanied with the politic (considered in its liberties and privileges), and these must not be severed. Thirdly: as in the King the natural capacity dies but the politic dies not . . . so in the people . . . their politic respect or capacity must still remain inviolable. . . .

Notwithstanding this distinction between King and people, yet seeing the King and people though distinct as head and members make up but one body politic, and [seeing that what makes them one] can be no other than consent of law and mutual utility, which is *forma populi* (the very essence of the people and commonwealth), . . . hence it follows that the preserving of this bond must be the chiefest law . . .

*Obj.* But what (some will say), shall not the safety of the people, as distinguished from the King, be esteemed as the chiefest law?

*Ans.* . . . I nothing doubt but a people may in a legal way stand upon their laws and liberties, and by force of arms defend them too if need require. . . . If in the ruin of their laws and liberties the ruin of the whole be involved – as it is undoubtedly [now] – then, it being the supreme law of nature to save the whole, they are bound by the same law to preserve their laws and liberties, that the whole may be thereby preserved.

## 3.6 A PLEA TO RECOVER THE 'ANCIENT WAYS OF PROCEEDING'

From Prynne, *A plea for the Lords* (1648), Ep. Ded: Wing P 4032.

Here Prynne (see headnote to [2.2]) expresses the faith which led him to make a remarkable series of collections of materials for the history of English law and the English constitution, and which led to his becoming Keeper of the Records in the Tower at the Restoration (Pocock 1957). The *Plea for the Lords* itself illustrates his collecting bent. The first edition, quoted here, ran to about 90 pages in 1648; the second edition of 1658 is more than 550 pages long. The expansion was entirely due to Prynne's industry in collecting and publishing further records to show the Lords' continual role in the legislative and judicial activities of English government. The extract printed here makes the political force of his activity clear: it is a conservative–restorationist one.

And truly, were all our Parliament Rolls, Pleas and Journals faithfully transcribed and published in print to the eye of the world, as most of our Statutes are, 'by the authority of both Houses of Parliament' . . . . it would not only preserve them from embezzling and the hazards of fire and war to which they are now subject, but likewise eternally silence [and] refute the Sectaries' and Levellers' ignorant false allegations against your honours' parliamentary jurisdictions and judicature, resolve and clear all or most doubts that can arise concerning the power, jurisdiction and privileges of both or either House, keep both of them within due bounds (the exceeding whereof is dangerous and grievous to the people, except in cases of absolute necessity for the saving of the kingdom, whilst that necessity continues and no longer) [and] chalk out the ancient, regular ways of proceeding in all parliamentary affairs whatsoever, whether or war or peace, civil or criminal, concerning King or subject, natives or foreigners; [it would] over-rule [and] reconcile most of the present differences between the King and Parliament, House and House, Members and Members; [it would] clear many doubts and rectify some gross mistakes in printed Statutes, lawbooks and our ordinary historians; [it would] add much light, lustre and ornament to our English annals and the common law, and make all lawyers and Members of both Houses far more able than now they are to manage and carry on all businesses in Parliament when they shall, upon every occasion almost, have former precedents ready at hand to direct them, (there being now very few Members in either House well read or versed in ancient Parliament Rolls, Pleas or Journals, the ignorance whereof is a great remora to their proceedings and oft-times a cause of great mistakes and deviations from the ancient, methodical rules and tracts of Parliament, now almost quite forgotten and laid aside by raw, inexperienced Parliamentmen, to the public prejudice, and injury to posterity).

## 3.7 THE KING'S FINAL WORD: 'I SPEAK NOT FOR MY RIGHT ALONE'

From three pamphlets reporting the trial of the King: C. W., *A perfect narrative of the whole proceedings* (1649): Wing W 9; *A continuation of the narrative* (1649): original Wing entry (C 5968) cancelled in Wing's second edn – because it is a continuation of W 9?; *The charge of the Commons against Charles Stuart* (1649): Wing E 2537.

While a conservative Parliament continued to treat with the King at Newport in the Isle of Wight even after the second war, the radical leadership in the New Model and in Parliament determined on bringing Charles Stuart, 'that man of blood' to justice for his crimes. (Crawford 1977). To accomplish their ends they had to purge Parliament and lean heavily on the often-reluctant members of the High Court of Justice whom they had appointed (Wedgewood 1964). The King here questions the authority of the Court and asserts his indubitable legal rights. As was by then his habit he insists that to override his legal rights is to override all legality whatsoever. The High Court, it will be noted, claims populist legality.

Saturday, 20 January, 1649
*Mr [John] Cook, Solicitor-General*: My Lord, in behalf of the Commons of England and of all the people thereof, I do accuse Charles Stuart, here present, of high treason and high misdemeanours; and I do, in the name of the Commons of England, desire the charge may be read unto him.
*The King*: Hold a little.
*Lord President*, [*John Bradshaw*]: Sir, the Court commands the charge to be read. If you have anything to say afterwards, you may be heard . . .
*Which the clerk then read as followeth*: That the said Charles Stuart, being admitted King of England, and therein trusted with a limited power to govern according to the laws of the land and not otherwise; and by his trust, oath and office being obliged to use the power committed to him for the good and benefit of the people and for the preservation of their rights and liberties; yet nevertheless out of a wicked design to erect and uphold an unlimited and tyrannical power to rule according to his will and to overthrow the rights and liberties of the people (yea, to take away and make void the

foundations thereof and of all redress and remedy of misgovernment, which by the fundamental constitutions of this kingdom were reserved on the people's behalf in the right and power of frequent and successive parliaments or national meeting in Council) he, the said Charles Stuart, for accomplishment of such his designs, and for the protecting of himself and his adherents in his and their wicked practices to the same ends, hath traitorously and maliciously levied war against the present Parliament and the people therein represented.

Particularly, upon or about the 30 June 1642, at Beverley in the county of York, [and from then until 1645 at York, Nottingham, '(where he set up his standard of war)', Edgehill, Keinton Field, Brainsford, Caversham Bridge, Gloucester, Newbury, Copredy Bridge, Bodmin, Leicester and Naseby]... and at many other places in this land at several other times within the years aforementioned and in the year 1646, he, the said Charles Stuart, hath caused and procured many thousands of the free people of the nation to be slain. And by divisions, parties and insurrections within this land, by invasions from foreign parts (endeavoured and procured by him) and by many other evil ways and means, he, the said Charles Stuart, hath not only maintained and carried on the said war both by land and sea during the years before mentioned, but also hath renewed, or caused to be renewed, the said war against the Parliament and good people of this nation, in this present year 1648... By which cruel and unnatural wars... much innocent blood of the free people of this nation hath been spilt, many families have been undone, the public treasury wasted and exhausted, trade obstructed and miserably decayed, vast expense and damage to the nation incurred, and many parts of the land spoiled, some of them even to desolation.

And for the further prosecution of his said evil designs, he... doth still continue his commissions to the [Prince of Wales] and other rebels and revolters, both English and foreigners, and to the earl of Ormond and to the Irish rebels and revolters associated with him, from whom further invasions upon this land are threatened, upon the procurement and on the behalf of the said Charles Stuart.

By all of which it appeareth that he, the said Charles Stuart, hath been and is the occasioner, author and contriver of the said unnatural, cruel and bloody wars, and therein guilty of all the treasons, murders, rapines, burnings, spoils, desolations, damage and mischief to this nation acted or committed in the said wars, or occasioned thereby. And the said John Cook, by protestation...

doth, for the said treasons and crimes, on behalf of the said people of England, impeach ... Charles Stuart as a tyrant, traitor, murderer, and a public and implacable enemy to the Commonwealth of England, and pray that the said Charles Stuart may be put to answer all and every the premises, that such proceedings, examinations [and] trials, sentence and judgement may be thereupon had as shall be agreeable to justice. ...

*The King*: I would know by what power I am called hither. I was not long ago in the Isle of Wight. How I came there is a longer story than I think is fit at this time for me to speak of, but there I entered into a treaty with both Houses of Parliament with as much public faith as it's possible to be had of any people in the world. I treated there with a number of honourable lords and gentlemen, and treated honestly and uprightly. I cannot say but they did very nobly with me. We were upon a conclusion of the treaty. Now I would know by what authority – I mean lawful (there are many unlawful authorities in the world, thieves and robbers by the highways) – but I would know by what authority I was brought from thence and carried from place to place, and I know not what. And when I know what lawful authority, I shall answer. Remember I am your King – your lawful King – and what sins you bring upon your heads, and the judgement of God upon this land. Think well upon it, I say, think well upon it, before you go from one sin to a greater. Therefore let me know by what lawful authority I am seated here and I shall not be unwilling to answer. In the meantime I shall not betray my trust. I have a trust committed to me by God, by old and lawful descent. I will not betray it to answer a new, unlawful, authority. Therefore resolve me that, and you shall hear more of me.

*Lord President*: If you had been pleased to have observed what was hinted to you by the Court at your first coming hither, you would have known by what authority – which authority requires you in the name of the people of England, of which you are elected King, to answer them. ... If you acknowledge not the authority of the Court, they must proceed.

*The King*: .... England was never an elective kingdom, but an hereditary kingdom for near these thousand years. Therefore let me know by what authority I am called hither. I do stand more for the liberty of my people than any here that come to be my pretended judges; and therefore let me know by what lawful authority I am seated here and I will answer it. Otherwise I will not answer it. ... Here is a gentleman (Lieutenant Colonel Cobbot). Ask him if he

did not bring me from the Isle of Wight by force. I do not come here as submitting to the Court. I will stand as much for the privilege of the House of Commons, rightly understood, as any man here whatsoever. I see no House of Lords here that may constitute a Parliament; and the King too should have been [a part of it]. Is this the bringing of the King to his Parliament? Is this the bringing an end to the treaty, in the public faith of the world? Let me see a legal authority, warranted by the word of God (the scriptures) or warranted by the constitutions of the kingdom, and I will answer.
*Lord President*: Sir, you have propounded a question and have been answered. Seeing you will not answer, the Court will consider how to proceed. In the meantime, those that brought you hither are to take you back again.

The Court desires to know whether this will be all the answer you will give, or no.
*The King*: Sir, I desire that you would give me and all the world satisfaction in this. Let me tell you it is not a slight thing you are about. I am sworn to keep the peace by that duty I owe to God and my country, and I will do it to the last breath of my body; and therefore you shall do well to satisfy first God, and then the country, by what authority you do it. If you do it by a usurped authority you cannot answer it. There is a God in heaven that will call you, and all that give you power, to account. Satisfy me in that and I will answer. . . . For I do avow that it is as great a sin to withstand lawful authority as it is to submit to a tyrannical or in any otherways unlawful authority. And therefore satisfy me in that and you shalt receive my answer.
*Lord President*: The Court expects you should give them a final answer. Their purpose is to adjourn till Monday next. . . .

Monday, 22 January
*The King*: . . . . If it were only my own particular case, I would have satisfied myself with the protestation I made last time I was here against the legality of this Court, and that a King cannot be tried by any superior jurisdiction on earth. But it is not my case alone; it is the freedom and the liberty of the people of England; and do you pretend what you will, I stand more for their liberties. For if power without law may make laws, may alter the fundamental laws of the kingdom, I do not know what subject he is in England that can be sure of his life or any thing he calls his own. . . .
*Lord President*: Sir, I must interrupt you, which I would not do, but that what you do is not agreeable to the proceedings of any

court of justice. You are about to enter into argument and dispute concerning the authority of this Court, before whom you appear as a prisoner and are charged as an high delinquent. If you take it upon you to dispute the authority of the Court, we may not do it, nor will any court give way unto it. . . . It is fit there should be law and reason, and there is both against you. Sir, the vote of the Commons of England assembled in Parliament, *it* is the reason of the kingdom, and they are these that have given . . . that law according to which you should have ruled and reigned. Sir, you are not to dispute our authority. . . it will be taken notice of that you stand in contempt of the Court and your contempt will be recorded accordingly.

*The King*: I do not know how a King can be a delinquent. But by any law that ever I heard of, all men (delinquents or what you will) . . . may put in demurrers against any proceedings, as [il]legal; and I do demand that, and demand to be heard, with my reasons. If you deny that you deny reason.

*Lord President*: . . . . Sir, neither you or any man are permitted to dispute that point. You are concluded. You may not demur the jurisdiction of the Court. If you do, I must let you know that they over-rule your demurrer. They sit here by the authority of the Commons of England; and all your predecessors, and you, are responsible to them.

*The King*: I deny that. Show me one precedent. . . .

*Lord President*: Sir, you are not to have liberty to use this language. How great a friend *you* have been to the laws and liberties of the people, let all England and the world judge.

*The King*: Sir, under favour, it was the liberty, freedom, and laws of the subject that I ever . . . defended . . . with arms. I never took up arms against the people, but for the laws.

*Lord President*: The command of the Court must be obeyed. No answer will be given to the charge.

Saturday, 27 January

*The Lord President*: then proceeded to the grounds of the sentence: . . . that the law was [the King's] superior, and that he ought to have ruled according to the law. The difference was, who should be the expositors of the law (whether he and his party, out of the Courts of Justice, or the Courts of Justice, nay the sovereign and high court of justice, the Parliament of England, that is not only the highest expounder of the law, but the sole maker of the law); and that for him and those that adhere to him to set themselves against it, was not law; that what some of his own party had said, *rex non habet parem in regno*, was granted, but though he was *major singulis*, yet he was *universis minor*; that the barons of old, when the Kings played the tyrants, called them to account, that they did *frenum ponere* [put a bridle on them]; that if they did forbear to do their duty now, and were so mindful of their own honours and the kingdoms' as the barons of old were, certainly the Commons of England would not be unmindful of what was for their preservation and safety; that if the King went contrary to that end, he must understand that he is but an officer in trust, and they to take order for the punishment of such an offending governor; that this is not a law of yesterday, upon the division of him and his people, but of old, and that the King's oath implied as much; and where the people could not have any other remedy, the Parliament were to do it, who were ordained to redress the grievances of the people. (The Parliaments were to be kept, we find in old authors, twice in the year, that the subject might, upon any occasion, have remedy)... that it was no new thing to cite precedents where the people, when power was in their hands, have made bold to call their Kings to account; that it would be too long a time to mention either France, Spain, the Empire, or other countries... and what the Tribunes of Rome were heretofore, and the Ephori of the Lacedemonian state, that was the Parliament of England to the English state; that he needed not to mention those foreign stories: if he looked but over Tweed... no kingdom had more plentiful experience than [Scotland] hath of the deposition and punishment of their offending and transgressing Kings (and to go not too far for example, the King's grandmother set aside, and his father, an infant, crowned). And there wants no examples here in England, both before and since the conquest, as King Edward II and Richard II were so dealt with by the Parliament... And for succession by inheritance, it was plain, from the conquest, that of twenty-four Kings, one half of them came in by the State...

After the Lord President had cited many things to this purpose in relation to the power of Kings and their being called to account for breach of trust, and expressed in what sense this present King had been guilty, according to the charge of being a tyrant, traitor, murderer and public enemy to the commonwealth, [he said that it was their duty] to do that which the law prescribes. They were not there *jus dare*, but *jus dicere*, [not to make law but to state what it was]... We may not acquit the guilty. What the sentence of law affirms to a traitor, a tyrant, a murderer and a public enemy to the country: that sentence he was to hear read unto him.

*Then the clerk read the sentence drawn up in parchment*: That whereas the Commons of England in Parliament had appointed them an High Court of Justice for the trying of Charles Stuart, King of England, before whom he had been three times convented, and at the first time a charge of high treason and other crimes and misdemeanours was read, in the behalf of the Kingdom of England, etc. (here the clerk read the charge). Which charge being read unto him as aforesaid, he, the said Charles Stuart, was required to give his answer, but refused to do so . . . For all which treasons and crimes, this Court doth adjudge that he, the said Charles Stuart, as a tyrant, traitor, murderer and public enemy, shall be put to death by the severing of his head from his body.

*Part four*
# ROYALISTS AGAINST RESISTANCE, 1642–1643

## 4.1 THE ORTHODOX CASE AGAINST REBELLION

From John Bramhall, *The serpent-salve* (1643), 52–3: Wing B 4236.

Bishop Bramhall (1594–1663) is perhaps most famous as one who wrote against Hobbes's politics (Bowle 1951) and his philosophical–theological doctrines of materialism and the necessitation of the will (Minz 1970). He was a member of the Court of High Commission, then chaplain and helper of Strafford in Ireland, before he was made bishop of Derry in 1643. He joined the Earl of Newcastle's northern royalist army as Newcastle's chaplain when the war broke out, and went in to exile with Newcastle on its defeat in 1644. He was rewarded at the Restoration with the archbishopric of Armagh. His moderate royalist constitutionalism stands in contrast to the hectoring, impatient suprematism of his fellow Irish bishop, Williams (see headnote to [2.1]; Daly 1971; Sanderson 1974), but nevertheless he would allow no resistance, even to a supreme power which breached the law and threatened religion. In this he echoed the Tudor homilies on *Obedience* (1547) and *Rebellion* (1571). This was the orthodox teaching of the Anglican Church and was repeated endlessly by royalist clerics (Morris 1953; Figgis 1896). Bramhall makes the case very briefly compared with many.

There is the law of God, there is the last will and testament of our Saviour, by which we hold our hopes of happiness, which to Christians must be as the pillar of fire to the Israelites, a direction when to go, where to stay. Here we read of tyrants and of the sufferings of the Saints, but not a word of any tacit trusts and reservations, or of any . . . rebellion against nature, or dispensation with oaths, nor of any resistance by arms. Certainly there is no one duty more pressed upon christians by Christ and his apostles than obedience to superiors. *Give unto Caesar that which is Caesar's*, saith our Saviour. *Submit yourselves to every ordinance of man for the Lord's sake* saith S. Peter. *Put them in mind to be subject to principalities and powers* saith S. Paul – and in that well known place to the Romans: *Let every soul be subject to the higher powers; whosoever resisteth the powers resisteth the ordinance of God, and they that resist shall receive to themselves damnation*. . . .

But is there no remedy for a christian [in case of tyranny]? Yes: three remedies.

The first is to cease from sin . . . A good King is God's right hand; a bad his left hand, a scourge for our sins. As we suffer with patience an unfruitful year, so we must do an evil prince sent by God . . . Said Aquinas, 'Remove our sins, and God will take away his rod.' The second remedy is prayers and tears. *In that day you shall cry unto the Lord because of your King* (*1 Samuel* vii. 18). S. Nazianen lived under five persecutions and never knew other remedy. He ascribed the death of Julian to the prayers and tears of christians. Jerem[iah] armed the Jews with prayers for Nebuchadnezar, not with . . . daggers. S. Paul commands to make prayers and supplications for Kings, not to give poison to them. S. Peter could have taken vengeance with a sword as well on Herod as Ananias, but that he knew that God reserves Kings for his own tribunal. . . . And when Saul had slain the priests of God and persecuted David, yet saith David: *Who can stretch forth his hand against the Lord's anointed and be guiltless*? (*1 Samuel* xxvi. 9). It was duty, and not a singular desire of perfection that held David's hand. Who can stretch out his hand? No man can do it. The third remedy is flight. This is the uttermost which our Master hath allowed. *When they persecute you in one city, fly unto another* (*Matthew* x. 23). But a whole kingdom cannot fly! Neither was a whole kingdom ever persecuted by a lawful prince; private men tasted of Domitian's cruelty but the provinces were well governed; the raging desires of one man cannot possibly extend to the ruin of all. Nor is this condition hard for subjects: *This is thankworthy, if a man for conscience towards God endure grief* (*1 Peter* ii. 19); and *If a man suffer as a christian, let him glorify God on this behalf* (*1 Peter* iv. 16). This way hath ever proved successful to the christian religion. The blood of the martyrs is the blood of the church.

## 4.2 'TOUCH NOT THE LORD'S ANOINTED'

From [John Spelman], *Certain considerations upon the duties both of prince and people* (Oxford, 1642), 13–16: Wing S 4937.

Sir John Spelman (1594–1643), lawyer, antiquary and MP, was knighted in 1641 and was himself the eldest son of a famous antiquary and knight, Sir Henry Spelman. One of the more talented royalist propagandists and a member of the King's inner circle at Oxford during the first war, he died of camp fever. Here he glosses a favourite royalist biblical story from *1 Samuel* xxiv and xxvi, and *2 Samuel* i. The figure of David was to haunt the debates concerning the legitimacy of the Rump and of Cromwell's assumption of power in 1653: anointed himself, and a 'type' of the redeeming Christ, David at once pronounced authoritatively against resistance yet came to power himself by the sword. He was as much of the 'type' of the guerrilla and mercenary as of the Prince of Peace (Pocock 1973a). The sins of obvious revolutionaries, like Korah and those with 'itching ears', were much more unambiguous.

Saul was King, but misgoverning himself and the kingdom, became as bad as excommunicate and deposed, for he was rejected of God, and David was by God's express command anointed to be King. All which notwithstanding neither David nor the people ever sought to depose him, to renounce obedience unto him, to combine against him, question his government, or so much as meddle with ordering any of the affairs that belonged to the King. Nay, Saul after this persecuted David unjustly, and in the midst of his unjust and hostile persecution was delivered into David's hand, and it was of necessity that David should take advantage and kill him for he could not otherwise have any assurance of his own life. David did then but even cut the skirt of Saul's garment, to the end it might witness his faithful loyalty, because it made it manifest he could as easily have cut the thread of his life. And even for this, his heart so smote him as that he cries out: *The Lord forbid that I should do this thing to my master the Lord's anointed, to stretch forth my hand against him*... Now whatsoever Saul was, or whatsoever he had done, neither his falling from God, nor God's declaring him rejected, nor David's anointing by God's command, nor Saul's unjust persecution of David (the Lord's anointed [as future king]) could dissolve the duty of his subjects nor make it lawful for them to lay their hands on him, no not when he was in wicked hostility against them. But Saul, in David's account, was still the Lord's anointed, still a sacred person, still David's master notwithstanding the circumstances which might seem to have discharged the ties of duty which David and the people did formerly owe unto him.

Neither is the anointing of Kings a thing sacred as to their own subjects only, but the regard thereof is required at the hands of strangers also because of the profanation and sacrilege that in the violation of their persons is committed even against God. Wherefore we see that though the Amalekite were a stranger and made a fair pretence that he had done Saul a good office when, at his own request, he despatched him of the pain of his wounds and of the pangs of approaching death, yet David . . . makes a slight account of the causes which he pretended, as a frivolous extenuation of an heinous fact, and condemns him, though a stranger, as an heinous delinquent against the majesty God. *How wert thou not afraid . . . to stretch forth thy hand and destroy the Lord's annointed*? Neither his being a stranger nor any other circumstances were so available, but that his blood fell deservedly upon his own head. . . . And therefore all actions of subjects, that in the progress of them tend or by the way threaten to arrive at that upshot, are unlawful, foul and wicked – and not only the actors themselves wicked, but their assistants, favourers, those that wish them well. [They], as St. John speaks, *that bid them God speed, are partakers of their evil deeds*.

But error in this point has made such impressions in the minds of many as that they will never be persuaded but that they may disobey and resist authority if ever they find it faulty, or the commands thereof not agreeing with their consciences. They will grant that they may not disobey authority in the lawful commands therefore, neither do evil that good may come thereon. But then they themselves will be the judges what commands are lawful, and what, not; what things are good, and what evil; and so they make obedience arbitrary, and government – by pretending conscience – at the discretion of the subject. Yea, though the things wherat they take check be of their own nature indifferent or doubtful (and therefore not matters of faith) yet will not they submit themselves nor their opinions unto any . . . But they from the authority of their own opinions or from the authority of such preachers as they themselves have chosen to be their guides, they will both censure, disobey and revile the ordinances of their church and the governors thereof, so secure in opposing imaginary or at least unproved superstition as they will not see how incompatible self-will, presumption, disobedience, arrogance and railing are with true religion. Nor [will they see] that the false teachers and their disciples, which our Saviour and his Apostles foretold should be in the last and perilous times and which St. Peter calleth *cursed children*, are not only described by this: (that they *have the form of Godliness but deny the power thereof; that they are in sheep's clothing but are inwardly wolves*; . . . that their way of working is after the way of private *insinuation, creeping* *into houses and leading silly women captive*; having *itching ears*;... that they be *they that separate themselves*, and the like) but they are especially described to be *traitorous, heady, high-minded*, to be such as *despise government*, as are *presumptuous, self-willed*, and not afraid to *speak evil of dignities*. And they *perish in the gainsaying of Korah*.* Now we know that the sin of Korah was that he, being a Levite and countenanced by an hundred and fifty princes of the Assembly... and at least 14,700 of the people, upon his own private opinion, to which his followers adhered (that both he, and all the congregation were holy, and might offer incense before the Lord as well as Aaron [the chief priest, as head of the family of Levi]) charged Moses and Aaron that they took too much upon them and that they exalted themselves above the congregation of the Lord. And therefore they holding themselves in a parity of authority with them, would not appear on their summons nor be obedient unto them. Yet (as if these passages in scripture nothing concern our times) we are nothing shy of those things whereof they do admonish us.

## 4.3 THE 'GOLDEN CHAIN' OF SUBORDINATION

From Peter Heylyn, *The rebells catechism* (Oxford, 1643), 15–17: Wing H 1731.

Difficulties were presented to the royalist position by the Calvinist and parliamentarian – originally Lutheran (Skinner 1978, II) – claim that subordinate magistrates were owed obedience as much as superior ones, and that if Charles acted outside his authority they might command the people to resistance against him (see [5.2] and headnotes below esp.). Heylyn (1600–62) had already proved himself a waspish and learned champion of high-flying royalism and Anglicanism, when, as one of Charles' chaplains, he joined the King at Oxford. A royalist analogue of Parliament's John Milton – he was rapidly going blind – he was to issue a stream of propaganda in books and pamphlets and as editor of the royalist newsbook, *Mercurius Aulicus*. He argued his case against resistance most fully in his *Stumbling-block of disobedience* which was published in 1658 but written during the first civil war. Here, in the *Rebells catechism*, he answers the worrying part of Parliament's case, marrying the scholastic logic of classification taught in the universities with normal royalist exegesis of *Romans* xiii.

*Ques*. Perhaps we may so far agree with you as to disable private persons from bearing arms and lifting up their hands against Kings

* Spelman quotes the following passages in the margin: 2 *Timothy* iii. 5–6; 2 *Peter* ii. 10; *Jude* 8, 11; and (on Korah) *Numbers* xvi.

and princes of their own authority. But think you that inferior magistrates are not enabled by their offices to protect the people and arm them (if occasion be) in their own defence?

*Ans.* 'Tis true that some divines of the reformed churches, who either lived in popular states or had their breeding at Geneva or thought the discipline by them defended could not otherwise be obtruded upon Christian princes than by putting the sword into the hands of the people, have spared no pains to spread about this dangerous doctrine, in which they have not wanted followers in most parts of Christendom. But S. Paul knew of no such matter when he commanded every soul to yield obedience and *subjection* to the *higher powers*, and upon no occasion to *resist* those *powers* to which the Lord had made them *subject*. So that although inferior magistrates may expect obedience from the hands of those over whom and for whose weal and governance they are advanced and placed by the prince in chief, yet God expects that they should yield obedience to the powers above them, especially to the highest of all, than which there is not any higher. There is a golden chain in polities, and every link thereof hath some relation and dependence on that before. So far forth as inferior magistrates do command the people according to that power and those instruments which is communicated by them the supreme prince, the subject is obliged to submit unto them without any manner of resistance. Men of no public office must obey the Constable, the Constable is bound to speed such warrants as the next Justice of the Peace shall direct unto him, the Justices receive the exposition of the law from the mouth of the Judges, the Judges have no more authority but what is given them by the King. And thereupon it needs must follow that though the Judges direct the Justices, and the Justices command the Constables, and the Constables may call the people to their aid if occasion be, yet all must yield a free obedience without reluctancy or resistance to the King himself. The reason is because, as Kings or *supreme magistrates* are called *God's ministers* by S. Paul, so the inferior magistrates are called the King's ministers by S. Peter. *Submit yourselves* [Peter says] *to the King as unto the supreme*, next, to such *governors as are sent* (or authorised) *by him for the punishment of evil doers*. Besides there is no inferior magistrate of what sort soever but as he is a public person in respect of those that are beneath him, so is he but a private man in reference to the powers above him, and therefore as a private person, disabled utterly (by your own rules) from having any more authority to resist his sovereign or bear arms against him, as any other of the common people. The government of states may be compared most properly unto Porphiry's tree, in which there is one *genus summum*, and many *genera subalterna*. Now 'tis well known to every young logician who hath learned his *predicables*, that [a] *genus subalternum* is a species only as it looks up to those above it, a genus in relation unto those below it. If you have so much logic in you as to make application of this note to the present case, you will perceive inferior magistrates to be no magistrates at all as they relate unto the King, the *genus summum* in the scale of government, and therefore of no more authority to resist the King or call the people unto arms than the meanest subject.

*Part five*
# PARLIAMENT'S RESISTANCE, 1642–1644

## 5.1 PARLIAMENT'S MINIMAL CLAIM

From Charles Herle, *An answer to Doctor Ferne's reply* (1643), 47: Wing F 1552; and his *A fuller answer to a treatise written by Doctor Ferne* (1642), 1–2: Wing F 1558.

A Presbyterian minister, Herle (1598–1659) was one of Parliament's more effective propagandists, turning the doctrine of mixed government against a King who was responsible for reviving it (headnotes to [3.4] and [8.5]). He was trusted by Parliament to license books on divinity, and was nominated Prolocutor of the Westminister Assembly on the death of its first head, Dr William Twiss. Restrained in his hatreds, and a constitutionalist, he could not stomach the events of 1648–49 and retired to Lancashire, where it is said he sheltered his old patron, James Stanley, 7th Earl of Derby, after the earl's disastrous attempt to recoup the royalist military losses of the second war. In these extracts he set out the claims he made on behalf of Parliament, indicates their source, and shows their relationship with those of other parliamentarian writers.

### *5.1.1 Herle's fuller answer*

1. A Parliament of England may with good conscience, in defence of King, laws and government established, when imminently endangered, especially when actually invaded, take up arms without and against the King's personal commands, if he refuse [to defend them].
2. The final and casting result of the States' ['Estates'] judgement concerning what these laws, dangers and means of preservation are, resides in the two Houses of Parliament.
3. In this final resolution of the States' judgement the people are to rest; and in obedience thereto may with good conscience, in defence of the King, laws and government, bear and use arms

### *5.1.2 Herle's answer*

The truth is, I, it may be more than the rest, declined the making use of self-defence as the main ground of arms being taken up, as – however questionless a ground sufficient, and every day more and more discovering its warranty – yet liable to . . . exceptions, such as are apt to fall within those limits of *justa & inculpata* [blameless justification] which the casuists add to *sui tutela* [self-defence]; and [I] therefore chose rather to insist on that power which the laws of the land – as His Majesty confesses in . . . his *Answer to the nineteen propositions* – places . . . . in the Court of Parliament . . . . As His Majesty doth not, so no man can question but that they are without his actual concurrence able . . . . by way of judgement as a Court to pursue delinquents to justice, if need be with arms, beyond any restraint of His Majesty's either commands or engagement.

## 5.2 THE SCRIPTURAL WARRANT FOR RESISTANCE

From [Herbert Palmer, etc.], *Scripture and reason pleaded for defensive armes* (1643), 3–5, 9–10: Wing P 244; William Bridge, *The wounded conscience cured* (1642), [15]: Wing B 4476.

### *5.2.1 Palmer*

*Scripture and reason*, by 'divers reverend and learned divines', was in the main the work of Herbert Palmer (1601–47). Palmer was already the author of a catechism as authoritarian as any displayed in Part 1, and in fact was to play the leading role in the production of the Westminster Assembly's Shorter Catechism with its orthodox rendering of the duties required by the Fifth Commandment. Here, however, in defence of Parliament, ordered printed by Parliament itself, he and his clerical colleagues may be observed adumbrating the doctrine that political authority inheres in the office and not the man, and that, moreover, the officers are limited in their rights to command obedience by the purpose for which the office they fill exists. Nevertheless, Presbyterians of Palmer's stamp were vigorously to assert in 1649 that their intentions had been 'not to bring his majesty to justice, as some now speak, but to put him in a better capacity to do justice' (*the dissenting ministers justification*); and Palmer's old colleagues disavowed any connection with the seclusions, purges and illegal actions of the revolutionary Army and Parliament. The 'presbyterians', as Milton famously alleged in his *Tenure of kings and magistrates* (1649), had nevertheless produced a theory which could be used to justify king-killing. Whether they intended it or not they were 'monarchomachs'.

Thus the case I suppose is understood . . . by the general of those that take the King's part against the Parliament: that neither the King in person, nor any of his officers and soldiers that have a commission from him may be resisted, because that were to resist the King, which say they all, the Apostle forbids and threatens [damnation as a sanction]. But here I blame [Dr Ferne's] negligent handling of that place, upon divers considerations: . . . .

The first verse begins . . . *Let every soul be subject to the higher powers*. Here are two questions: what is meant by 'subject'; what is meant by 'higher powers'. By being 'subject' is meant yielding obedience, either active or at least passive – i.e. doing or forbearing according to command or [else] submitting and suffering when one does otherwise. It cannot be denied but both these are parts of subjection and that so much is commanded by the word υποτασσεσθω [hypotassestho = 'subject itself']. . . . But the second question: what is meant by 'higher powers' will clear in what cases either of these is required. By the 'higher powers' is meant all civil and legal authority, which in S. Peter's phrase is of the *King as supreme*, or *governors* (for these [governors] are higher than the people though lower than the King). But it is to be observed that the word is in the abstract, 'powers', which notes the authority wherewith the person in authority is legally invested and not the person in the concrete, lest that might be understood as the personal commands, without or beyond, or even against, his authority. Which conceit the Apostle doth greatly prevent [by] using the word 'power', which he doth also all the while he treats of this matter, except only that once he names 'rulers', verse 3 of [*1 Peter* ii].

It is to be observed that the things about which authority (and so subjection) in this place is conversant are civil matters belonging to the Second Table . . . Not that I deny magistrates to have authority to command things belonging to the First Table, and that subjection is due to them in such commands concerning religion (so that it be according to the word of God). But I say that this is to be fetched from texts other than this. My reason is, because the Roman magistrates, of whom properly the Apostle speaks, were so far . . . from commanding things for religion that they commanded things against religion and the First Table. And therefore the active subjection at least here required is limited to civil matters.

And now that so much as I have said is required (active obedience to the legal, civil authority [of] all magistrates in their legal commands in civil matters – or at least passive yielding to the penalty of the laws in case of not obeying actively – and neither further than to legal commands of legal authority) appears in the

Apostle's reason in this first verse. *For there is no power but of God*, which he redoubles in the second phrase, *the powers that be are ordained of God*... Every soul must be under their order... because they are ordered by God under him, his deputies and vicegerents in their order and degree, higher and highest. This is true of all powers, and therefore to all must subjection be performed. And to none hath God ordered or ordained any authority but legal... None will deny [this] of other governors besides the supreme. So can none with reason affirm that *any* hath more authority than the laws, whether specific or general, written or unwritten, have allotted them.... And this our Doctor [actually] confesses... [regarding] active obedience: that [it] is no more due but according to the laws of God and the established laws of the land. Only he argues for passive obedience beyond this, everywhere, because he argues against resistance even of tyranny. But... if he be bound to be subject to tyranny... by virtue of the commandment here, then tyranny is the ordinance of God or magistrates have power ordained of God to use tyrannous violence....

Till God's ordinance can be proved allowing tyranny (which it never can be) or undeniably ordaining a man to suffer it (which is nowhere in His word... though often it is so in His providence, when He affords no means of resistance) this text of the Apostle will in no way condemn resisting by arms tyrannous and outrageous violences.

Who may not be resisted? The text saith, *the power*, any magistrate acting with lawful authority legally. The Doctor would restrain it to the supreme because he thinks it was hard to assert all governors irresistible, though tyrannous. But I say... the governor or magistrate may be no more resisted than the monarch. And the King is resisted in resisting the meanest officer. Even high treason may be committed by taking up arms with some circumstances against a magistrate who is not supreme. The laws cannot be obeyed but by obeying other governors in the King's absence (who cannot be everywhere); and so obstinate disobedience (which is resistance) may be when only a petty officer or magistrate is present but commands according to law...

The Apostle's reasons against resisters are:

1. *For rulers are not a terror to good works but to evil*: Now, is this a reason why I may not resist a tyrant? Who can be more terror to good works and not to evil than he that is bent to subvert religion, laws and liberties? *Ergo*, of such a resistance of a tyrant the Apostle speaks not, but of that ruler who goes altogether according to laws

and liberties . . .

2. A second reason or enforcement of the Apostle's argument against resistance is: *Wilt thou then not be afraid of the power? Do that which is good and thou shalt have praise of the same.* Now doth this argue a tyrant is not to be resisted? Is there no cause of fear of him (while a man does that which is good) that is bent to subvert religion, laws and liberties? Or shall a man have praise, in doing good, of such a tyrant? . . . .

4. The Apostle adds: *If thou do that which is evil, fear, for he beareth not the sword in vain: for he is the minister of God, a revenger to execute wrath upon him that doth evil* . . . A tyrant secures those that do evil (so they will join with him and serve him in his tyranny) from fear. And he bears the sword not only in vain, in reference to any good end intended by God's ordinance, but altogether contrary to it. [He] is so far from being the minister of God that he is . . . the minister of his own lusts, to shelter those that do evil, and to pursue with all wrath and revenge he that doth good and will not be a slave to his lawless designs and desires . . . Of such a tyrant S. Paul argues not that he may not be resisted, but him that he describes, which is a just governor, and so upon no terms to be resisted . . .

7. Finally, he concludes this matter with saying: *Render all their due.* By what law of God or man may a tyrant subvert religion, laws and liberties, or even be let alone in so doing? I am sure the Apostle hath not expressed any such thing hitherto. It is *ergo* but the Doctor's mistake though I confess it hath been many wise and good men's before him . . . All [the Apostle's] reasons go quite contrary unto, as describing the power and ruler that is to be subjected to and not resisted [as] altogether cross to tyranny; and his interpretation and assertion is altogether cross to the Apostle's.

## 5.2.2 *Bridge*

Originally suspicious of separation from a national church, though he stood for an anti-episcopal reformation, William Bridge (1600?–70) announced himself an 'independent' as co-author of the *Apologetical narration* (1644) in which the 'dissenting brethren' of the Westminister Assembly pleaded against an imposed uniformity of church doctrine, worship and discipline (printed and discussed in Haller 1934). Here, in 1642, Bridge replies to the royalist Dr Henry Ferne (headnote [7.1]) in an exchange on another familiar biblical text on resistance. Ferne had held that Elisha's example showed only that 'personal defence is lawful against sudden and illegal assaults of . . . messengers' (*Resolving of conscience*, 5–6). Bridge, in a passage of Protestant casuistry in the service of Parliament, shows that this 'case' teaches far otherwise. Wallace (1968) discusses the casuistical temper of the civil war debates.

Then the Doctor saith Elisha's example speaks very little, [only] . . . 'that personal defence is lawful against the sudden and illegal assaults of such messengers, yea of the prince himself, thus far [as] to ward off his blows, to hold his hand and the like' . . . .

If you may ward his blows and hold his hands, this is more than praying and crying and suffering. Suppose the King has an army with him? How can you hold an army's hand without an army? . . . This instance of Elisha tells us that messengers sent by the King to take away any man's life may be taken prisoners. Is not that a resistance? For Elisha said: *see you that son of a murderer hath sent to take away my head? Look, when the messenger cometh, shut the door, and hold fast at the door* (*2 Kings* vi. 32).

Then the Doctor distinguisheth betwixt a personal defence and a general resistance by arms. He saith a personal defence may be without all offence and doth not strike at the order and power that is over us, as a general resistance by arms doth.

But why was Elisha's defence personal? Because he was one person that was defended? Then if one man defend himself against a thousand in arms, that is personal defence? Or was it personal because only the person of the prophet made defence and had none to assist him? Not so, because he spake to the elders to shut the door and hold him fast. And if that act of Elisha's was contrary to the King's command why did it not immediately strike at the order and power that was over him, as our resistance doth now? Indeed if subjects, as private men strengthened with no authority, should gather together in a rude multitude to oppose laws and governors, then that work should strike immediately at the order and power and life of the state. But that the state should send out an army to bring delinquents to be tried in the highest Court of the kingdom that justice and judgement may run down like water which hath been staunched up, is rather to confirm and strengthen the order and power and authority.

And so it is in our case.

## 5.3 THE LEGAL RIGHT TO RESIST

From [Henry Parker], *A political catechism* (1643): Wing P 416. The tract is fully reprinted in Weston (1965, App. II).
Herle, Prynne and others often argued that the law provided that

Parliament might resist the illegal encroachments of Kings [6.2; 8.5]. In *Scripture and reason*, 'To the Reader', it had been suggested that the reader might 'peruse' the King's *Answer to the XIX propositions* [3.4], 'as one of which a political catechism might be drawn to instruct the people'. Palmer had seen that there the King seemed to have made (and admitted) a legal case for Parliament's right to resist, and one much less clumsy than was required in the reproduction of ancient precedent and rehearsal of legal opinion. Henry Parker (1604–52), Parliament's most effective controversialist, and, together with Philip Hunton, the most gifted in the skills of logic (Allen 1938; Judson 1936; Jordon 1942) seems to have taken up the challenge. His point, that Parliament was admitted to have a legal power 'more than sufficient to resist tyranny', was to be endlessly iterated in parliamentarian tracts.

*Ques. 22* But if there be an attempt (or danger) that the King's favourites and followers go about to change this regulated monarchy into an arbitrary government, and so into a tyranny, is there authority in the Houses sufficient . . . to remedy this?
*Ans.* Power legally placed in both Houses is 'more than sufficient to prevent and restrain the power of tyranny' (p. 20).
*Obs[ervations]*

1. Then at least whatever power is necessary to prevent or restrain the power of tyranny is confessed to be legally placed in both Houses, for else there is not power sufficient, much less 'more than sufficient'.

2. Then it is lawful for the two Houses to raise arms to defend themselves in case an army be raised against them, for else they have not power sufficient to restrain the power of tyranny. There is no greater power of tyranny than to raise arms against the Houses of Parliament; and there is no way to restrain this tyranny but by raising arms in their own defence. Less than this cannot be sufficient.

3. If a legal power be placed in them not only to 'restrain' but to 'prevent' the power of tyranny, then they are the legal judges when there is danger of tyranny; and they have legal power to command their judgement to be obeyed for prevention as well as restraint of tyranny.

4. Then it is lawful for them to provide for their own and the Kingdom's safety and they have a legal power to command the people to this purpose, not only when arms are actually raised against them but when they discern – and accordingly declare – a preparation made towards it. For if they let alone altogether the exercise of their power till arms are actually raised against them, they

may in all likelihood find it too late not only to prevent, but even to restrain the power of tyranny . . .

6. Then they have legal power to levy monies, arms, horse [and] ammunitions upon the subjects in such cases of danger, even without or against the King's consent. For it cannot be imagined that in such cases when the King's favourites and followers have gotten commands from him to protect them in their delinquencies and attempts to introduce tyranny, that he will ever consent to levies of monies against those favourites and followers or to be raising arms against them, specially he being still in their hands and among them, and not with his Parliament . . .

7. They that have made the *Protestation* to maintain and defend the power and privilege of Parliament may see in all these things . . . what is that power and what the privileges of Parliament, which they have so solemnly in the presence of Almighty God vowed, promised and protested to maintain.

8. And finally, since the two Houses of Parliament have so often and fully declared their intentions in settling the Militia, securing Hull and the magazine there, and the navy at sea – with the ports and forts – and afterward in raising arms under the command of the Earl of Essex, and last of all, levying monies by voluntary contributions and assessments, they have only used that legal power which is in them for the punishment of delinquents and for the prevention and restraint of the power of tyranny, of all of which, they are the legal judges. And all the subjects of this kingdom are bound by the laws to obey therein, and those doubly bound who that have made the late *Protestation*.

## 5.4 THE REASONABLENESS OF RESISTANCE

From *A few propositions shewing the lawfulnesse of defence against the injurious attempts of outrageous violence* (1643), [1]–[4]. [5]–[6], [9]–[10]: Wing F 836.

Ordered printed by Parliament on 8 June 1643, this anonymous pamphlet appeals to the 'law of nature' and to 'reason' as the grounds of resistance. It leaves scriptural exegesis to the divines and the legal case to the *Political catechism*. The formal and substantive characteristics of the law of nature and the nature and teachings of 'reason', were as much disputed in this period as any other (Woodhouse 1951; Sirluck 1959), but this much was clear: that it was easier to use them against a party in arms than it had been against the King before the wars began. Earlier, Charles could claim – with at least a colour of truth – to be ruling according to the positive law of the realm; but the war inevitably generated clear atrocities on both sides. The author, it will be noticed, does not mind 'private resistance' to violence, but the authority to command and organize it he envisages basically to remain with Parliament. His substantive teaching is that of Herle, Bridge and Parker, even though he appeals to a set of rules formally quite distinct from positive law, and partially distinguished from scriptural injunction.

1. By the law of nature it is lawful for anyone to defend themselves against any private person that assaults them to take away their lives or puts them in danger. Neither can it be that the law of any country can justly deny this; for all just laws are with respect to common safety, which is none at all if the lives of particulars may not be by themselves defended from private violence.

2. By the same law of nature it is lawful to defend themselves against any private man that would offer violence to their chastity. Neither can any law of any country justly deny this; for chastity is an inherent good, of which there can be no pretence why any should be robbed or deprived of it. And in one respect it is more inviolable than life; for there may be, and are, many cases wherein it is lawful to deprive others of their lives and for a man to yield up his own life patiently, but none wherein it is lawful to deprive them of their chastity or to yield that up, it being ever a sin against the law and life of nature.

3. By the law of nature also, it is further lawful for any to defend their goods from any private person that offers to take them violently away. And no law of any country can justly deny this defence of goods altogether; for otherwise they expose all the country to rapine and spoil. Only it must be remembered that in this case of goods (as also in lesser injuries to a man's person) Christian meekness, recommended and charged upon us by our Saviour (*Matthew* v. 39–40) requires that sometimes we suffer to some degree rather than defend ourselves even by law civil, and therefore much rather than by our own hand; namely, when our defence might endanger more harm to be done by us than we are like to suffer or to hazard our own suffering worse, and when our suffering may give hopes of overcoming evil with good or the like. But otherwise God nowhere disallows absolutely the defence of our very goods, and so of our persons, from the outrages of any private violence.

4. Moreover in any one of these cases [any]one may defend them-

selves against any officer or inferior magistrate that without all authority of law offers injurious assaults of outageous violence. No law of any country can justly deny this neither; for though there is no absolute necessity of this or that formality of law where the officer and his authority are known to all and there is an evidence notorious of the fact for which (by way of justice and punishment) the goods or life of any is taken away, yet otherwise such an officer or magistrate is no more privileged to do . . . any such act, altogether beyond the bound of his lawful office, than a private person is. But even any such officer and inferior magistrate is liable to punishment (even capital) for his robbery or murder practised or attempted by him as well as any private person when legally convicted of it. Though therefore there is (which is to be remembered) a constant honour due to every officer and magistrate according to his degree so long as he carries himself not altogether contrary to his office, yet when he attempts to do any such acts altogether contrary to his office . . . it cannot but in reason and justice be equally lawful to defend oneself against him and his assaults as against any private person.

5. The command of the supreme magistrate, without due process of law, to take away one's goods (unless his authority be absolute to lay what taxes he pleases upon any at any time) and much more the life of any, or (upon any pretence whatsoever) their chastity, can in no sort authorise any private person or even any officer or inferior magistrate so to do, or deprive the assaulted persons of their just defence before argued for. Neither can the law of any nation be supposed to contradict this: for as for goods, if the law subject them to the supreme magistrate's pleasure it makes or declares him then to be an absolute monarch and then his will any way manifested is sufficient process of law; but for life, there is not (neither can be justly), no not in the hand of the greatest monarch, any absolute authority to command the taking away the life of any merely at his own will and pleasure. For all monarchy, and even all authority among men, is primarily and principally for God's glory and then for the good of the whole society, and but subordinately for the honour and greatness of the monarch. But as it cannot be conceived how it should be to God's glory who hath so peremptorily forbidden the shedding of innocent blood, so is it not imaginable that it should be for the good of the whole society that any one man should have absolute power of the life of all the rest (or even of any one) merely at his own pleasure. [There is] no true good to the monarch himself, none to the commonwealth, and least of all to the

person of such a subject that should be put to suffer it; so that no such thing can in reason be liable to a command, but that still for all, [if] any should command against him in that sort, there is still the just liberty of defence by the law of nature forenoted. Whereunto may be added that no man can pretend any authority but what God in nature or scripture hath certainly given, or subjects have consented unto – at least in their ancestors – and it is certain that God hath given no man in nature or scripture any such authority to take away the lives of others at their own mere wills and pleasures. And neither can any nation, by the allowance of God in nature or scripture, consent that any should have such absolute power over their lives at pleasure. For they have it not themselves, and none can give another that power which they never had themselves . . .

11. Those that are appointed officers in any nation by law to preserve the peace are specially authorised by their places and offices to defend the innocent against such injurious assaults and . . . to charge all those that are under them . . . to join together in such defence, and moreover, for the apprehension of such malefactors as disturb the peace by such attempts of violence. Also, those that are under authority are bound . . . to join with such officers who legally charge them to help them keep the peace. And all this notwithstanding any pretended command from the supreme magistrate or his very presence offering to warrant violent outrages . . . No laws of any nation can be supposed to contradict even this wholly, for though laws may possibly make void all inferior officers' commands in the presence of the supreme, or in case any command from him prohibit them in any particular case, yet at least as private persons . . . they may defend themselves and their neighbours. And if the law of the nation doth not wholly suspend their authority upon the pleasure of the supreme, then even as officers they may defend and call to defence as aforesaid, as being the proper end of their offices . . .

19. When in any kingdom or commonwealth there are States ['estates'] or Parliaments which represent the whole body of the subjects, they are not only the public watchmen and Great Council of the kingdom but the great officers and chiefest Court of Justice of the whole kingdom, and so entrusted and charged above all others with the keeping of the peace and defence of the innocent all the kingdom over. And so their authority reaches throughout the whole kingdom . . . to command all inferior officers and magistrates and private persons to do their duties respectively . . . for the necessary defence of themselves, neighbours and the whole king-

dom, and to this end to arm themselves and march orderly into any part of the kingdom for the suppressing and preventing and apprehending of all notorious violators of the peace, or suspected practicers against it. No law of a kingdom that hath such State, such a Parliament, can rationally be supposed to deny them this authority . . .

20. . . . Whence it also follows undeniably that they may in such exigents of necessity appoint captains and other officers of war, and a General over all whose wisdom and authority may manage their authority to the right ends and purposes of it; and such they may invest with all necessary authority for the right ordering of their soldiers and all others for the common good – and this specially when the ordinary officers of justice, or captains of the soldiers . . . either will not join in such just and necessary defence, or have not skill to manage and conduct the forces. No law that yields to all that went before can be supposed to refuse this, which were utterly to disappoint the defence undertaken and reduce them into a worse condition than before . . . .

Thus far to show what the law of nature allows to all and the law of nations doth not deny to any, nor can be supposed rationally to forbid it. And this under what government soever, being but the voice of nature and nations. If any desire further to see how this agrees with the particular constitution of government in this nation I shall refer him for that to the *Political catechism* and the *Kingdom's case*.

## 5.5 THREE PARLIAMENTARIANS ON THE RIGHTS OF THE PEOPLE TO RESIST

From Herle, *A fuller answer*, 20–1 (see headnote to [5.1]; Bridge, *Wounded conscience*, [7], 24, 36–7 (see headnote to [5.2]); Jeremiah Burroughes, *A brief answer to Doctor Ferne's book* [1643], 2–3, [7]–[8], [10]–[11]: Wing B 6059.

Bridge and Herle, like most parliamentarians, were sensitive to royalist claims that Parliament's principles implied that 'the people' – the 'headless multitude' – might not only resist any magistrate they took to be a tyrant, but *ipso facto* had a power to constitute whom they would, if they would, to rule over them [7.1; 7.6; 7.8]. In these extracts they deny that this is the correct inference to draw. Jeremiah Burroughes (1599–1646), however, an 'independent' in religion, and co-author with Bridge of the *Apologetical narration*, was less squeamish. Tuck (1974) has discussed Burroughes's *Brief answer* as an example of how the civil war years saw a distinct movement away from the idea that magistrates had authority simply because they were legally entitled to their office, and towards the view that the particular actions of each magistrate must be examined to see whether they accorded with the purpose for which their authority existed. If they did not, then the magistrate might be resisted, whether he had title to act or not. In the extract below, Burroughes may be seen developing this new view, already evident enough in Palmer, Herle and Bridge; but it is only Burroughes who does not hesitate to draw the royalist inference: that if the actions of authorities are to be scrutinised there is no reason to deny that 'the people' should be the scrutineers. Nor is there any reason why they should not constitute authority anew if they find it necessary. Clearly, to be an 'independent' was not a sufficient condition for admitting the constitutive power of the people; but it helped, and (despite Franklin 1978) they did claim this. Others, more radical, were to follow them in this [10.4; 10.5; 11.4]. Herle exiled himself from the centre of power in 1648; Bridge later found he could live with the revolution, while opposing, it is true, the excesses of popular millenarianism. Palmer and Burroughes were dead by then, but it is hard to envisage Palmer approving the constitutional revolution, or Burroughes opposing it.

### *5.5.1 Herle*

A . . . question begged [by Ferne and other royalists] is, 'that in case the King and the Parliaments should *neither* discharge their trust, the people might rise and make resistance against both' – a position which no man I know maintains. The Parliament *is* the people's own consent, which once passed, they cannot revoke . . . We acknowledge no power can be employed but what is reserved, and the people have reserved no power from themselves in Parliament . . . . This reassumption of power is like the Pope's reassumption of the house of Loretto, a mere castle in the air of the Doctor's brain.

### *5.5.2 Bridge*

*Objection*: But if the power of the prince be derived from the people, then they may take away that power again.
*Response*: It follows not. Neither shall the people need to think of such an inference. Indeed if the power were derived from the people to the prince firstly, and that the people were so straight-laced that they would have no power left to defend themselves in case of danger when the prince is misled or unfaithful, then the people might be occasioned to think of deposing their prince. But that the power of the prince be originally from them, yet if they have so

much power left as in times of danger to look to their own preservation, what need they think of any such matter?
*Objection*: Why [not]? ... If the people give the power, then, if abused, they may take it away also.
*Response*: No, that needs not, seeing they never gave away that power of self preservation ... This position, of any, is the only way to keep people from such assaults, whereby the power of the prince is more fully established; whereas if people were kept from power of self-preservation which is natural to them, it were the only way to break all into pieces. For 'nothing violating nature lasts'.

.... There is not the same reason why the people should be so ready to think that the Parliament do neglect their trust, being that they are very many chosen out of the kingdom for their faithfulness, approved every way for their goodness and wisdom; whereas a prince may be born to the Crown, and so by virtue of his inheritance may rule though he be known to be vicious. As also because it is received by all the kingdom that we ought to be governed by laws, and the people well know that Parliament are better able to judge of the law than the prince is. As also because the people do actually elect and trust the Parliamentmen with the present affairs of the kingdom. Now [though] the prince indeed be trusted by our forefathers whereunto the people do now consent, yet there is not that actual election or designation of him unto the *present* affairs of the kingdom as there is of Parliamentmen chosen for these particular businesses ... and therefore the people take themselves bound to stand by their arbitrament. Neither can they think that they are at a like liberty to renounce their arbitrament and sentence as they are for denial of their prince's commandment ... If a people upon surmises that the Parliament do not perform their trust should call in their trust and their power then they should have left themselves naked of all authority and should be private men. But now that they look to themselves in this time of danger – and in *that* sense to reassume their power which they have derived to their prince – they are still led on by authority....

We desire all the world should know that we now take up arms as an act of self-preservation, not endeavouring or intending to thrust the King from his office, though for the present, [the] State sets some under the King at the stern till the waters be calmed.

### *5.5.3 Burroughes*

The Apostle says expressly *whosoever resists shall receive damnation.*

But he do not say expressly, whosoever resists the highest men should receive damnation, but whosoever shall resist the power. *Let everyone be subject* not to the wills of the highest men, but *to the higher power*. There is a good deal of difference between these two. The higher power, i.e. that authority that God and man hath put upon such a man, it is εξουσια [exousia = 'authority'], not δυναμις [dynamis = 'strength'], that must be subjected to, not resisted. We profess against resisting power, [in the sense] 'authority', though abused. If those who have power to make laws shall make sinful laws, and so give authority to any to force obedience, we say here that there must be either flying or passive obedience. But if one that is in authority command out of his own will and not by law, I resist no power, no authority at all if I neither actively nor passively obey; no, I do not so much as resist abused authority. This may seem strange at first, but if you think of it, you will believe it. The Doctor thinks the answer to this place is only from the limitation of the person or the cause of resisting, as if we held that no particular men upon any cause, but [only] States [i.e. estates] may resist upon such and such causes. Whereas we do not answer so, but we distinguish between the man that hath the power and the power of that man, and say [that] although the power may not be resisted according to the letter and the sense of the text, yet the illegal will and ways of the man may be resisted without the least offending against the text. . . . [This] is not resisting abused power, for it is resisting no power at all. Abused power is the ill use of what is given to men; but the ill use of what was never given to them more than to any other is abuse of their wills but not of their power. By 'power', I do not mean 'strength', but 'authority'. . . .

But if Parliament should so degenerate and grow tyrannical, what means of safety could there be for a state? I confess the condition of such a state would be very dangerous, and like to come to confusion. Parliament then could not help themselves, and the whole state ought to suffer much before it should help itself by any ways of resisting. But if you can suppose a Parliament so far degenerate as they should all conspire together with the King to destroy the kingdom, and to possess the lands and riches of the kingdom themselves; in this case, whether the law of nature would not allow standing up to defend ourselves, yea to reassume the power given to them, to discharge them of the power they had and set up some other, I leave to the light of nature to judge . . . The servant does not resist the 'power' of his master where he upon just grounds leaves him and goes to another, if he be such a master as is his master by his own choice, for such-and-such ends and purposes, and had his power limited by agreement.

I know this will be cried out as of dangerous consequence, wherefore God deliver us (as I hope He will) [from] ever making use of such a principle. It is hard to conceive it possible that a Parliament can so degenerate as to make our condition more grievous by unjust acts than it would be if the power in a kingdom should return to the law of nature from whence at first it rose.

## 5.6 THE PEOPLE IN THE MILLENIAL 'LAST DAYS': A ROYALIST–PARLIAMENTARIAN EXCHANGE

From Jeremiah Burroughes, *A brief answer* [16] (see headnote to [5.5]); Henry Hammond, *Of resisting the lawful magistrate upon colour of religion* (Oxford, 1644), 27–9: Wing H 557. This is the expanded version of the 1643 edition. I use the copy at the Bodleian, Pamph. D. 65 (30).

Millenial imagery, in which visions of the 'last days' of the war against Antichrist that would precede the rule of the 'Saints' on earth, had been commonly conjured up to exhort the parliamentarian host to battle. Burroughes's *Glimpse of Sion's glory* (1641) is a fine example of the genre (extracts in Woodhouse 1951; Prall 1968; attribution, Christianson 1978). Here Burroughes again adopts the millenial mode. It required a much more freely analogising method of scriptural interpretation than his casuistic exegesis of *Romans* xiii in [5.5.3]. Casuistry and millenarian analogising, though, supported the same conclusion. Dr Henry Hammond (1605–60), whose *Of resisting the lawful magistrate* is mainly devoted to normal royalist arguments against resistance, turned his attention to Burroughes's millenarianism in his last two pages, and in doing so showed some of the difficulty of fixing on precise contemporary denotations for the figures of *Revelations*: 'the merchants', the 'Kings', 'the whore', the 'voice of many waters', etc. Hammond became a royal chaplain in 1645, and was often with Charles in his last years. Millenarianism may have been an establishment mode of thought before the wars (Lamont 1969); but its dangers were all too evident to moderates and conservatives by 1642. No longer a weapon against popery and foreigners alone, it greatly extended its range of fire throughout the civil wars and interregnum ([10.7; 10.8]; Capp 1972; Toon 1970; Cohn 1962).

### *5.6.1 Burroughes*

There is a necessity in these times people's consciences should be further satisfied in their liberties . . . than formerly, because the time is (we hope) at hand for the pulling down of Antichrist. And we find by scripture that work at first will be by the people. *Revelation* xviii. 1–4: *The angel came down from heaven and cried mightily in a strong voice, Babylon the great is fallen, is fallen: And I heard another voice from heaven, saying, come out of her my people* . . . And so to the ninth verse [where] her destruction is threatened. Now verse nine . . . says: *The kings of the earth who have committed fornication and lived deliciously with her, shall bewail her, and lament for her, saying,* [verse 10] *alas, alas;* [and verses eleven and fifteen say:] *And the merchants of those things that were made rich by her shall stand weeping and wailing.* No marvel then that so many Proctors get together to seek for peace on any terms.

Here you see Babylon must fall down, and yet the Kings lament her fall. Who must pull her down but the people? Not that the people can raise a war merely for religion. But God will so order things that the papists shall by their malice be put upon such plots and enterprises that they shall make themselves liable to the justice of the law, so the Kings shall have no legal power to rescue them from it, but the inferior magistrates assisted by the people shall in a just way fall upon them, even then, when the Kings of the earth and their merchants shall lament them. Hence [in] *Revelation* xix. 6, the *Hallelujah* that is begun upon the Lord God Omnipotent's reigning is begun by the people: *I heard the voice as of many waters, saying, Hallelujah.* Now the scripture frequently sets forth the people by 'waters', as [in] *Revelation* xvii. 15 . . . Surely the right knowledge of these liberties God hath given the people will much help forward the great things God hath to do in this latter age.

Let Babylon fall; let the Church prosper; it is enough. Our lives are not much worth.

### *5.6.2 Hammond*

As for the evidence of that Revelation-rule that the commonalty, in opposition to their Kings, must have the great stroke in executing God's judgement on Antichrist (proved *Revelation* xviii. 4, 6, 9), I must answer that I never wonder enough at the power of prejudice evinced in this Objector by what he hath put together to this purpose to prove that the people, contrary to their Kings, shall destroy Antichrist. This is thought by him sufficient evidence, that, 'the people are commanded to go *out of her*' (verse 4), when (verse 9) it follows that the *Kings of the earth shall bewail her, and lament for her.* The unconcludingness of this argument I shall not insist on, but only look forward to another place which he cites immediately,

*Revelation* xvii. 17, where the *ten Kings* are said to *hate the Whore, and make her desolate*.... Where it is for the Objector's turn, the *Kings of the earth* must signify their persons in opposition to their people; but where it is not for his turn (*Revelation* xvii), there the word 'Kings' must signify the people, or any but the King. Would not the spirit of meekness have easily compounded this business and have given the word 'Kings' leave in both places to signify both their persons and their realms, and to have reconciled the places so that some kings with their kingdoms should bewail her, and some again hate her? They bewail her that continued with her until her destruction, when they see the smoke of her burning (xviii. 9); and others hate her who had once tasted of her filthiness and repented and left her before. This were very agreeable to the texts (if we had not peremptorily resolved to fetch some other sense out of them). That first place, alone by itself, concludes only thus much: that good men come or are exhorted to come out from Antichrist and avenge the Whore; and earthly men that love her, bewail her; but not that either the first are all common people – for sure, Kings may be called God's people, or be in that number – or the second none but Kings....

It seems Antichrist must never be cast out of a kingdom till the people do it in spite of the King! And therefore it is concluded that it was not done here in the days of King Edward, nor Queen Elizabeth, nor King James; and now, since the new revelations have assured men that Antichrist must now be cast out utterly from amongst us, it is become necessary that our sovereign should be a papist, and as much zeal and as solid arguments used to persuade our friends that indeed he is so (though his constant words and actions evidence the contrary) as are produced to maintain any other article of our new Saints' belief. One of the most suspected and hated heresies of these days is to doubt of the popish affections of our superiors, especially the King. Well, by this doctrine, if the King should chance not to be a papist, he must turn to be one, or else popery cannot be cast out in his time. If so he should do (turn papist on purpose to prepare or dispose his kingdom to turn Antichrist out) this might be answerable to God's hiding of truths to that end, to help Antichrist in. But should His Majesty prove so malicious to prove protestant in earnest, then what would become of that sure word of prophecy that so many have been persuaded to depend upon, that Antichrist must now be cast out of this kingdom? (which, saith the Objector, cannot be, unless the people do it, while the King bewails).

*Part six*
# SOVEREIGNTY

## 6.1 THE NECESSARY NATURE OF SOVEREIGN POWER

From Thomas Hobbes's translation of his Latin *De Cive* (1642) – *Philosophical rudiments concerning government and society* (1651), Part II, Ch. 6, extracted from Molesworth (1839–, vol. 2). (Howard Warrender is preparing a new edition of *De Cive*, which will supersede all others.)

Thomas Hobbes (1558–1679) is justly the most celebrated of English political thinkers and the object of many studies (e.g. Oakeshott 1946; Macpherson 1962; Brown 1965, Goldsmith 1966; McNeilly 1968; Pocock 1971; King 1974; Tuck 1979). Two features of his doctrine of sovereignty are worth noting here. First, that he entirely eschews recourse to legal or historical argument to demonstrate the rationally necessary nature of sovereignty. He deduces it from the universal desire of self-preservation among men taken in conjunction with a brilliantly expounded detailing of what life would be like where there was no sovereign power. In the extract printed the reader can observe the deductive process at work, though he stated the axioms elsewhere in much the style of his acquaintance, Dudley Digges [7.7]. Philosophical controversy rages as to whether he built normative force into his axioms, and historical controversy as to what social factors influenced his view of human nature. The second thing to notice is that it was not the outbreak of war that led him to his axioms or conclusions. His doctrine of absolute sovereignty was stated in pretty well its mature form in manuscript in 1640, and was only to be repeated in his famous *Leviathan* of 1651 (Goldsmith 1980). Of course, as Hobbes insisted there: 'as the nature of foul weather lieth not in a shower or two of rain, so the nature of war consisteth not in actual fighting, but in the known disposition thereto'; but it is salutary to be reminded that political absolutism does not need evident disorder for its production, and more generally, that the relationship between political thought and practice is not a simple one. Sir Robert Filmer had already written his *Patriarcha* – another absolutist tract – by 1639 (I remain unconvinced by Wallace 1980), and his *Anarchy of mixed and limited monarchy*

(1648[7.8]) was to add nothing important to his Hobbesian doctrine of the nature of sovereignty. Of course Filmer derived his doctrine in a different way, but the powers he attributed to a sovereign were the same.

There was, however, a difference between the two which illustrates the difficulty in defining Hobbes's politics by reference to the usual partisan positions and argumentation of his day. Before the revolution of 1649, Filmer argued that sovereignty was lodged by divine ordinance in the legitimate kings of England: Hobbes that sovereign power was his or theirs who could wield it. In a series of ground-breaking articles, Skinner has reminded us that Hobbes should not be regarded in isolation from his contemporaries as a 'political philosopher', but as one, who like some of his contemporary ideologues, especially from 1648 to 1652, was concerned to argue a politics the basic doctrine of which was the rationalist one that obedience was owed to a government (and *any* government) that could protect the subject. The affinity between the Hobbes of *Leviathan* and Ascham [11.3] is clear. Nor are they atypical of the times (Skinner 1965, 1966, 1972a, b). Yet for all that, Hobbes thought all available doctrines of legitimate rule but his were wrong well before others, and, responding to a crisis in which none of the old formulae would work, came to the view that obedience rested on the ability to protect (Wiener 1974). His politics were agnostic as regards accepted formulae of legitimacy. He would not have a bar of legitimist royalism, divine right royalism, royalist and parliamentarian constitutionalisms, presbyterian doctrines of resistance, moderationist trimming, or the liberationisms of the sects. Accordingly, his foul reputation as a political ideologist among his contemporaries (Bowle 1951) is as explicable as the respect with which he was regarded by those (mostly foreigners) who took political philosophy seriously and by his 'engager' allies of 1649–52.

It is not enough to obtain . . . security, that every one of those who are now growing up into a city do covenant with the rest, either by words or writing, not to steal, not to kill, and to observe the like laws; for the pravity of human disposition is manifest to all, and by experience too well known how little (removing the punishment) men are kept to their duties through conscience of their promises. We must therefore provide for our security not by compacts but by punishments; and there is then sufficient provision made when there are so great punishments appointed for every injury as apparently to prove a greater evil to have done it than not to have done it. For all men, by a necessity of nature, choose that which to them appears to be the less evil.

Now the right of punishing is then understood to be given to anyone when every man contracts not to assist him who is to be punished. But I will call this right, the sword of justice. But these kinds of contracts men observe well enough for the most part, till either themselves or their near friends are to suffer. Because therefore – for the security of particular men, and by consequence, for the common peace – it is necessary that the right of using the sword for punishment be transferred to some man or council, that man or council is necessarily understood by right to have the supreme power in the city. For he that by right punisheth at his own discretion, by right compels all men to all things which he himself wills – than which a greater command cannot be imagined.

But in vain do they worship peace at home who cannot defend themselves against foreigners; neither is it possible for them to protect themselves against foreigners whose forces are not united. And therefore it is necessary for the preservation of particulars that there shall be some one council or one man who hath the right to arm, to gather together, to unite so many citizens in all dangers and on all occasions as shall be needful for common defence against the certain number and strength of the enemy – and again, as often as he shall find it expedient, to make peace with them. We must understand therefore that particular citizens have conveyed their whole right of war and peace unto some one man or council, and that this right – which we may call the sword of war – belongs to the same man or council to whom the sword of justice belongs. For no man can by right compel citizens to take up arms and be at the expense of war, but he who by right can punish him who doth not obey. Both swords therefore, as well this of war as that of justice, even by the constitution itself of a city, and essentially, do belong to the chief command.

But because the right of the sword is nothing else but to have power by right to use the sword at his own will, it follows that the judgement of its right use pertains to the same party: for if the power of judging were in one, and the power of executing in another, nothing would be done. For in vain would he give judgement who could not execute his commands; or if he executed them by the power of another, he himself is not said to have the power of the sword, but that other, to whom he is only an officer. All judgement therefore in a city belongs to him who hath the swords, that is, to him who hath the supreme authority.

Furthermore, since it no less (nay, it much more) conduceth to peace to prevent brawls from arising than to appease them being risen; and that all controversies are bred from hence: that the opinions of men differ concerning *meum* and *tuum*, just and unjust, profitable and unprofitable, good and evil, honest and dishonest and the like (which every man esteems according to his own judgement), it belongs to the same chief power to make some common rules for all men, and to declare them publicly, by which every man may know what may be called his, what another's, what just, what unjust, what honest, what dishonest, what good, what evil – i.e., summarily: what is to be done and what to be avoided in our common course of life. But those rules and measures are usually called the civil laws, or laws of a city, as being the command of him who hath supreme power in the city. And the civil laws (that we may define them) are nothing else but the commands of him who hath the chief authority in the city for the direction of the future actions of his citizens.

Furthermore, since the affairs of the city, both those of war and peace, cannot possibly be all administered by one man or one council without officers and subordinate magistrates, and that it appertaineth to peace and common defence that they to whom it belongs justly to judge of controversies, to search into neighbouring councils, prudently to wage war, and on all hands warily to attend the benefit of the city, should also rightly exercise their offices, it is consonant with reason that they depend on and be chosen by him who hath command both in war and peace.

It is also manifest that all voluntary actions have their beginning from, and necessarily depend upon, the will; and that the will of doing or omitting aught depends on the opinion of the good and evil of the reward or punishment which a man conceives he shall receive by the act or omission; so as the actions of all men are ruled by the opinions of each. Wherefore by evident and necessary inference, we may understand that it very much concerns the interest of peace that no opinions or doctrines be delivered to the citizens by which they might imagine that either by right they may not obey the laws of the city – i.e., the commands of that man or council to whom the supreme power is committed – or that it is lawful to resist him, or that a less punishment remains for him that denies, than him who yields, obedience. For if one command somewhat to be done under penalty of death, another forbid it under pain of eternal death – and both by their own right – it will follow that the citizens, although innocent, are not only by right punishable, but that the city itself is altogether dissolved; for no man can serve two masters; nor is [that other, spiritual commander] less, but rather more a master, than he whom we obey for fear of temporal death. It follows therefore that this one, whether man or court, to whom the city hath committed the supreme power, have also this right: that he both judge what opinions and doctrines are enemies unto peace, and also that he forbid them to be taught.

Last of all, from this consideration, that each citizen hath submitted his will to his who hath the supreme command in the city – so as he may not employ his strength against him – it follows manifestly that whatsoever shall be done by him who commands shall not be punished. For as he who hath not power enough cannot punish naturally, so neither can he punish him by right who by right hath not sufficient power.

It is most manifest by what hath been said, that in every perfect city (i.e., where no citizen hath right to use his faculties at his own discretion for the preservation of himself, or where the right of the private sword is excluded) there is a supreme power in some one (greater than which cannot by right be conferred by men, or greater than which cannot by men be conveyed on a man) we call absolute. For whosoever hath so submitted his will to the will of the city, that he can, unpunished, do anything – make laws, judge controversies, set penalties, make use at his own pleasure of the strength and wealth of men – and all this by right: truly he hath given him the greatest dominion that can be granted. This same may be confirmed by experience in all cities which are, or ever have been; for though it be sometimes in doubt what man or council hath the chief command, yet ever there is such a command, and always exercised, except in time of sedition and civil war; and then there are two chief commands made out of one. Now those seditious persons who dispute against absolute authority do not so much care to destroy it, as to convey it to others. . . .

## 6.2 THE 'SOVEREIGN POWER OF PARLIAMENTS'

From William Prynne, *The soveraigne power of parliaments* (1643), I, 46–8, 92, 104: Wing 4088.

Despite their hesitation and unwillingness to embrace a theory of the sovereignty of the two Houses of Parliament, parliamentarians like Prynne, Parker and Herle were led to do so (Allen 1938; and esp. Judson 1936, 1949). Here Prynne, like others of his generation using Jean Bodin's definition of sovereignty as his touchstone (Salmon 1959), interprets English law and history as demonstrating what the title of his book calls the 'sovereign power of parliaments'. Poor Lamont (1963) has an unavoidably difficult time bringing the mass of contradictory doctrine in the book to some semblance of order; and Allen cannot help remarking on Prynne's 'very extensive reading to singularly little purpose'. In fact, Prynne argued the sovereignty of King-in-Parliament, *and* in the two Houses, *and* in the Commons, *and* in no one at all. Lamont judiciously concludes that he argues like a lawyer, to a brief – the brief being simply that of persuading as many as possible to support the Parliament against the King. In the passage following, though, Prynne clearly argues for the sovereignty of the two Houses and their right to set up, vary and disestablish all other governing powers. Equally clearly, the people (Franklin 1978) are decidedly not the constitutive power.

The Parliament, as our lawbooks and writers resolve, is 'the most high and absolute power, the supremest and most ancient Court of the Realm of England, and hath the power of the whole Realm, both head and body. And among other privileges this is the highest: that it is above the law itself, having power upon just grounds to alter the very common law of England, to abrogate and repeal old laws and to enact new laws of all sorts, to impose taxes upon the people . . . It hath power to declare the meaning of doubtful laws, and to repeal all patents, charters, grants and judgements whatsoever of the King or any other Courts of Justice if they be erroneous or illegal, not only without, but against the King's consent, so far as finally to oblige both King and subjects'. Now it is clear, on the contrary side, that the King hath not the power of the whole Realm vested in his person, that he and his prerogative are not above, but subordinate, to the law of the realm . . . [and that he cannot do those things Parliament can which have just been listed] without or against his people's joint consent in Parliament . . . Jean Bodin, that great lawyer and politician, resolves (*De Republica*, book 1, chap. 10): that, 'the mark of an absolute and sovereign prince is to give laws to all his subjects in general, and to every one of them in particular, without consent of any other, greater, equal, or less than himself. For if a prince be bound not to make laws without the consent of a greater than himself, he is a very subject; if not without an equal, he then hath a companion;' (as Bracton and others say our English King *hath*, namely his earls and lords, thence styled *comites*) 'if not without the consent of his inferiors, whether it be of his subjects or of his Senate or of his people, then he is no sovereign'. Whence it follows that the Kings of England . . . are no absolute sovereign princes (as some royalists and court divines falsely aver them to be) but mere mixed, politic kings, inferior to the laws and Parliaments. [In fact, Parliaments] are the sole lawmakers [and] law alterers, though not against but with the King's assent (considered not abstractively as [the] King's, but copulatively as a branch and member of Parliament). And indeed... though the King's royal assent be generally requisite to pass and ratify laws, yet I humbly conceive that the original, prime legislative power of making laws to bind the subjects and their posterity rests not in the King's own royal person or jurisdiction but in the kingdom, and Parliament which represents it.

For first, admit the King should propound any laws to his people... yet those laws would no ways oblige them unless they voluntarily consented and submitted to them in Parliament. And the sole reason why our acts of Parliament bound subjects in former times and bind us at this day is not because the King willed them but because the people gave their general consents unto them in Parliament – as Sir Thomas Smith in his *Commonwealth of England*, Holinshed, the prologues to the most ancient statutes ('the King, by the advice and assent of the Lords Spiritual and Temporal, and Commons, and at the special request of the Commons in Parliament assembled, and *by the authority of the same Parliament*, doth grant and ordain, etc.'), the King's Coronation Oath (*quas vulgus elegerit*) and all our lawbooks resolve. And [all this] upon a received maxim of law: *quod omnes tangit ab omnibus debet approbari* (what concerns all ought to be approved by all)... The King in passing bills doth but, like the minister in marriage, declare it to be a law, but it is the parties' consents which make it the marriage, and the people's only that makes it a law to bind them...

All public acts are the whole kingdom's laws, not Kings' alone, made principally and solely for the subjects' benefit if good, their prejudice if ill. Therefore the whole kingdom (represented by both Houses not the King) knowing much better what is good and bad for themselves than the King alone, it is just and reasonable that they, not the King, should be the principal lawmakers....

The King hath little or no hand in making, but only in assenting to laws when they are made by the Houses, as the usual form of passing acts ('the roy le veult' – the King wills or assents to it – not before, but after they have passed both Houses) imports. [This] assent of his, if the bills be public and necessary for the public good, is not merely arbitrary at the King's will, but the King by oath and duty is bound to give it. And the Lords and Commons may in justice demand it....

[Prynne then discourses on the history of the Coronation Oath, the history of how Kings have been deposed and Crowns disposed of by Parliaments; and he relates how Parliaments have removed, 'bridled', and even appointed Kings' servants, both 'great' and 'menial'.]

There is one clear demonstration yet remaining to prove the supreme power of Parliaments above Kings themselves, which is this: that the Parliament is the highest Court and power to which, 'all appeals are finally to be made from all other Courts and Judges whatsoever, yea from the King's own personal resolution, in, or out of any other of his Courts: and such a transcendant tribunal from which there is no appeal to any other Court or person, no not to the King himself, but only to another Parliament' (Smith, *Commonwealth*, Book 2, Chs 1–2). If any erroneous judgement be given in the King's Bench, Exchequer Chamber, Chancery, Court of Wards or any other Court within the realm or in the Parliament of Ireland, it is finally to be determined in Parliament. . . . If any sentence be unjustly given by any Ecclesiastical Courts . . . the final appeal for redress must be to Parliament. Illegal sentences in the now exploded, extravagant, Courts of Star Chamber and High Commission, injuries done by the King and his Privy Council at the Council Table are examinable and remediable in this High Court. Nay, if the King himself should sit in person in the King's Bench or any other Court . . . and there give any judgement, it is not obligatory or final, but that the party against whom judgement is pronounced may appeal to Parliament for relief . . . But if the Parliament give any judgement, there can be no appeal to any higher tribunal. . . .

[Prynne then relates the history of Parliaments' settling disputes as to rights of succession to the Crown as showing again that Parliament must be the High Court.]

By all which acts (worthy the reading and consideration) the Parliament's supreme power of settling and disposing the descent and inheritance of the Crown and giving authority even to the King himself, to dispose of it upon condition . . . will easily appear. . . . It is a clear case without dispute that if the King should die without any heir, the Crown would escheat to the whole kingdom and Parliament, who might dispose of it in such a case to what person they pleased. [They could] quite change that form of government if they saw good cause, no particular kind of rule being so simply necessary by any divine right or law in any state or kingdom, but that, as it was first instituted, so it may in such a case, be changed by the whole kingdom's general consent, upon sufficient grounds. The like we read of [German] Emperors deceasing without heir, [and] of some of our Saxon and British Kings before the conquest, and of others in Castile, Aragon and other kingdoms where the Crown has been transferred from one family to another by the kingdom's consent, for want of heirs. . . .

### 6.3 THE KING'S SUPREMACY

From John Bramhall, *Serpent-salve*, 60–63 (see headnote to [4.1])

Here Bramhall has recourse to the normal royalist arguments showing regal supremacy. They hint at a view of English history much different from Prynne's, and incorporate a legalistic rehearsal of the King's powers presented with an aplomb equal to Prynne's opposing view of the legal position. He provides, finally, a brief gloss on the doctrine of *salus populi* as expressed by the royal counsel in the Ship Money Case and as used to Parliament's benefit by Henry Parker, against whose *Observations* [8.3] he is arguing.

The . . . last error is to tie the hands of the King absolutely to his laws. First: In matters of grace the King is above his laws. He may grant especial privileges by charter to what persons, to what corporations he pleaseth, of his abundant grace and mere motion. He may pardon all crimes committed against the laws of the land, and all penalties . . . imposed by the same. The perpetual custom of this kingdom doth warrant it. All wise men desire to live under such a government where the prince may with a good conscience dispense with the rigour of the laws. . . .

Secondly: In all acts of regal power and justice his majesty may go besides or beyond the ordinary course of law by his prerogative. New laws for the most part – especially when the King stands in need of subsidies – are an abatement of royal power. The sovereignty of a just conqueror who comes in without pactions is absolute and bounded only by the laws of God, of nature, and of nations. But after he hath confirmed old laws and customs, or by his charters granted new liberties and immunities to the collective body of his subjects or to any of them, he hath so far remitted of his own right, and cannot in conscience recede from [them]. I say, 'in conscience': for though human laws (as they are human) cannot bind the conscience of a subject – and therefore *a fortiori* not of a King who is the lawgiver – yet by consequence of the law of God, which saith *submit yourselves to every ordinance of man for the Lord's sake* . . . they do bind. (Or to speak more properly, God's law doth bind the conscience to the observance of them.) This is that which divines do use to express thus: that they have power to bind the conscience *in se sed non a se* [in themselves, but not from themselves] *non ex authoritate legislatoris sed ex æquitate legis* [not from the authority of the lawgiver, but from the equity of the law]. Many who do not grant that to violate the law of man is to sin universally, yet in case of contempt or scandal do admit that it is sinful. So then the laws and customs of the kingdom are limits and bounds to his majesty's power. But there are not precise laws for every occurrence; and even the laws themselves do often leave a latitude and pre-eminence to his majesty, not only for circumstances and forms of justice, but even in great and high privileges. These we call the prerogative royal – as to be the fountain of nobility, to coin money, to create magistrates, to grant possession to his debtors against their creditors, to present to a benefice in the right of his ward (being the youngest coparcener) before the eldest, not to be sued upon an ordinary writ but by petition, and many others which are beyond the ordinary course of common law – being either branches of absolute power, or prerogatives left by the laws themselves.

Thirdly: in case of evident necessity where the whole commonwealth lies at stake, for the safety of the King and kingdom his majesty may go against particular laws. For howsoever fancied and pretended invisible dangers have thrust us into real dangers and unseasonable remedies, [and] have produced our present calamities, yet this is certain: that all human laws and particular proprieties must veil and strike top-sail to a true public necessity. This is confessed by the Observer himself where in this treatise [he saith, p. 4], 'that *salus populi* is the trancendent acme of all politics; the law paramount that gives law to all human laws', and [that] 'particular laws cannot act contrary to the legislative intent, to be a violation of some more sovereign good introducable or some extreme and general evil avoidable, which otherwise might swallow up both Statutes and all other sanctions'.

*Part seven*
# ROYALIST ARGUMENTS, 1641–1648

## 7.1 THE FIRST CHAMPION OF THE KING'S CAUSE

From Henry Ferne, *The resolving of conscience* (Cambridge, 1642), 11–15, 21: Wing F 800.

Henry Ferne (1600–62), the 'Doctor' in many parliamentarian arguments already presented here, produced the first of the royalist pamphlets raised on the foundation of the manifestos that had passed between King and Parliament and on which a superstructure of parliamentarian writing was already being raised by such as Henry Parker, the 'Observator' in the extract. Ferne was a cleric with a living in Leicestershire in 1642; but his life was to change dramatically when he first impressed the King with a sermon at Leicester and then in the autumn produced his *Resolving of conscience*. He was to become a royal chaplain, negotiator and polemicist; at the Restoration he was rewarded with the mastership of Trinity College, Cambridge; in 1662 he was consecrated bishop of Chester, but he died soon after. In the *Resolving of conscience* and later writings he was to insist on the divine origin of 'power', the duty of non-resistance, the non-contractual origins of the English constitution, and the logical impossibility of legitimacy's being based on contract. In doing so he was partly addressing himself to what his opponents had said and partly rendering normal royalist *credenda*. The royalist–parliamentarian debate has never been exhaustively studied, but there is much in Allen (1938), Daly (1966, 1971, 1978, 1979a, b), Figgis (1896), Gooch (1898), Gough (1955), Jordon (1942), Judson (1949), Pocock (1957, 1975), Schochet (1974), Sirluck (1959), Wallace (1968, 1980), Weston (1965, 1970, 1980), Wormald (1951), Wormuth (1939) and Zagorin (1954).

However the 'fundamentals of government' are much talked of, this is, according to [the parliamentarians'] reason, the fundamental in *all* kingdoms and governments. For they say power was everywhere from the people at first . . . This will serve no more for the power of resistance in England than in France and Turkey. But if this *must* be the fundamental, it is such an one as upon it this government cannot be built but confusion and anarchy may readily be raised, as shall appear by the clearing of these two particulars: whether the power be so originally and chiefly from the people as they would have it; then, whether they may upon such causes [as where the King will not 'discharge his trust'] assume that power.

First, of the original of power, which they will have so from the people that it shall be from God only by a kind of 'permissive approbation' (as we may see from the Observator and all other that plead for the power of resistance). We must distinguish here what the writers of the other side seem to confound, to wit, the power itself (which is a sufficiency of authority for command and coercion in the governing of a people), from the designing of the person to bear that power and the qualification of that power according to the divers ways of executing it in the several forms of government. And *then* we grant that the designing of the person is sometimes from the people by choice, and that the power of the prince (receiving qualification by joint consent of himself and the people) is limited by laws made with such consent. But the power itself is of God originally and chiefly, which we prove by scripture and reason.

The Apostle [Paul] speaks it expressly: the *powers* are *of God* and *the ordinance of God* (*Romans* xiii. 1–2). St Peter (*1 Peter* ii. 13) indeed saith, *every ordinance of man*; but 'of man' there and 'of God' [in St Paul], is much differing. [In Peter] it is 'of man' *subjectivè*: i.e., every ordinance or power set up amongst men; but [in Paul] it is of God *causaliter*: i.e. from Him, His ordinance. And if in that 'of man' there be implied any creation or causality or invention of man, it respects the qualification of the power according to the forms of several governments and offices in them which are from the invention of man. It doth not make the power itself the creation of man. [That] is the constitution and ordinance of God; and men are not only naturally bent to society but are also bound, as they are reasonable creatures, to set up and live under government, as under an order of that providence by which the world is governed.

[A ruler] is called the *minister of God* (Romans xiii. 4); but if so from the people and no otherwise from God than they would have him, he should be 'minister of the people' rather. He is indeed their minister for their *good* – which makes the people to be the end of this governing power, not the fountain and original of it. Therefore the necessity of subjection urged hath a double ground (verse 5): the *ordinance of God*, whose ministers rulers are (there's the fountain and original power to govern) then the people's *good* upon which rulers ought to attend (that's the end of the governing power). To the same purpose speak those other places: *By me Kings reign* (*Proverbs* viii) and *I have said ye are Gods* (*Psalms* lxxxii. 6), in relation to which our Saviour saith (*John* x. 34–5) *They are called Gods to whom the word of God came.* That *dixi*, that word, is the command, the issuing out as it were, of the commission for the setting up of a governing power among the people.

These places cannot be satisfied with that poor part they on the other side leave to God in the setting up of power for the governing of men: i.e., to approve it when the people hath created or invented it. Indeed, if we consider the qualifications of this governing power and the manner of executing it according to the several forms of government, we granted it before to be the invention of man. And when such a qualification or form is orderly agreed upon we say it hath God's permissive approbation. And therefore the imputation is causeless which the pleaders on the other side do heedlessly and ignorantly lay upon us divines as if we cried up monarchy [as] the only government to be *jure divino*. For although monarchy hath this excellency, that the government God set up over his people in the person of Moses, the Judges and the Kings was monarchical, yet we confess that neither that, nor aristocracy, or any other form is *jure divino*. But we say the power itself (i.e., that sufficiency of authority to govern) which is in monarchy or aristocracy, abstractly considered from the qualifications of either form, is an efflux or constitution subordinate to that providence, an ordinance of that *dixi*, that silent word by which the world was at first made and is still governed under God. . . .

So is it also suitable to reason, because God doth govern all creatures, reasonable as well as unreasonable. The inferior or lower world he governs by the heavens or superior bodies according to those influences and powers he hath put into them. And the reasonable creatures, men, he governs by others set up in his stead over them, for which they are called Gods because in his stead over the people. And the powers are said to be not only *from God* but also [*ordained*], as orders ranked by him and under him too, subordinate to that providence by which all creatures are governed. These ministers He sometimes designed immediately by himself: as Moses, the Judges, Saul, David, etc. Now he designs his vicegerents, on earth mediately, as by election of the people, by succession, or inheritance, by conquest, etc. To conclude: the power itself of government is of God, however the person be designed or that power qualified according to the several forms of government by those laws that are established or those grants that are procured for the people's security.

Thus much for the original of power. Now we come to the forfeiture (as I may call it) of this power. If the prince, say they, will not discharge his trust, then it falls to the people or the two Houses (the representative body of the people) to see to it, to reassume that power and therefore resist. This they conceive to follow upon the 'derivation of power' from the people by virtue of election, and upon the 'stipulation or covenant' of the prince with the people, as also in regard of those 'means of safety' which every state should have within itself. . . .

Concerning the derivation of power: first, if it be not from the people as they will have it, and as before it was cleared, then there can be no reassuming of this power by the people. That's plain by their own argument. Secondly, if the people should give power so absolutely as they would have it, leaving nothing to God in it but approbation, yet could they not therefore have right to take that power away. For many things which are altogether in our disposing before we part with them are not afterward in our power to recall, especially such in which there redounds to God an interest by the donation, as in things devoted (though afterward they come to be abused). . . . Thirdly, how shall the conscience be satisfied that this their argument, grounded upon election and derivation of power from the people, can have place in this kingdom, whenas the Crown not only descends by inheritance but also hath been settled by conquest in the lines of Saxons and Normans? In answering to this they look beyond these and say [that] the right is still good to the people by reason of their first election. I answer: so then that first election must be supposed here, and supposed good against all other titles, or else this power of resistance falls to the ground. It is probable that Kings at first were by choice here as elsewhere among the heathens. But can conscience rest upon such remote probabilities for resistance or think that first election will give it power against princes that do not claim by it? We tell them that the Roman Emperors were not to be resisted (*Romans* xiii. 2). They reply . . . that they were absolute monarchs. Was it any otherwise than by force of arms, the way the Saxons and Normans made themselves masters of this people? And was not the right of the people as good against them for the power of resistance by virtue of the first election as well as of the people of this land against their Kings after so many conquests? This I speak, not as if the Kings of this land might rule as conquerors – God forbid – but to show this slender plea of the first election can no more take place against the Kings of this land than it could against the Roman monarchs (especially according to their argument that hold all power originally from the people and that . . . to be the fundamental of all government). Therefore whether Kings were in this land at first by election or no, we acknowledge what belongs to the duty of a prince in doing justice and equity: what grants, also laws [and] privileges have since those conquests been procured or restored to the people. Unto all those the King is bound, but yet not bound under forfeiture of his power to the people.

In the next place . . . that capitulation or covenant and the Oath which the prince takes to confirm what he promiseth are so alleged as if the breach or non-performance on the prince's part were a forfeiture of his power. But . . . the words 'capitulation' or 'covenant' are now much used to make men believe the King's admittance to the Crown is altogether conditional (as in the merely elective kingdoms of Poland, Sweden, etc.) whereas our King is King before he comes to the coronation, which is sooner, or later, at his pleasure, but always to be in due time in regard of that security his people receive by his taking the Oath (and he again mutually from them) in which performance there is something like a convenant – all but the forfeiture. The King there promises, and binds himself by oath to performance. Could they in this covenant show us such an agreement between the King and his people, that in case he will not discharge his trust then it shall be lawful for the states of the kingdom by arms to resist and provide for the safety thereof, then it would be something to give conscience warrant for resistance (but not sufficient in my opinion, such conditions being altogether unreasonable). [first six words in bracket transposed]. . . .

This power of resistance when used and pursued is accompanied by the evils of civil war. Former times show it; and how little was gained by it beside the expense of blood. . . . And at this day we feel and groan under the evils brought upon us through this power of resistance: the law silenced, the property and liberty of the subject everywhere invaded, and the Lord knows when or how we shall be restored to them . . . We see the danger if (as is now said for the justifying of this power of resistance, the King will not discharge his trust and therefore it falls to the representative body of the people to see to it . . .) the people being discontented, and having gotten the power, shall say 'the members of the two Houses do not discharge the trust committed to them; they do not do that for which they were chosen and sent for'. Then may the multitude by this rule and principle now taught them, take the power to themselves, it being claimed by them, and say to their rulers (as *Numbers* xvi. 3) *Ye take too much upon you*, or as Cade and Tyler, boast themselves reformers of the commonwealth, overthrow King and Parliament, fill all with rapine and confusion, draw all to a Folkmoot and make every shire a several government. These are dangers and evils not conceived in fancy, but such as reason tells us may follow and experience hath often.

## 7.2 THE GRACE OF A LEGAL MONARCH

From John Spelman, *The case of our affaires, in law, religion, and other circumstances* (1643), 1–3, 6–7, 12–13: Wing S 4935. The full tract has been reprinted by the Rota, 1975.

Here Spelman (headnote to [4.2]) states the moderate royalist position as to the supremacy of a King who is nevertheless bound by the laws he himself has created of his own 'grace'. He may legally rescind them, but he has moral (i.e. religious) obligation not to depart from his word – which he would if he did so. Like most royalists in the controversy, Spelman had to spend a lot of space arguing that Charles could and should be trusted to rule as a 'legal monarch' (Daly 1966), and that it was the parliamentarians who were acting illegally. This would have been a reasonable line to take had Charles been worthy of trust, but moderates had a King who continually gave the lie to their words.

Our State of England, even by the declaration of our laws, is a kingdom, an empire, a well-regulated monarchy, the head thereof a supreme head, a sovereign, a King whose Crown is an imperial Crown, the kingdom *his* kingdom, *his* realm, *his* dominion, the people *his* people, the subject[s] *his* subject[s] not only as they are single men, but even when being in Parliament assembled. They make the body representative of the whole kingdom considered apart without the King, so that the very Parliament itself is called *his* Parliament. The King alone by law hath power to call together in Parliament that representative body, and at his pleasure to dissolve it. He personally hath homage and oath of fidelity of all the peers and *his* barons; and all the Commons in Parliament do by law swear allegiance to him as to the, 'only supreme governor', and 'to assist and defend all jurisdictions, privileges, pre-eminences and authorities belonging to him, his heirs and successors, or annexed to the imperial Crown of the realm'. By the same oath also is every officer of considerable trust in church and commonwealth assured to his majesty – and not only they, but every single man of twelve years of age ought by law in some or other of his majesty's Leets to swear allegiance to his majesty. . . .

This sovereignty in the King appears not only by that Oath of Supremacy, but by the constant acknowledgement of our Acts of Parliament both ancient and modern, which always style the King, 'our sovereign Lord the King', i.e. not sovereign Lord to every single man only (as the Observer traitorously and foolishly would make it) but the universality of us, even to our body representative in Parliament. . . . Our very Acts of Parliament [declare] this State to be a right 'imperial kingdom'; a kingdom we know consisteth of no more than two formal parts only, that is to say, a sovereign head and a subject body; and then it clearly followeth that what co-operation soever there be of any members with the head for the doing of any necessary act of State, whatsoever necessity there be of the concurrence of those members, and howsoever they may seem to be parties, orders or states co-equally authorised in the power of acting with the head, yet plainly there neither is nor can be any co-ordination nor co-equality of any estate, order or degree of the subject with the sovereign, nor any competition of the subjects' power . . . with the virtual and primary influence of the sovereign's power, but a plain subordination and subjected ministration of the one under the sovereignty of the other. . . .

We see the sovereignty of this State clearly vested in the King, by law established in him, and inseparably annexed to his person, by which he hath also inseparably both the sovereign power and the sovereign judgement. But, as in judging and determining matters of private interest his power is not absolute but is restrained to judgement (not judgement arbitrary in his own person but judgement to be administered by the proper sworn Judges of his Courts of law), so in matters of public affairs, for so much as concerns the making of law, his power and judgement are restrained to the concurrence of the nobles and commons in Parliament, as that he cannot make any settled law without their consent. But then in all other things that are not expressly restrained by any law [like an emergency power of dictatorship, powers of peace and war, powers to regulate the sitting of Parliament, powers of honouring, rewarding, pardoning, etc] . . . the sovereignty both of judgement and power ever hath been and still is in the King alone . . .

Now this restraint, being at first collateral and accidental to the sovereign power, did not in the beginning otherwise bind our princes than by their voluntary and pious submission of their wills, till, constant custom becoming a law made the usage which was at first of their will become an absolute and inevitable limitation of their power, so as that at this day no positive law can now be made by the King without the consent of the Peers and of the Commons. And yet, for all this necessity now of their concurrence and consent, not any part of the sovereignty (to which the legislative power is inseparably incident) is in any sort transferred or communicated unto them: but, as in our copyhold estates, the copyholder of a mere tenant-at-will comes by custom to gain a customary inheritance and so limit and restrain the will and power of the Lord as that he cannot make any determination of the copyholder's estate otherwise than according to the custom of the manor, yet he does not deprive the Lord of his lordship in the copy-hold, nor participate with him in it, neither yet divest the fee and frank-tenement out of the Lord, but they still remain in him and are ever parcel of the Lord's demesne....

Apparently therefore, the sovereign or regal power being... in matters of private interest restrained to the rule, jurisdiction and administration of law as well by inferior courts as by the House of Lords, and in the public affair of making the law restrained to the concurrence of the Peers and Commons, is not so properly said to be 'restrained' as 'regulated'. For neither is any of the King's just and necessary power to the prejudice of the Crown taken from him (for the law in no sort suffers any diminution of the just and due sovereignty), neither is any partnership of the supremacy thereby thrust upon the King when the law, notwithstanding the restraint, expressly declares him, 'the only supreme governor'. Neither yet is any of the irregular and exorbitant absoluteness which the law separates from the regality any way transferred to the Court or persons that are the instrumentals of the regulation; but the law, separating all irregular licentiousness from the regality, utterly annihilates and makes null all practice and exercise thereof. In sum, all that is effected by this regulation is, the King as he ever was so still remains, wholly and solely sovereign of the kingdom, only not of a licentious and illegal but of a regular and legitimate dominion... We are further to observe that in point of making of law, the law restraining... the sovereign power to the consent of the Peers and Commons, the more that by this regulation it purged it from destructive exorbitancies, the more tender it grew of the just and legitimate rights thereof remaining; and therefore, considering the person of the sovereign to be single and his power counterpoised by the opposite wisdom of the two numerous bodies of the two Houses, it allowed unto the King power to swear unto himself a body of counsel of State (which our laws sometimes call his Grand Council), and to swear unto him also counsellors at law, even the Judges themselves and others learned in the law, faithfully to advise him in his government, that he may be perpetual. And if upon a general pretence of evil counsel, without any instance in what, his majesty be deprived of the use and assistance of any of his sworn counsel (especially in Parliament time when the sovereignty may be so easily overmatched), it will make such a breach of privilege of the first of the three orders in Parliament as will destroy the true frame of Parliaments, diminish the power of the Crown, and bring the settled estate of the kingdom into the calamitous innovation of an unsettled and ever-changing form of government, and so into all manner of misery and confusion.

## 7.3 CONQUEST AND THE GRACE OF KINGS

From Henry Ferne, *A reply unto several treatises* (Oxford, 1643), 18–27: Wing F 799

By the time Ferne (headnote to [7.1]) wrote his *Reply* he was in Oxford at the King's side. His problem in the extract produced here will be obvious: he is anxious to deny the parliamentarian myths of original contract and Anglo-Saxon freedoms; and he is equally anxious to deny that he claims that the current title of modern English Kings lies in conquest and that the subject is subject merely to the sword. He accordingly marries royalist historiography – which recognised conquest as a fact (Skinner 1965) – with the legal theory of royal grace as expressed by Spelman in [7.2]. The role of conquest in royalist thought has been the subject of a recent controversy among scholars (Wallace 1968; Skinner, 1965, 1966, 1972a, b). The controversy is interesting partly because in writing of the English past as if conquest had irrupted the ancient customary and 'fundamental' law royalists left the way open for radicals to criticise parts or even the whole of the constituted laws (Hill 1958), partly because they forged a weapon which could in turn be used against a defeated royal line in the 'engagement controversy' of 1649–51, and partly because it is really far from clear just what they were claiming the normative force of past conquest to be and how often they appealed to conquest anyway. Clearly Ferne's position is at least that conquest can extinguish old rights and titles to power; but it is not clear whether he claims more than that conquest can provide a *de facto* basis on which a new structure of legitimacy might come to rest but not depend on for legitimacy. The whole seventeenth-century controversy illustrates a tendency – nicely described by Pocock (1957 and further explored in the eighteenth-century, 1968) – to clothe political rationalism in the guise of interpreting the past.

I will conclude this section with a brief consideration of what [Hunton] delivers concerning monarchy by conquest. First, 'If the invasion', saith he, 'be made upon pretence of title, and the pretender doth prevail, it is not conquest properly but a vindication of title. And then the government is such as the title is by which he claimed' (*Treatise of Monarchy*, p. 21). I will not dispute whether a people so standing out do forfeit those privileges and liberties they formerly enjoyed, or whether a prince so forced to vindicate his title by subduing the people be not free from the former limitations to which princes, peaceably entering, bind themselves, and whether he may use such a people as a conqueror. I would commend the clemency and piety of that prince that would not, but I do not see the injustice if he should so use them.

Secondly, he blames the censure which [Herle, in] the *Fuller answer* [p. 10] gave of conquest ('that the title of it was such as plunderers have', etc.), and tells us 'the right of conquest is such as the precedent war is. If that be lawful, so is the conquest. Yet it is not the conquest that makes them morally bound but their own consent in accepting of the government.' (*Treatise*, p. 22) Well . . . a forced conquest will suffice, and such will scarce be wanting to a conquest! And they that plead title of conquest do not divide it from such a forced consent of the people, but from a free and limiting election.

Thirdly, he grants that while their natural sovereign is in being the people cannot by consent devolve a right to the conqueror. But suppose they have not that tie upon them? May they perpetually stand out against the conqueror; or rather, are they not bound to consent and yield to his yoke after they see they are wholly subdued and he has settled a frame of government among them? He tells us, 'Conquest may give title and power to dispose of the country, goods and lives of the conquered; but still it is in the people's choice to come to a moral condition of subjection. If they will suffer the utmost of violence from the conqueror rather than consent to any terms of subjection (as Numantia in Spain) they die, or remain a free people. Nor do they resist God's ordinance if at any time of advantage they use force to free themselves from so violent a possession. . . . It is an uncontrollable truth in policy that the consent of the people, either by themselves or their ancestors, is the only mean in ordinary providence by which sovereignty is conferred upon any person or family.' (*Treatise*, pp. 22–3) . . . *Answer*: That consent of the people is the 'only mean' in [his] sense may be an 'uncontrollable' truth in the policy lately framed. But it is certain that God has power to dispose of us in ordinary providence without expecting our consents and choice. It is plain by scripture that conquest is a mean of translating kingdoms and disposing of people in the way of ordinary providence. It was so when God gave Egypt to Nebuchadnezzar as an hire for his service done upon Judah, also when the Ammonites and Edomites were subdued by David... Had these no right over those conquered nations but by expecting their consent? Yea, will [Hunton] say a right to dispose of their lands and goods and lives but not to challenge their moral consent? Well we doubt not but such conquerors could force their consent; but I ask, were they not *bound* to yield it? Is there no way for that providence which translates kingdoms to discover itself but by the consent of the conquered people, that if they please to be obstinate, His providence shall give no right, His setting up a King by conquest over such a people shall be no institution or ordinance? This is good policy but bad divinity. I conceive it an 'uncontrollable' truth that when the invading prince has perfectly subdued a people (there being no present sovereign or heir apparent of the Crown to whom they are bound) and has settled and disposed all things and constituted a frame of government, then I say providence doth sufficiently discover itself, and such a people ought to submit, and consent, and take the prince as set over them by the hand of providence, so that if they will persist finally to resist... they resist the ordinance of God. If he will not believe me, let him hear Calvin, who doth enforce obedience to that prince which is over us by reason drawn from that providence of God which disposeth kingdoms and sets up over us what Kings He please, and from the example of Nebuchadnezzar doth infer [the same] (Calvin, *Institutes*, book 4, chap 20, sects 26 and 27).

....I had twice occasion in my first treatise (*The resolving of conscience*) to speak of the beginning of this government in the arms of the Saxons and Normans, which was not... to prove our King absolute... but... by way of answer to what was spoken by [parliamentarians] touching a right in the people by virtue of such a capitulating election at first as they suppose to have given beginning to this monarchy. In both places, I expressly intimated those conquests were not mentioned to win an arbitrary power to the King but only to exclude resistance and such a supposed election.

The beginning of this English monarchy and the root of succession of the monarchs we must fetch from the Saxons, and [Hunton] bids us look so far back, when (to cut off the advantages that may be had against him from the Normans' entrance) he tells us that 'Duke William came upon the old, limited title whereby the English Saxon kings, his predecessors held this kingdom.' (*Treatise*, p. 35) How the Saxons entered this kingdom is well known. They made themselves masters of this kingdom by arms, which, although it doth not infer our Kings are now absolute . . . yet it doth plainly overthrow such an original mixture in the sovereign power as this author has fancied . . . I shall be briefer in my answer to [him, because I have already answered a similar point made in Herle's *Fuller answer* in my *Conscience satisfied*, sect. 3].

First, this author saith, 'It was not a conquest that the Saxons made, but an expulsion.' (*Treatise*, p. 35) This is neither true nor greatly material . . . Not true because it cannot be imagined but a greater part of the Britons remained under the Saxon yoke, [and] so Mr Camden tells us . . . Nor is it greatly material; for if we imagine that the Britons were not brought under the yoke but expelled, yet we cannot imagine that the government of those Saxon Kings (being made by the acclamation of their soldiers, as when the praetorian guard or some army abroad saluted a Roman Emperor) was at first any other than is the government of generals over their soldiers, i.e. unlimited, much less so 'limited' and 'mixed' as this author fancieth it . . . [He] doth admire their wisdom . . . that had the contriving of it. But can anyone suppose such a platform laid that considers the beginning of the Saxon monarchy, or imagine such admirable wisdom, 'more than human', in those rude and violent beginnings?

But he tells us in the second place: 'the Saxons planting themselves here under their commanders no doubt continued the freedom they had in Germany, and so changed their soil, not their government'. (op. cit. p. 35) But what proof to put this out of doubt? A conjecture out of Tacitus, that wrote of the Germans some hundreds of years before this entrance of the Saxons . . . But why should we rest upon such dreams and uncertainties as these men would put us upon? This is certain: that the Saxons being entered, and having vanquished the Britons, did by degrees . . . raise seven kingdoms or monarchies independent, yet so as that still one of them, the most powerful, was monarch of all, or King of England, as Mr Camden and others show out of Bede . . . At length the King of the West Saxons, Egbert, vanquished the rest and settled the sole monarchy in his line and those that should come after him. Now I would fain know how this author [Hunton] or any other of their best fancies can conceive that such a mixture as joins nobles and commons in the sovereign power with the monarch (for so they would have it) can possibly consist with such a beginning of government? . . . .

[Hunton] indeed tries what his fancy can do . . . 'Suppose a people (nobles and commons) set over themselves by a public compact one sovereign, and resign up themselves to him and his heirs to be governed by such and such fundamental laws. Then suppose them covenanting with their sovereign that if cause be to constitute any other laws he shall not do it by his sole power, but they reserve at first, or afterwards it is granted them (which is all one), a hand in concurrence therein, that they will be bound by no laws but what they join with him in the making of. (*op. cit.* p. 44)' And so he goes on . . . but . . . he must have a strong fancy that can conceive . . . this consistent with the beginnings of the Saxon government, as if it could be laid in such a platform . . . [And where] he would lay this platform up to the view, he brings up the Houses to this power they have by steps of time . . . [and] speaks doubtingly of the original contriving of this government, 'whether', saith he, 'done at once or by degrees found and perfected'. (loc. *cit.*) But this contriving must be made once and at first when they choose the first King, or else they cannot have this power and authority radically their own. And we cannot imagine but Bede and other historians would have observed such [a] convention of nobles and commons . . . for the contriving of this government, in which they demeaned themselves with such admirable wisdom. Or if they could not tell us of such a convention of them at first for the contriving and beginnings of government, they could not but observe some meetings of them after, for the use of this power in the managing of the government.

Assemblies doubtless there were for representing of grievances to the monarch and for giving advice in the redress (and among the orders . . . were *procurators cleri*, the representatives of the clergy) . . . But here we are called by this author to believe (or rather 'suppose') an assembly consisting of nobles and commons vested with part of the sovereign power by original constitution, whenas neither his nor any other author could bring any other record for it above the Norman conquest; and those histories or chronicles which mention the beginning of Parliaments as they now stand in authority do not rise so high as those times . . . The Parliament itself (24 Henry VIII *c.* [12]) doth declare that, 'This realm of England has been ever accepted for an empire governed by one supreme head', and tells us that histories and chronicles show as much. Why should these chronicles be so many ages silent in the original constitution by which this author gives the two Houses their power from the beginning of this monarchy if either such a constitution ever was, or indeed could consist with 'this Empire' and this 'one supreme head'? . . . .

We need not after all this . . . seek advantage from the entrance of the Norman conqueror. Yet this we can say (and it appears out of several authors cited by Mr Camden in his *Britannia*, sect. 'Norman'), that the Conqueror . . . . 'as a trophy and memorial of his conquest', disposed of the lands of the conquered, changed their tenure, abrogated what English laws and customs as he pleased, and gave them what laws he thought good. And unto this his people were content to yield. . . . So that [Hunton] speaks but his own fancy when he concludes thus upon William the Conqueror, 'By granting the former laws and government, he did equivalently put himself and his successors into the state of a legal monarch. And in that tenure have all the Kings of this land held the Crown unto this day . . .' (*op. cit.* p. 37) How far Duke William made use of his title by conquest, and how he granted the former laws and government appears by that which was spoken even now out of Mr Camden, i.e., he made use of it so far forth as he pleased, and granted what laws he pleased of the former government; and what new ones he pleased, those he imposed upon the people, and unto this they agreed (willingly or unwilling it matters not as is sometimes granted by this author). But [Hunton says that] by this he did, 'equivalently put himself and successors into a state of legal monarchs'. He did it so in a good sense, but not as this author means it. For we know . . . that his meaning is that Duke William by granting such laws did put himself in such a condition as if at first he had been limited by the people, they reserving to themselves the power of resisting his exorbitances which should be destructive of those limititations and laws. This is a 'legal monarch' in his sense. But we say he became a legal monarch, i.e., bound himself to rule according to such laws as he had granted. Nor do we rake up a title of conquest for his successors or would have them any other than legal monarchs. But . . . it appears that the root of succession, whether English or Norman, sprang up by conquest, and that the privileges and powers wherewith we see the subject invested were of an after-spring, (i.e., of after-agreement or by condescendent of the monarch), which powers and privileges, grants [and] liberties, though not original yet they are irrevocable. The prince is bound to observe them because of the oath of God [made to God in the Coronation Oath.]

## 7.4 THE DIVINE ORDINANCE FOR KINGS

From John Maxwell, *Sacro-sancta regum majestas: or the sacred and royal prerogative*. (Oxford, 1644), 81–96: Wing M 1348. I use a Bodleian copy not noted in Wing: 4°G 10 Th (6).

Dr John Maxwell (1590–1647) was a Laudian Scottish bishop. One of an endangered species, he was deposed by the General Assembly and made his way to Oxford and the King's camp via service as a cleric in Ireland. He was made archbishop of Tuam in 1645. He is said to have died 'on his knees' when he heard of the more constitutionalist Scots surrendering their prisoner Charles to the much less accommodating English. From a scholarly point of view, *Sacro-sancta regum majestas* has the virtue – like the parliamentarian work of a fellow Scot, Samuel Rutherford – of being explicit and lengthy on many points which his southern allies were content rather to indicate than to argue. The extract printed here illustrates this. God's ordinance for government, the patriarchal pattern of authority, the undesirability of democracy, etc. are all made clear. It also reproduces an argument which Allen (1938) finds rather to state than solve a problem. It seems to me that the psychology revealed in the passage about the necessitated 'vehement desire and inclination to submit to government' might well stand as typical of the period: no one liked government at all, but they found it hard to conceive of living without it. Even Winstanley, who came closest to working out a politics of anarchy, later receded from that position in a search for 'true magistracy' headnotes and [10.8).

That God is the author of all government amongst his creatures, and especially of the government of mankind, appeareth by reason. The same who is the author of all creatures in their being and existence must be the author of their subsistence and preservation in that being and existence. It is an infallible maxim in the schools, in nature [and] in scripture . . . [that] he that giveth being is the same that preserveth the being. Creation is begun conservation and conservation is a continued creation.

We assume [that] things made existent by creation cannot subsist and have continuance but by order, by government; from whence naturally it followeth God must be the author of this order and government, and consequently hath not left it arbitrary to man by composition and consent to do it. Authority strengtheneth this reason. . . . It is not arbitrary (in S. Augustine's mind) to man whether [there is] government or not. . . . In his judgement . . . it is a commanded, a necessary thing, and that . . . by an inevitable, irrepealable ordinance which nothing temporary can make void . . . . He that disclaimeth the *jus naturae* (the dictate of nature) to be *jus divinum* (the law and ordinance of God) hath made a divorce betwixt himself, and nature and reason, and sound divinity....

I humbly entreat those who are contrary-minded to consider seriously how Almighty God, in the creation of man (before woman was made of him and for him), and before he had any child or subject to govern, fixed authority and power for government in the person of Adam.... It is not to be controverted, if Adam had never fallen, aristocracy or democracy or mixed government had never been existent or apparent in the world. What specie of government had been then? I pray you tell me it... If then, in *statu instituto*, in the state of innocency and perfection, God Almighty did establish government and fix it in Adam before his wife was created, or a subject born, is it not by this evident, that God judged it in His wisdom better that neither woman nor posterity should be, than that one should not be to rule over all?.... If it was necessary in the state of innocency to establish it thus by God's decree, how much more in *statu peccati*, in our decayed and corrupted state by sin?.... After the fall it is declared transmissible from Adam to the first born (*Genesis* [iii. 16]). [And as for women; *To her he said*]... *Thy desire shall be to thy husband, and he shall rule over thee*. Let any man judge then whether or not with reason it can be said that this establishment of *sub* and *supra*, subject and sovereign, be [only the] constitution of man. And withall (by the way) let any indifferent man judge what may be said for monarchy, its excellency and conveniency above other species of government....

Because of men's sins, and by God's judgements following sin, a multitude may be divided from their natural sovereign (be dispersed by a war, a persecution or some other necessity imaginable) and yet meet in a strange land or some territory not inhabited. This case presupposed, I demand whether or not this *populus inconditus* [disordered multitude] would not condescend presently and necessarily to some sovereign power to govern and protect them. Who can deny it? Again, if all these were descended from one, or sprung up from one root, and their common father were with them, would not [nature], equity and humanity necessitate them to submit to him, and that from him it should be hereditarily transmitted to his first born, and so forward?.... I change the case. Take them not only as *inconditus populus*, [but as]... a confused mixture of more nations, more families [which] have not one common father. If they condescend that one shall have sovereign power over all, and so by consent shall be surrogated in the place of a common father and that this sovereignty shall be transmitted to his eldest son and so forth: from whence this power? Necessity forceth them to a government. Without it they can have neither society, nor safety, nor peace, nor happiness. But all their part is only to design or declare the man (which is only *potestas designativa, potestas deputativa*) but the power is only from Almighty God, the *potestas collativa*. The authority, the sovereignty is *of God, from God*, God's. The reason is evident. The substitute must have it by the same hand, by the same means [that] he had it in whose place he was substituted. By what is said, he cometh in the place of a common father; and the father's right is immediately from God, and of God. . . .

It is a ruled case in law that . . . 'the way by which we came to have . . . the right to anything' (provided it be lawful, otherwise that maxim is of undoubted truth . . . 'long possession cannot secure an unjust title' . . . ) . . . 'is not prejudiced by the way by which we obtain it'. The jurists give the reason of this: 'If a man come at anything by a legal title by the law of nations' (i.e. by the law of common equity) 'the possession or apprehension is entire and valid.' Now apply all this. When a people disordered are without a government and destitute of a governor to whom by a title and right of nature it is due condescend to design and choose one for their ruler, why shall he not, *should* he not, enjoy, inherit the right of, the deficient proprietor? And seeing the right proprietor had this right by God, by nature, how can it be but, howsoever the designation of the [new] person is from the disordered community, yet the collation of power is from God immediately and from His sacred and inviolable ordinance? And what can be said against *modus aquirendi*, the way by which such a one elected obtaineth this right? For seeing God doth not now send Samuels and Elishas to anoint or declare Kings, we are in His ordinary providence, to conceive the designation or election of the person as the manifestation of God's will, *voluntas signi* [a sign of His will], as the schools speaketh (just so as when the church designeth one to sacred orders). . . .

*Chapter VIII*

If there were no more to disprove this popular tenet 'that sovereignty in a King is by derivation from the community', this is more than enough: that it is built upon a false ground; for it presupposeth and taketh as granted that in the community, whether collective of all individuals, or virtual and representative by some in place of all, there is an inherent *potestas activa rectiva* (a ruling, active power), which is most false. . . . How is it imaginable that in all the people in gross, in common, this *potestas activa regiminis*, or *potestas activi regiminis* (this power of activating government) is seated as in its prime, principal and most proper seat and subject? Government intrinsically, essentially includes in it a specific distinction of *regentes* and *recti* [rulers and ruled]: some to be governors, some to be governed. If all and every one hath this power abovementioned, where then are those that are to be ruled and governed?

If they would speak rationally, there can no other power be conceived to be inherent in the community, naturally and properly, but only *potestas passiva regiminis* (a capacity or susceptibility to be governed by one or more). This capacity in the community is attended with an *appetitus naturalis* and *necessarius ad regimen* (a natural necessity and vehement inclination and desire to submit to government) by which it is to be stated into an happier and safer posture and condition. (Just so . . . as the 'first matter', of which natural philosophy speaketh, hath a desire to be united to some form, by which receiving a particular determination to a specific and individual entity, it is actuated and perfected). . . . This capacity in the community, being natural, and common to all, and having from it issuing out a vehement desire to actual government, obliges all . . . by the law and dictate of nature to submit to actual government. [This] desire or propension, if you reflect on it . . . is not merely and properly *voluntary*; because, howsoever nature dictates that government is necessary for the maintenance of society, for happiness, for safety and protection, yet every singular and individual person, by corruption and self-love hath . . . a natural averseness and repugnancy to submit to any. . . . It is despair to attain at government that makes the greatest and most part to submit to government, and that they see and feel that without government none can enjoy society or safety. This forceth that natural repugnancy, which is singularly and severally in every one, to give way to that universal, natural and necessary propension of nature to government.

This *appetitus universalis* and *naturalis*, this vehement necessary propension and desire to government, is not unlike that act of the understanding by which it assenteth to the first principles of undeniable, uncontrollable truth, which are evident *ex vi terminorum*, by evident appearance in the essential connection of the terms. Or it is not unlike to that first act of man's will by which necessarily *fertur in summum bonum*, it is carried to its chief good. Both of these in sound philosophy are not . . . free acts of the understanding and will, but *necessarii*, such as cannot otherwise be. Just so, this consent and submission to government...is...not so free as it may choose or reject, but in some kind it is *necessarius*, elicited by force, constraint or necessity, [so] that all and every one are necessitated to it by that necessity of obedience nature hath laid upon them.... [It] followeth that this consent in the community and every individual is not *pure activus*, purely and simply active, but hath more alliance with *consensus passivus*, a necessary and necessitated consent. From this then, it is more than apparent that by that our new statists call the 'voluntary consent of the people', nothing is bestowed upon him or them in whom the sovereignty is fixed. Nor can the community be a donor of any right or power, but in submission and subjection. It will puzzle infinitely our new state philosophy to make anything, in its kind passive, really active and collative of positive acts and effects....How dare they be so impertinent, so impudent to say that 'in the people there is an underived majesty'? [Quoting Parker, *Observations*, p. 15] It is right down contradictory to scripture (*Daniel*, ii. 37; v. 18). It is said *God giveth kingdom, power, strength, glory and majesty*. More absurd is that that they with brazen face affirm: this majesty in a King is derived only *cumulativè, communicativè*, so that the people are not divested of it but... in some cases (which if they be not real, people shall fancy them at pleasure) this same sovereignty and majesty is resumable. An old philosopher would laugh at him who would presume to say that a matter passive, actuated and perfected by union with a form, could at pleasure shake off the specific and individual form and marry itself to another. They may with as good reason say that a husband has marital power from his wife, and (to gratify that sex, with which they are very prevalent) they may endow every wife with that power to resume her freedom and to marry another at pleasure!....

A [further] argument against this popular error and deceit is this. If all sovereignty and supreme power were originally inherent in the people and from thence derived to the King, then undoubtedly democracy were the best of all governments. The reason is pregnant. That species and kind of government which cometh nearest its original must be sounder and more perfect...The nearer to the fountain, the stream runneth more pure and clear. This argument cannot be well taken off; and it is a strong argument... for monarchy. It proveth the excellency of monarchy above all governments because it approacheth nearest the government of God, and God Himself who is the author of all government....[And] howsoever all writers of politics in many things concerning policy disagree among themselves (as clocks, or our Sectaries) yet all unanimously accord and agree in this: that of all government, democracy and popular government is the worst, and [they]... prefer aristocracy to it by many stages. [This] likewise enforceth our argument for the excellency of monarchy. For the farther you recede from monarchy (as in democracy) the worse the government is; and the nearer you approach it (as in aristocracy) the government is the better....

## 7.5 THE ROYALIST HISTORY OF PARLIAMENT

From [Robert Filmer], *The freeholders grand inquest* (1648), 6–11: Wing F912. The full text is printed in Peter Laslett (ed.), *Patriarcha and other political works of Sir Robert Filmer* (Oxford, 1949).

It has recently been suggested (Weston 1980) that Sir Robert Filmer (*c.* 1588–1653), infamous as the victim of John Locke's *First treatise*, was not the author of *The Freeholder's grand inquest* (1648). However that may be – and it is hard to see that Laslett's (1949) attribution can yet be laid aside – the work demonstrates the importance of learned historiography to the royalist–parliamentarian controversy. If Filmer were right, and the medieval 'Parliaments' were the 'creatures' of Kings, then the constitution was not immemorial, it had not existed 'time out of mind' [8.5], and the 'ancient ways of proceeding' [3.6] did not teach an interdependence of the parts of the constitution and the rights and liberties of the people. The powers and duties of Parliaments might be specified by their creator and the King was author of the people's rights. Parker had after all argued that whatever created a thing was greater than that thing [8.3], and the widespread use of genetic argument (Schochet 1975) suggested the same conclusion: that if the King was the creator and sustainer of Parliament, then Parliament was subservient to him. This brief extract seeks only to illustrate Filmer's inexorable piling on of the evidence; his argument is discussed in Pocock (1957), in one of the most satisfying pieces of intellectual history ever written. For more on Filmer, see [7.8] below.

For clearing the meaning and sense of the writ, and satisfaction of such as think it impossible but that the Commons of England have always been a part of the Common Council of the kingdom, I shall insist upon these three points: 1. That anciently the barons of England were the Common Council of the kingdom. 2. That until the time of Henry I the Commons were not called to Parliament. 3. Though the Commons were called by Henry I, yet they were not constantly called, nor yet regularly elected by writ until Henry III's time.

For the first point, Mr Camden, in his *Britannia*, doth teach us that in the time of the English Saxons, and in the ensuing age, a Parliament was called *Commune Concilium*, which was, saith he... 'the presence of the King, Prelates, and Peers assembled'. No mention of the Commons. The prelates and peers were all the barons. The author of the chronicle of the church of Litchfield, cited by Mr [John] Selden, saith...'After King Edward was King, by the Council of the barons of England he revived a law which had lain asleep threescore and seven years; and this law was called the Law of St. Edward the King.' In the same chronicle it is said that William the Conqueror [at London in the fourth year of his reign] had... a Council of his barons. And it is of this Parliament that his son, Henry I, speaks, saying: 'I restore you the laws of King Edward the Confessor, with those amendments wherewith my father amended them by a Council of his barons.'

In the fifth year, as Mr Selden thinks, of the Conqueror.... [and so Filmer continues, to give six further examples of there being no Commons before the time of Henry I]...At the coronation of Henry I, all the people of the kingdom of England were called, and the laws were then made; but it was... 'by the Common Council of my barons'. In his third year, the peers of the kingdom were called without any mention of the Commons; and another, a while after... 'by the consent of the earls and barons'.... [twelve more citations follow]....

32 Henry III. The King commanded all the nobility of the whole realm kingdom to be called to treat of the state of the kingdom...

49 Henry III. The King had a treaty at Oxford with the peers of the kingdom...

At a Parliament at Marlborough, 55 Henry III, statutes were made by the assent of the earls and barons.

Here the place of Bracton, Chief Justice in this King's time, is worth the observing: and the rather for that it is much insisted on of late to make for Parliaments' being above the King. The words in Bracton are, 'The King hath a superior, God; also the law by which he is made King; also his Court, viz. the earls and barons.' The Court that was said in those days to be above the King was a court of earls and barons. Not a word of the Commons, or the representative body of the kingdoms being any part of the superior Court. Now for the true sense of Bracton's words, how the Court of earls and barons are the King's superiors. They must of necessity be understood to be superiors so far only as to advise and direct the King out of his own grace and good will only. [This] appears plainly by the words of Bracton himself, where, speaking of the King, he resolves thus: . . . 'Nor can any man put a necessity upon him to correct and amend his injury unless he will himself, since he hath no superior but God. It will be sufficient punishment for him to expect the Lord an avenger.' Here the same man who (speaking according to some men's opinion) saith the law and Court of the earls and barons are superior to the King, in this place tells us himself the King hath no superior but God! The difference is easily reconciled. According to the distinction of the schoolmen, the King is free from the *co-active* power of the laws or counsellors, but he may be subject to their *directive* power according to his own will. That is, God can only compel; but the law and his Courts may advise him. . . .

These precedents show that from the conquest until a great part of Henry III's reign (in whose days it is thought the writ for election of Knights was framed) which is about 200 years – and above a third part of the time since the conquest to our days – the barons made the Parliament or Common Council of the Kingdom. Under the name of barons, not only earls but bishops also were comprehended, for the Conqueror made the bishops barons. Therefore it is no such great wonder that in the writ we find the Lords only to be the counsellors, and the Commons called only to perform and consent to the ordinances. . . .

## 7.6 THE ABSURDITY AND DANGER OF BASING OBLIGATION ON CONSENT

From John Spelman, *A view of a printed book intituled Observations* (Oxford, 1643), 14–15, [25], [29], [31]: Wing S 4941; Maxwell, *Sacro-sancta regum majestas*, 98–9, 101. (see headnotes to [4.2], [7.4].

The parliamentarians continually claimed that the two Houses should be followed in war because they 'represented' the people – since political obligation was based on consent and to be represented precisely was to have consented. There was (and is) a lot wrong with this line of argument: first, Parliament 'represented' the people only in a highly conventional way, as stipulated in law; second, if obligation is based on consent, when and how did each individual consent to government and (if that can be answered satisfactorily) why cannot any individual withdraw consent? Filmer is well known as a precursor of David Hume as a critic of the consent theory of obligation (Schochet 1975; Allen 1928b), and the reader will find his criticisms below [7.8]. Many other royalists, however, were quick to pounce on the obvious fictions and illogicalities of the parliamentarian position. Here are two.

### *7.6.1. Spelman*

I should rather think if regal power were originally conveyed from the people, they by conveying it over have divested themselves of it. If it were conveyed upon conditions, then under those conditions it may be held against them; if absolutely, then it may be held absolutely over them. It was necessary by the law of nature that they should convey over a power unto some, for, willy-nilly, a people cannot be without a government; or, were the conveyance voluntary, have they therefore a power over it at pleasure to revoke it, although it were often ratified by Oaths of Allegiance and Supremacy? Doth not this doctrine destroy not only monarchy but all government whatsoever? The people, [Parker says], are the authors and efficient causes of that power that the Parliamentmen have by conveyance from them. May the people therefore conclude themselves to be above Parliament and at their pleasure revoke and control their power? May Newcastle, or any particular borough or county disauthorise those they have empowered? Or if any particular borough or county cannot remove their proxies, yet the major part of the electors throughout the kingdom, may, according to this doctrine, revoke the trust and authority that all members have. If so . . . how can any obedience be required to their votes, whenas it is doubtful whether the major part of the freeholders do not disavow their proceedings? . . . . You see whereunto the Observator's principles do lead; and if you desire to know the fountain from whence he drew these goodly doctrines, that little treatise entitled *Puritano-jesuitismus* will point [it] out unto you . . .

[You, Parker, say] the Parliament is supreme . . . in matters of state and law. But again I must consider. [You say] '. . . the Lords and Commons' . . . [are] . . . 'virtually the whole kingdom'. Why do you put the Lords in . . . ? The Lords vote in respect of their baronies derived from the Crown; the Commons vote in the right of their electors whom they represent. At least nine parts of the kingdom neither do nor may vote in their elections: the clergy in respect of their spiritual livings may not, nor the most substantial copyholders, farmers or lessees for years, nor inheritrixes, jointresses nor reversioners. Heirs apparent and men that live upon interest are excluded, and all that have not 40/- *per annum* freehold land (which I imagine cannot be above a tenth part of the kingdom). Tell me, good Sir, you that list to unsettle principles (power being, you say, nothing else but the 'might and vigour' which a society of men contains in itself) why should the 'might and vigour' of those, being far the major part, be overmastered and concluded by the votes of those that are deputed by a minor number of the people? Or why should half the kingdom, in which there are a few boroughs, be equalled and overborne in voting by two counties out of which many burgesses are chosen? Old Sarum shall have as many votes in Parliament as the city of London or county of Wiltshire, by which it seems the Commons are not sent with equality from all parts, nor sent by all. How do they represent all? What reason is there that the kingdom should sit down with their votes? The truth is, the King, Lords and Commons are virtually the whole kingdom for that all the people did at first submit themselves to their determination. 25 Hen 8 cap 21: 'Your Royal Majesty and your Lords and Commons, representing the whole realm in this, your most High Court of Parliament, have power, etc.'; so that in the King principally, but yet in conjunction with the Lords and Commons, is the virtue and power of the kingdom contained. . . .

This doctrine (of the people's power to judge of danger against the commands of the sovereign, and upon that to take up defensive arms) if it should be admitted, will be [no] more pernicious to kingly government out of Parliament than it will be to Parliaments themselves. For, as the people may preserve themselves against a wilful seduced prince that would destroy them, so may they send against an ordinance of the Lords and Commons if they shall judge it to tend to the destruction of the kingdom or subversion of government. The charter of nature by its supreme law entitles all to seek their safety, and against this it will be of little purpose for you to tell the people, 'that next to renouncing God, nothing is more pernicious than to forsake their representatives', when they shall judge their representatives forsake their trust and would lead them on to anabaptism or any other way to destruction. . . .

I would gladly be instructed how this power [of command] is derived unto them, either from the King or people, or whether we must think they above all other men were naturally born to it.

### *7.6.2 Maxwell*

[Another] argument to prove that sovereignty in a King is not from the community or multitude is this: If this sovereignty be natively inherent in the multitude, it must be proper to every individual of the community. If it be so, *Quisque nascitur liber* (every one is born a free man in the forest), then it will necessarily follow that the generation and posterity of those who have first contracted with their elected King are not bound to that covenant...Upon their native right [they] may start aside, appoint another King, and that without any breach of covenant or any just title in the King of their fathers to force or reduce them to his obedience (an excellent way devised to preserve King and kingdom in peace and safety).... There can be no civil commerce, no true faith in dealing, in bargaining, if you open this back door: that when a man hath contracted [or] covenanted to his disadvantage he may resume it and put himself in *statu quo*. If it were granted that royalty in a King were by a contract betwixt him and his people, and revocable by the people upon the appearance of disadvantage, it cannot stand but in all inferior contracts of less concernment the like should hold. Is there any act more freely done than when a woman, not subject to paternal authority, of perfect age, under no guardian, maketh choice of an husband as she fancieth? And, I pray you, may she afterward shake him off at pleasure? God forbid....

Buchanan, one of their greatest authors, holds that if a Parliament determine in a matter of law, it can establish nothing but a...preparatory precognition, and the influence of the legislative power is not, till it be approved and admitted by the community. The Observator, fearing this tenet of Buchanan may make void the orders of the House, leaveth here his master, and averreth 'that the right of the gentry and commonalty is entirely in the Knights and Burgesses of the House of Commons and will have their orders irrevocable'. A wonder it is that they are so favourable in their own case and so unjust and unequal in the King's case. For if it were granted...that all power in the King were by a trust devolved upon him from the people, what is the reason of the difference that *he* shall not have the right as entirely, as irrevocable as the commissioners of the counties and corporations?

## 7.7 CONSENT AS A ROYALIST BASIS

From Dudley Digges, *The unlawfulnesse of a subjects taking up armes* (Oxford, 1644), 1–6: Wing 1462.

Dudley Digges the younger (1613–43) died at Oxford, like Spelman, of camp fever. A member of the Tew circle who met at Viscount Falkland's house at Great Tew in the 1630s, he was an associate not only of moderate royalists like Edward Hyde and Falkland himself, but of men like John Selden and the (pre-1642) Hobbes, men who believed that it was possible to renounce, by contract, the 'natural right' of self-preservation (Tuck 1979). But why should they renounce it?

Here Digges, in a very Hobbesian vein (Sirluck 1959), depicts that 'natural state' from which it would be rational to recede. 'Law', the will of the sovereign, would then supervene upon natural right, and all would be obliged, by an enforced contract, to obey. Hobbes, Chapter XIII of whose *Leviathan* of 1651 contains the most famous discussion of the 'state of nature', was to end at a less drastic conclusion: men could not give up their natural right; they could, and should, make it extremely difficult for themselves to exercise it by arming their sovereign so well; but if the sovereign could no longer protect them they were no longer obliged to obey. In his posthumous *Unlawfulness of a subject's taking up arms*, from which this extract is taken, Digges had recourse to many other more conventional religions and legal arguments, and on these grounds, too, would not be accused, like Hobbes, of arguing that *any* successful usurper should be obeyed. He argued for the sovereign power of the Stuarts, and not just for sovereign power in general. Obviously, though, the doctrine that obligation is based on consent was not just a parliamentarian or radical position.

He that will endeavour to make the yoke of government more easy . . . . shall be sure to find many favourable readers, because the greater part of mankind . . . . are easily prevailed upon to make a truce with conscience, and eagerly prosecute what appears most profitable. And the chiefest cause of our miseries is that they do not rightly apprehend what is truly advantageous. . . . They rule their actions and desires but by one syllogism and look upon the immediate consequence – which is the satisfaction of some particular ends and serving some present turn – and have not ordinarily so much depth of understanding as to be able to discern the future evils which will inevitably spring from the same fountain. . . .

[I] instance two main principles by which the seduced multitude hath been tempted to catch at an empty happiness, and thereby have pulled upon themselves misery and destruction.

The first is a doctrine craftily instilled into the minds of the people upon no other foundation but a mistake in the meaning of true and profitable liberty: that the law of nature doth justify any attempt to shake off those bonds imposed upon them by superiors, if inconvenient and destructive of native freedom – the fallacy of which is easily discerned by understanding men. It is true, if we look upon the privileges of nature (abstracting from paternal dominion), freedom is the birthright of mankind and equally common to everyone as the air we breathe in or the sun which sheds his beams and lustre as comfortably upon beggars as upon the Kings of the earth. This freedom was an unlimited power to use our abilities according as will did prompt – the restraint of which would questionless have been very grievous, but that experience did demonstrate it was not so delightful to do whatever they liked as it was miserable to suffer as much as it pleased others to inflict. For any that was stronger than his neighbour had it in his power to hinder him from enjoying the benefits of liberty. Nor yet could the most powerful man among them take any extraordinary comfort in this as yet hostile state, because his mind was distracted with continual fears, since there was not any so contemptibly weak but that if he despised his own life or desired to enjoy it with more uncontrolled pleasures, he might make himself master of any other man's – though not by force, yet by subtlety and watching advantages. Or at least a few, combining, might destroy the strongest and might be tempted so to do for their fuller security.

This was their unhappy condition amidst fears and jealousies, wherein each single person looked upon the world as his enemy and doubted . . . . lest the hand of every man might be upon him. . . . I will add the unavoidable occasions of quarrel, extremely opposite to the prime dictate of nature (the preservation of ourselves) and to the means that conduce thereto (a peaceable enjoyment of the comforts of this life). For whilst everyone had a right to all, nobody could with safety make use of anything; since when some would take to themselves what others delighted in, their desires and rights being equal, there was no title but that of greater force which could determine to whom it ought to belong; and this could not be determined but by fighting; and this right reason abhored, as by which men would either be exposed to famine in the midst of plenty or else be forced daily to hazard the loss of their lives out of a natural desire of conserving them.

The sense of these calamities quickening their understandings to find out, easily prevailed with their wills to entertain a remedy of so great evils, which, manifestly proceeding from division, the ready cure was to make themselves one, because no body is at variance with itself. There being no way to effect this naturally, they reduce themselves into a civil unity by placing over them one head and by making his will the will of them all, to the end there might be no gap left by schism to return to their former confusion. Because the wills of men, though the fountains of voluntary actions, yet are not themselves the objects of choice (for we cannot

* Original version: '. . . (for we cannot will to be willing, (this would be infinite) but to performe what is commanded) and so are not capable of being obliged by compacts; therefore this submission . . .'

will to be willing – this would be infinite), [we] are not capable of being obliged by compacts, [only of agreeing] to perform what is commanded. Therefore this submission* of all to the will of one, or this union of them agreed upon, is to be understood in a politic sense – and signifies the giving up of every man's particular power into his disposal so that he may be able to enforce those who are unwilling, upon some private ends, to be obedient for the common good. Otherwise they would enjoy the benefits of others' faith in observing laws, and the advantage of their own violations and breaches, which may probably be prevented if penalties be appointed much greater than the profit which can come by their disobedience – because, as men are naturally tempted by hopes of good, so they are as naturally deterred by a certain expectation of greater evils.

Thus, also, by transferring every particular man's power into the hands of one is not meant a real laying down and natural translation of their strength (because nerves and sinews are not transferable, as [are] their money and goods), but a consent and mutual obligation, as of all to one (whether he be King as in a monarchy, or some nobles – for they are [one] too – as in aristocracy, so of everyone to each other) of not using their natural power but only as the law shall require, i.e. of not resisting that body in which the supreme power is placed, as likewise of aiding him or them by virtue of that promise or of that oath, according to the nature of the contract whence he or they summon their strength.

By what is laid down may be discovered the weakness of their second principle . . . . that the law of nature will defend us, whomsoever we kill (though the King) in our own defence; and we are acquitted by that principle *vim vi* [that force may be resisted with force]. (Nay some go higher and make it unlawful *not* to resist even the highest authority, it being a sin against nature etc. [These], the examples of the holy martyrs and of Christ himself do clearly confute . . .). I will briefly answer it. . . .

It ceases to be lawful after we have made ourselves sociable parts in one body, because we have voluntarily and upon agreement restrained ourselves from making use of this native right. And the renouncing this power by mutual compact will appear very consonant with sound reason, whether we look upon the benefits ensuing thereby or the mischiefs avoided; for it is a more probable means to the attaining that very end in the relation to which they plead for it: the preservation of particular persons. Upon this condition of obliging ourselves not to resist public authority, in requital for this submission of our private strength we are secured by the united power of all, and the whole kingdom becomes our guard. And it is most likely we should be less exposed to injuries when that impartial and equal measure of right, the known law, is by this means maintained. The evils which would flow from this licence to resume our power against contract are infinite. Our own feelings too fully instruct us in the sad effects; and I doubt not but the weariness of our present sufferings and the expectation of growing mischiefs will be powerful beyond rhetoric to persuade us to value highly the public tranquillity. I am confident, if the people of this land . . . . were able to deliver themselves from their 'defenders', we should suddenly be restored to happiness, and it would be as hard a matter to engage them in a civil war when they had again tasted the sweetness of plenty and quiet as it is to persuade them to agree to peace, who challenge a legal power by the title of war to dispose of the King's and subject's revenues at pleasure.

As reason induced men to enter into such a covenant and to lay a mutual obligation one upon another not to resist authority upon whatever grounds, whether of fancied or of real injustice, but to submit their actions and persons to the ordinary tribunal, though it might possibly happen that some particulars would be sentenced unjustly (because a far more considerable good could not be obtained unless by agreement patiently to submit to this possible evil, since the common peace and quiet cannot be effectually provided for if it shall be indulged to any to appeal from the laws themselves and to judge their judges) so honesty and religion strictly bind them to preserve their faith entire, and this contract inviolable.

The pains I have taken to lay open by way of introduction, to the view and examination of all that desire real satisfaction, the foundation upon which rule and subjection are built will not appear so delightful as it was necessary. . . . *Populi salus suprema lex* is the engine by which the upper rooms are torn from the foundation and seated upon fancy only, like castles in the air. For the safety of the people is really built upon government; and, this destroyed, the other . . . will soon be swallowed up in the common confusion. But this is evidently destroyed by these principles. For government is an effect, not of a people's divided powers, but as they are united and made one by civil constitution. For that when we call it 'supreme power', we impose an improper name and have given an occasion for mistakes (yet I shall not endeavour to alter the common use of speaking, but only to prevent a misunderstanding of it) because indeed this power is simply one; and when it doth express itself by one person or more (who yet are but several parts of one governor, according to different forms)† there is not left in the kingdom or commonwealth any civil (i.e. legal) power which can appear in resistance, because all of them have bound their natural hands by a politic agreement.

Hence it follows [that] those that will allow any power to subjects against their ruler, let it be one man or many united by one common form .... do thereby dissolve the sinews of government, by which they are compacted into one and which made a multitude a people, and ... break the commonwealth into as many pieces as they have set up opposers against it. For there cannot be two powers and yet the kingdom remain one .... I am fully persuaded no sober man can imagine the policy of this state is so defective as to open a necessary way to its own ruin, i.e. to divide the kingdom legally in itself; and therefore it must necessarily be granted, those that take up arms, being not authorised so to do by law, are guilty of rebellion and the consequences of it: murder and rapine. It is very easy to determine whom the law hath armed with power, because not any part of the people, not the two Houses, but the King alone is sworn to protect us, which is an evident argument he is enabled to effect this end, and that the necessary means to compass it, which is the *posse regni*, is at his disposal.

## 7.8 SOVEREIGNTY, PATRIARCHALISM AND THE ILLOGIC OF MIXTURE AND CONSENT

From Robert Filmer, *The anarchy of a limited or mixed monarchy* (1648), Preface, 1, 6–11, 19–23, 15–16. The full tract is reprinted in Laslett (1949).

This extract represents Filmer at his best, partly because it *is* an extract, and partly because the *Anarchy of a limited or mixed monarchy* (1648) digests the patriarchalism of his earlier, diffuse and disordered *Patriarcha*, and in any case concentrates on what he was best at: showing the weaknesses of others' cases. Here he attacks Philip Hunton [8.6] in particular. Filmer's patriarchalism has recently been studied at some length by Schochet (1975); and Daly has devoted almost a whole book to him (1979a). Both scholars record the wealth of literature that has sprung up since the later 1920s on this most unlikely candidate for fame. (To which should be added the 1980 pieces by Wallace and

† Original version: '... (according to different formes) who are yet but severall parts of one governour ...'

Weston.) A Kentish squire, respectable and well connected, but hardly a public figure in his own times, Filmer attempted to lie low during the civil wars, though he did suffer imprisonment at the hands of the parliamentarians. He took no part in the Kentish rising of 1648 which triggered off the second war (Laslett 1949). His fame was to come posthumously when he was republished during the crisis that was to end in the 'Glorious Revolution' of 1688. His *Patriarcha* was attacked by – among others – the Whig martyr, Algernon Sidney, and by the great John Locke (Laslett, 1960). Until the 1920s he was the paradigm of the stupid and fanatical Tory squire; but Dunn (1969), Schochet (1979) and Tully (1980) have shown why even his foolish-seeming patriarchalism may have elicited such a hysterical response. The power of the father in the Stuart household was a potent symbol of political power – though whether fathers any more than Kings actually succeeded in exercising that power may have been another matter.

We do but flatter ourselves if we hope ever to be governed without an arbitrary power. No: we mistake. The question is not whether there shall be an arbitrary power, but the only point is who shall have that power, whether one man or many? There never was nor ever can be any people governed without the power of making laws, and every power of making laws must be arbitrary: for to make law according to law is *contradictio in adjecto* [contradictory by definition]. It is generally confessed that in a democracy the supreme and arbitrary power of making laws is in the multitude; and so in an aristocracy the like legislative or arbitrary power is in a few, or in the nobility; and therefore, by a necessary consequence, in a monarchy the same legislative power must be in one. . . .

This ancient doctrine of government in these latter days hath been strangely refined by the Romanists, and wonderfully improved since the reformation (especially in point of monarchy) by an opinion that the people have originally a power to create several sorts of monarchy, to limit and compound them with other forms of government at their pleasure. As for this natural power of the people: they find neither scripture, reason, nor practice to justify it . . .

Since the growth of this new doctrine of the limitation and mixture of monarchy it is most apparent that monarchy hath been crucified, as it were, between two thieves, the Pope and the people. For, what principles the papists make for the use of the power of the Pope above Kings, the very same (by blotting out the word 'Pope' and putting in the word 'people') the plebists take up to use against their sovereigns. . . .

I cannot but reverence that form of government which was allowed and made use of for God's own people and for all other nations. It were impiety to think that God, who was careful to appoint judicial laws for His chosen people, would not furnish them with the best form of government, or to imagine that the rules given in divers places in the gospel by our beloved Saviour and his Apostles for obedience to Kings should now, like almanacs out of date, be no use to us because it is pretended that we have a form of government now, not once thought of in those days. It is a shame and scandal for us Christians to seek the original of government from the inventions or fictions of poets, orators, philosophers and heathen historians who all lived thousands of years after the creation and were . . . ignorant of it, and to neglect the scriptures which have, with more authority, most particularly given us the true grounds and principles of government.

There is scarce the meanest man of the multitude but can now in these days tell us that the government of England is a limited and mixed monarchy. (And it is no marvel, since all the disputes and arguments of these distracted times, both from the pulpit and the press to tend and end in this conclusion.) The author of the *Treatise of monarchy* hath copiously handled the nature and manner of limited and mixed monarchy and is the first and only man I know who hath undertaken the task of describing it. Others only mention it, as taking it for granted. . . .

I will now touch some few particular passages in the treatise. Our author first confesseth, 'It is God's express ordinance there should be government', and he proves it by *Genesis* iii. 16, where God ordained Adam to rule over his wife, and her desires were to be subject to his, and, (as hers) all theirs that should come of her. Here we have the original grant of government, and the fountain of all power placed in the father of all mankind. Accordingly we find the law for obedience to government given in terms of 'honour thy father': not only the constitution of power in general, but the limitation of it to one kind (i.e. to monarchy or the government of one alone) and the determination of it to the individual person and line of Adam. And all three are ordinances of God. Neither Eve nor her children could either limit Adam's power or join with others with him in the government; and what was given to Adam was given, in his person, to posterity. This paternal power continued monarchical to the Flood, and after the Flood to the confusion of Babel. When the kingdoms were first erected, planted or scattered over the face of the world, we find (*Genesis* x. 11) it was done by colonies of whole families, over which the fathers had supreme power, and were Kings. [They] were all the sons or grandchildren of Noah, from whom they derived a fatherly and regal power over their families. Now, if this supreme power was settled and founded by God himself in the fatherhood, how is it possible for the people to have any right or title to alter and dispose of it otherwise? What commission can they show that gives them power either of limitation or mixture? It was God's ordinance that supremacy should be unlimited in Adam and as large as the acts of his will. And, as in him, so in all others that have supreme power, as appears by the judgement and speech of the people to Joshua when he was supreme governor. These are their words to him: *All that thou commandest us we will do. Whosoever he be that doth rebel against thy commandment and will not hearken unto thy words in all that thou commandest him, he shall be put to death.* We may not say that these were evil counsellors or flattering courtiers of Joshua, or that he himself was a tyrant for having such arbitrary power. Our author, and all those who affirm that power is conveyed to persons by public consent, are forced to confess that it is the fatherly power that first enables a people to make such a conveyance: so that admitting (as they hold) that our ancestors did at first convey power, yet the reason why we now living do submit to such power is for that our forefathers (every one for himself, his family, and posterity) had a power of resigning up themselves and us to a supreme power. As the scripture teacheth us that supreme power was originally in the fatherhood without any limitation, so likewise reason doth evince it that if God ordained that supremacy should be, that then supremacy must of necessity be unlimited. For that power that limits must be above the power which is limited. If it is limited it cannot be supreme. So that if our author will grant supreme power to be the ordinance of God, the supreme power will prove itself to be unlimited by the same ordinance, because a limited power is a contradiction. The monarchical power of Adam, the father of all flesh, being by a general binding ordinance settled by God in him and his posterity by right of fatherhood, the form of monarchy must be preferred above all other forms, except the like ordinance for other forms can be shown. Neither may men .... prefer or compare any other form with monarchy....

To proceed with our author. In the third page he saith, 'The higher power is God's ordinance. That it resideth in one or more, in such or such a way, is from human designment. God by no word binds any people to this or that form, till by their own all bind themselves.' Because the power and consent of the people in government is the burden of the whole book, and our author expects it should be admitted as a magisterial postulation without any other proof than a naked supposition, and since others also maintain that originally power was or now is in the people and that the first Kings were chosen by the people, they may not be offended if they be asked in what sense they understand the word 'people', because this, as many other words, hath different acceptions, being sometimes taken in a larger, otherwhile in a stricter sense. Literally, and in the largest sense, the word 'people' signifieth the whole multitude of mankind. But figuratively and synecdochically, it notes – many times – the major part of a multitude, or sometimes the better, or the richer, or the wiser, or some other part; and oftentimes a very small part of the people (if there be no apparent opposite party) hath the name of 'the people' by presumption.

If they understand that the entire multitude or whole people have originally by nature power to choose their own Kings, they must remember that by their own principles and rules, by nature all mankind in the world makes but one people who they suppose are born alike to an equal freedom from subjection. And where such freedom is, there all things must necessarily be in common; and therefore, without a joint consent of the whole people of the world, no one thing can be made proper to any one man, but it will be an injury and a usurpation upon the right of all others. From whence it follows that, natural freedom being once granted, there cannot be any one man chosen a King without the universal consent of all the people of the world at one instant, *nemine contradicente*. Nay, if it be true that nature hath made all men free, yet it cannot seem reasonable that they should have the power to alter the law of nature; for if no man have power to take away his own life without the guilt of being a murderer of himself, how can any *people* confer such a power as they have not themselves upon any one man without being accessories to their own deaths, and every man become guilty of being *felo de se*?

If this general signification of the word 'people' be disavowed, and men will suppose that the people of particular regions or countries have power and freedom to choose unto themselves Kings, then let them but observe the consequence. Since nature hath not distinguished the habitable world into kingdoms, nor determined what part of a people shall belong to what kingdom and what to another, it follows that, the original freedom of mankind being supposed, every man is at liberty to be of what kingdom he please, and so every petty company hath a right to make a kingdom by itself – and not only every city but every village and every family, nay, and every particular man [hath] a liberty to choose *himself* to be his own King if he please. And he were a madman, that, being by nature free, would choose any man but himself to be his own governor. Thus, to avoid the having but of one King of the whole world, we shall run into a liberty of having as many Kings as there be men in the world, which, upon the matter, is to have no King at all but to leave all men to their natural liberty, which is the mischief the pleaders of natural liberty do pretend they would most avoid.

But if neither the whole people of the world nor the whole people of any part of the world be meant, but only the major part or some other part of a part of the world, yet still the objection will be stronger. For (besides that nature hath made no partition of the world, or of all the people into distinct kingdoms, and that without a universal consent at one and the same instant, no partition can be made) yet if it were lawful for particular parts of the world by consent to choose their Kings, nevertheless their elections would bind none to subjection, but only such as consented. For the major part never binds but where men at first either agreed to be so bound or where a higher power so command. Now there being no higher power than nature but God himself, where neither nature nor God appoints the major part to bind, their consent is not binding to any but only to themselves who consent.

Yet, for the present to gratify them so far as to admit that either by nature or by the general consent of all mankind the world at first was divided into particular kingdoms and the major part of the people of each kingdom assembled, allowed to choose their King, yet it cannot be truly said that ever the whole people or the major part – or indeed any considerable part – of the whole people of any nation ever assembled to any such purpose. For, except by some secret miraculous instinct they should all meet at one time and place, what one man or company of men less than the whole people hath power to appoint either time and place of elections, where all alike be free by nature? And without a lawful summons, it is most unjust to bind those that be absent. The whole people cannot summon itself. One man is sick, another is lame, a third is aged, and a fourth is under the age of discretion; all these at some time or other, or at some place or other, might be able to meet if they might choose their own time and place, as men naturally free should.

In assemblies that are by human politic constitution, the superior power that ordains such assemblies can regulate and confine them both for time, place and persons, and other circumstances; but where there is an equality by nature there can be no superior power; there every infant at the hour it is born in hath a like interest with the greatest and wisest man in the world. Mankind is like the sea, ever ebbing or flowing. Every minute one is born, another dies. Those that are the people this minute, are not the people the next minute; in every instant and point of time there is a variation. No one time can be indifferent for all mankind to assemble. It cannot but be mischievous always at least to infants and others under the age of discretion – not to speak of women, especially virgins, who have by birth as much natural freedom as any other, and therefore ought not to lose their liberty without their own consent.

But in part to salve this it will be said that infants and children may be concluded by the votes of their parents. This remedy may cure some part of the mischief, but it destroys the whole cause and at last stumbles upon the true original of government. For if it be allowed that the acts of parents bind the children, then farewell the doctrine of the natural freedom of mankind. Where subjection of children to parents is natural, there can be no natural freedom. . . . In nature there is no nonage. If a man be not born free, she doth not assign him any other time when he shall attain his freedom; or, if she did, then children attaining that age should be discharged of their parents' contract. So that in conclusion: if it be imagined that the people were ever but once free from subjection by nature, it will prove a mere impossibility ever lawfully to introduce any kind of government whatsoever without apparent wrong to a multitude of people. (It is further observable, that ordinarily children and servants are far a greater number than parents and masters; and for the major part of these to be able to vote and appoint what government or governors their fathers and masters shall be subject unto is most unnatural, and in effect to give the children the government over their parents). . . .

The main charge I have against our author now remains to be discussed. And it is this: that instead of a treatise of monarchy he hath brought forth a treatise of anarchy: and that by his own confessions shall be made good.

First, he holds [that] a limited monarch transcends his bounds if he commands beyond the law, and the subject legally is not bound to subjection in such cases.

Now if you ask the author who shall be judge whether the

monarch transcend his bounds, and of the excesses of the sovereign power, his answer is, 'There is an impossibility of constituting a judge to determine this last controversy . . . I conceive in a limited monarchy there can be no stated internal judge of the monarch's actions if there grow a fundamental variance between him and the community. There can be no judge, legal and constituted, within that form of government.' In these answers it appears there is no judge to determine the sovereign's or the monarch's transgressing his fundamental limits. Yet our author is very cautious and supposeth only a 'fundamental variance' betwixt the monarch and the community. He is ashamed to put the question home. I demand of him: if there be a variance betwixt the monarch and any of the meanest persons of the community, who shall be the judge? If the monarch himself judge, then you destroy the frame of the state and make it absolute, saith our author; and he gives his reason: for to define a monarch to a law and then make him judge of his own deviations from that law is to absolve him from all law. On the other side: if any, or all, the people may judge, then you put the sovereignty in the whole body or part of it, and destroy the being of monarchy. Thus our author hath caught himself in a plain dilemma. If the King be judge then he is no limited monarch; if the people be judge then he is no monarch at all. So farewell limited monarchy; nay farewell to all government, if there be no judge.

Would you know what help our author hath found out for this mischief? First he saith that a subject is bound to yield to the magistrate when he cannot *de jure* challenge obedience, if it be in a thing in which he can possibly without subversion and in which his act may not be made a leading case and so bring on a prescription against public liberty. Again he saith, if the act in which the exorbitance or transgression of the monarch is supposed to be, be of lesser moment and not striking at the very being of that government, it ought to be borne by public patience rather than to endanger the being of the state. The like words he uses in another place, saying if the will of the monarch exceeds the limits of the law, it ought to be submitted to, so it be not contrary to God's law nor bring with it such an evil to ourselves or the public that we cannot be accessory to it by obeying. These are but figleaves to cover the nakedness of our author's limited monarch, formed upon weak supposals in cases of lesser moment. For if the monarch be to govern only according to law, no transgression of his can be of small moment if he break the bounds of the law, but it is a subversion of the government itself and may be made a leading case and so bring on a prescription against public liberty. It strikes at the very being of the government and brings with it such an evil as the party that suffers, or the public, cannot be accessory to. Let the case be never so small, yet if there be illegality in the act it strikes at the very being of limited monarchy, which is to be legal...

Secondly our author tells us if the monarch's act of exorbitancy or transgression be mortal, and such as suffered dissolves the frame of government and public liberty, then the illegality is to be set open and redressment sought by petition – which, if failing, prevention by resistance ought to be. And if it be apparent, and appeal made to the consciences of mankind, then the fundamental laws of that monarchy must judge and pronounce sentence in every man's conscience; and every man... must follow the evidence of truth in his own soul to oppose or not to oppose, according as he can in conscience acquit or condemn the act of the governor or monarch.

Whereas my author requires that the destructive nature of illegal command should be set open, surely his mind is that each private man in his particular case should make a public remonstrance to the world of the illegal acts of the monarch, and then, if upon his petition, he cannot be relieved according to his desire, he ought, or it is his duty, to make resistance? Here I would know who can be judge whether the illegality be made apparent. It is a main point, since every man is prone to flatter himself in his own cause and to think it good, and that the wrong or injustice he suffers is apparent, when other moderate and indifferent men can discover no such thing.... Yet our author will have an appeal made to the conscience of all mankind; and that being made, he concludes [that] the 'fundamental laws' must judge. I would very gladly learn of him what a 'fundamental law' is, or else have any one law named to me that any man can say is a fundamental law of the monarchy. I confess he tells us that the common laws are the 'foundation' and the statute laws are 'superstructive', yet I think he dares not say that there is any one branch or part of the common law but that it may be taken away by an Act of Parliament. For many portions of the common law (*de facto*) have; and (*de jure*) any point may be taken away. How can that be called fundamental which hath and may be removed, and yet the statute laws stand firm and stable? It is contrary to the nature of 'fundamental' for the building to stand when the foundation is taken away....

Truly the conscience of mankind is a pretty large tribunal for the fundamental laws to pronounce sentence in. It is very much that laws, which in their own nature are dumb and always need a judge to pronounce sentence, should now be able to speak and pronounce sentence themselves. Such a sentence must surely be upon the hearing of one party only, for it is impossible for a monarch to make his defence and answer and produce his witnesses in every man's conscience in each man's cause who will but question the legality of the government. . . . For all this, the conclusion is, every man must oppose or not oppose the monarch according to his own conscience. Thus, at the last, every man is brought by this doctrine of our author's to be his own judge. And I also appeal to mankind whether the end of all this be not utter confusion and anarchy.

Yet after all this, the author saith this power of every man's judging the illegal acts of the monarch argues not the superiority of those who judge over him who is judged; and he gives a profound reason for it. His words are: 'It is not authoritative and civil, but moral, residing in reasonable creatures and lawful for them to execute.' What our author means by these words ('not authoritative and civil, but moral') I understand not (though I think I do). Yet it serves my turn that he saith that resistance ought to be made, and every man must oppose or not oppose according as in conscience he can acquit or condemn the acts of his governor. For if it enable a man to resist and oppose his governor, without question it is authoritative and civil. Whereas he adds that moral judgement is residing in reasonable creatures and lawful for them to execute, he seems to imply that authoritative and civil judgement doth not reside in reasonable creatures nor can be lawfully executed. Such a conclusion fits well with anarchy; for he that takes away all government and leaves every man to his own conscience (and so makes him an independent State) may well teach that authority resides not in reasonable creatures, nor can be lawfully executed. . . .

[His] mixed monarchy – just like the limited – ends in confusion and destruction of all government. You shall hear the author's confession. 'That one inconvenience must necessarily be in all mixed governments which I showed to be in limited governments. There can be no constituted legal authoritative judge of the fundamental controversies arising between the three estates. If such do arise it is the fatal disease of those governments for which no salve can be applied. It is a case beyond the possible provision of such a government. Of this question there is no legal judge. The accusing side must make it evident to every man's conscience . . . The appeal must be to the community as if there were no government. And, as by evidence consciences are convinced, they are bound to give their assistance.' The wit of man cannot say more for anarchy.

## 7.9 A NEW ROYALIST: CLEMENT WALKER IN 1648

From Clement Walker, *The history of independency* (1648), 64–72: Wing W 329.

Clement Walker (d. 1651) was, like Prynne, a 'recruiter' to the Long Parliament. (As the events of the civil wars thinned the ranks of Parliament, new MPs were recruited by election, and these two were among that number). Walker's *History of independency* is an important source of our knowledge of the last civil war years of the Long Parliament, and was much relied on by the great Victorian historians of the period, Gardiner and Firth. The *History* was also ideology. It is the work of one, who, like Prynne, could not approve of the radical 'independents' with whom he, a constitutional conservative and a 'presbyterian' who stood for a unified national church, was supposed to work. This extract represents Walker's reaction to the Army's alliance with the independents in early 1648, before Pride's Purge: force had already been threatened, and Walker lays out the lineaments of the case he and Prynne, now royalists after the Purge, were to make in future. Walker died a prisoner of the Rump. Prynne survived to remind the interregnum regimes of how they had acted illegally, reneged on the declarations of the earlier war years, and were merely oligarchies based on force. That these attitudes were widespread is attested by the recent historical work of Underdown (1971) and Worden (1974). Wallace (1964) has catalogued the 'engagement controvesy' of 1649–51 in which many conservatives objected to engaging – or promising – to obey the new regime.

The engaged party have laid the axe to the very root of monarchy and Parliaments. They have cast all the mysteries and secrets of government . . . before the vulgar, like pearl before swine, and have taught both the soldiery and people to look so far into them as to ravel back all governments to the first principles of nature. He that shakes fundamentals means to take down the fabric. Nor have they been careful to save the materials for posterity. What these negative statists will set up in the room of these ruined buildings doth not appear; only I will say they have made the people thereby so curious and so arrogant that they will never find humility enough to submit to civil rule. Their aim therefore from the beginning was to rule them by the power of the sword – a military aristocracy or oligarchy – as now they do. Amongst the ancient Romans, *tentare arcana imperii* (to profane mysteries of state) was treason, because there can be no form of government without its proper mysteries, which are no longer mysteries than while they are concealed. Ignorance, and admiration arising from ignorance, are the parents of civil devotion and obedience, though not of theological.

Nor have these grandees and their party in the Synod dealt more kindly with the church than with the commonwealth, whose reverend mysteries – their pulpits and holy sacraments, and all the functions of the ministry – are by their connivance profaned by the clouted shoe, the basest and lowest of the people making themselves priests and with blind distempered zeal preaching such doctrines as their private spirits . . . dictate to them . . . Yet the greatest wonder of all is that they suffer the Lord's Supper . . . to be so much neglected in almost all the churches of the kingdom. Is it because men usually, before they receive our Saviour . . . sweep the house clean, casting out of their hearts . . . pride, ambition, covetousness, envy, hatred, malice, and all other unclean spirits . . . [which] uphold those badges of factions and terms of distinction and separation: 'cavaliers', 'roundheads', 'malignants', 'well-affected', 'presbyterians' and 'independents'? Or is it because they fear if the church were settled in peace and unity it would be a means to unite the commonwealth, as a quiet and cheerful mind often cureth a distempered body?

That these grandees govern by power, not by love and the laws of the land . . . [also] appears by the many garrisons they keep up, and numerous army they keep in pay to overpower the whole kingdom – more than at first Parliament voted – [and] their compelling the Parliament to put the whole militia of England and Ireland, by land and sea, into the power of Sir Thomas Fairfax and their party. Nor do they think the laws of the land extensive enough for their purposes. Therefore they piece them out with arbitrary ordinances, impeachments before the Lords and martial law . . . . and by illegal accusations, blank impeachments, threatening remonstrances and declarations etc. fright away many members and compel the rest to vote and unvote what they please – whereby all the Parliament doth is void and null in law, *ab initio*, it being no free Parliament, but a sub-committee to the Army, living as the Egyptians did under vassalage to their own mamelukes or mercenaries . . .

Many honest men took part with this Parliament, seduced by those fair pretences of defending religion, laws and liberties, which they first held forth to the people, and being unwilling to have a Parliament conquered by the sword – not thinking it possible that a prevailing faction in Parliament should so far prevaricate as to conspire to enslave King, Parliament and kingdom, to subvert the laws, liberties and fundamental government of the land under which they and their posterity were, and were likely to be, so happily governed, and [to] betray religion unto heretics and schismatics, and share the spoils of the commonwealth between them... Many at the beginning much disliked that religion should be used as an ingredient to the carrying on of civil war and that schismatics should have so great a stroke in managing the business, yet were pacified with this consideration: that we must refuse no helps in our defence. If a man be assaulted by thieves on the highway, he will not refuse to join with schismatics or Turks in a common defence. [And] the same authority that then countenanced those schismatics (it was hoped) would be able to discountenance them again when the work was done. But the grandees of the Houses, having other designs, had so often purged the Houses that they left few honest men in them to oppose their projects, still bringing in schismatics and men of their own interests by enforced and undue elections into their rooms, and so by insensible degrees, new-modelled the House suitable to their own corrupt desires and new-modelled this Army accordingly.... The people, who had no intention to be entrusted so far, were step by step so far engaged before they were aware that they could not draw their feet back, and do now find... that the bit is in their mouths, the saddle fast girt upon their galled backs, and these rank riders mounted who will spur them not only out of their estates, laws and liberties, but into hell with renewed treasons, new oaths, covenants and engagements if they take not more heed... They have changed their old, honest principles and their old friends who bore the first brunt of the business, and have taken new principles and friends in their room, suitable to their present desperate designs. And now that they have squeezed what they can out of the King's party, they think of sequestering their old friends, because they adhere to their old principles....

I am not ignorant that there is at natural purging, a natural phlebotomy, belonging to politic as well as to natural bodies, and that some good humours are evacuated with the bad; yet I cannot but deplore what I have observed, that the honestest and justest men on both sides – such as, if they have done evil, did it because they thought it was good... have always fared worse than other men, as if this difference between King and Parliament were but a *syncretismus* of illusion against honest men. Nay I do further foresee that in the period and closing up of this tragedy they will fare worst of all, because they have not taken the liberty to enrich themselves with public spoils... but are grown lean and poor by their integrity....

I do here in the name and behalf of all the free commons of

England, declare and protest that there is no free nor legal Parliament in England, but the two Houses sit under a visible, actual, and a horrid force of a mutinous army, to destroy, expel and murder . . . the rest of their fellow members, who sat in Parliament doing their duty when the two Speakers with a small company of Members secretly fled away to the Army and sat in council with them, contriving how to enslave King, Parliament, city and kingdom, and how to raise taxes at their pleasure, which they share amongst themselves and their party, under the name and title of the 'Godly', the 'Saints'. And afterwards they brought the Army up to London against the Parliament and the city in a hostile manner . . . The two Houses have sat under the said force ever since the 6 August [1648], and therefore all they have done, and all they shall do in the condition they now stand in, is void and null in law.

*Part eight*
# PARLIAMENTARIAN ARGUMENTS, 1642–1644

## 8.1 THE RANGE OF POSSIBLE ORIGINS, AND THE CHOICE

From [Henry Parker], *Some few observations upon his majesties late answer to a declaration . . . of May 1642* [1642] 15–16: Wing P424? (The Bodleian copy used, Ash 991(8), 16pp, is dated 1643); Burroughes, *Brief answer*, [9]–[10] (see headnote to [5.5]).

Whatever their precise political colour, royalists and parliamentarians inherited the scholastic (Rommen 1945) assumption that political legitimacy was dependent on the origins of the regime in question. Patriarchalists like Maxwell and Filmer [7.4; 7.8] believed this no less than contractualists like Prynne, Parker, Herle and Hunton [8.2–8.6]. The parliamentarians, for their part, had recourse to Huguenot theories of origins developed in the latter half of the sixteenth century in France and transmitted to the Netherlands and Scotland in particular (Salmon 1959; Skinner 1978). The royalists were quick to point out their no lesser dependence on Catholic, especially Jesuit thought, as we have seen Filmer doing already ([7.8]; cf. Oakley 1962). English parliamentarian thought, no less than that of their mentors, oscillated between the three poles of asserting the immemorial origins of the constitution (Pocock 1957), claiming that it had been in gradual growth through historically ascertainable points of consent recorded in the legal records, and relying on the notion that there must have been some original contract in which the rights of governors and governed were irrevocably laid down (Höpfe and Thompson 1979). The variety and incoherence of these positions will be amply illustrated below. In the parliamentarian extracts here, their opening gambit, as it were, is indicated. The difficulties of further parliamentary play were perhaps no greater than the dilemma posed to the royalists by the gambit, as a close reading of Ferne [7.3] will have indicated.

### *8.1.1 Parker*

[S]ome courtiers do suggest that all supreme dignities are so founded by God's immediate hand alone as there remains nothing human in them, and that the public consent of such-and-such nations as to such-and-such limits and conditions is nothing at all requisite. This is the ground of all arbitrary unbounded sway. For if all nations, by common consent, can neither set limits or judge limits set to sovereignty, but must look upon it as a thing merely divine and above all human consent or comprehension, then all nations are equally slaves; and we in England are born no more by the laws of England than the asinine peasants of France are there (whose wooden shoes and canvas breeches sufficiently proclaim what a blessedness it is to be born under a mere divine prerogative). But I hope that prerogative, in defence of which the King intends to sacrifice his life, is that which is settled and bounded by the known laws of the land, and whose surest basis is the common consent, and whose most honourable end is the common good.

### *8.1.2 Burroughes*

I demand, what first invested such a family with real power more than another? It must be either God from heaven designing it, as [he did] David, or men appointing it, or taken by force. There is no *quartum* [fourth way]. It was not the first, and to say the third is the right is an extreme wrong to the King. If mere force can give a right, then whosoever is most forcible hath right. It must therefore be something else. What can that be but the consent of people to such a family? (which is in effect all one with election). You may give it what name you will; it is . . . a near certainty that even here [in England] Kings were at first either by choice, or by that which in effect is all one.

## 8.2 THE POPULAR BASIS OF KINGLY POWER: I

From Prynne, *Soveraigne power*, I, 36–7 (see headnote to [6.2])

With an insouciance born of utter conviction, Prynne here argues from Mario Salamonio's populist and scholastic *Sovereignty of the Roman patriciate* (1544); from the Jesuit, Juan de Mariana; from the doubtfully authentic *Mirror of Justices* and *Fleta* (Whittaker 1895); and from Bracton, who – as the royalists told him – also spoke of the King as having no superior in the realm and of being under none but God. Scholastic considerations of causality are mixed with assertions as to the proper end of government, and both are found to be expressed in the medieval English constitution. By 1648 [2.2; 3.6] Prynne's views had changed.

It is the unanswerable argument of Marius Salmonius (an incomparable civil lawyer and philosopher) [in the] first book of his *De Principatu* (Paris, 1578, pp. 17–27) to prove, 'the whole kingdom and people the sovereign power, greater than the prince, and the prince . . . inferior under them because he is not only their servant, but creature too, being originally created by and for them. Now as every creator is of greater power and authority than its creature, and every cause greater than its effect, so is the authority and power of the people which creates the prince and princely power and augments or limits it as there is cause . . . greater than the prince or royal power . . . Though he be greater than any private subject or magistrate over whom he rules, yet still he is inferior to all the people and the kingdom, whose servant and creature he is, and by whose authority he doth and manageth all things. And though principalities, generally considered, be of God, yet the constitution of princes and their several degrees of power are merely from men'. Likewise . . . John Mariana, a Spanish Jesuit, in his book *De rege et regis institutione*: ([1599], Book 1, chap 8): 'the whole commonwealth, kingdom and people are of greater authority and power than the King', as for other reasons, so for this, 'that he is but their creature [and] servant and derives all his royal authority from them alone, not for his own but their service and benefit who may enlarge or restrain it as they see fit'. And not to trouble you with foreign authorities on this point (which are infinite) I shall only acquaint you with the resolution of some eminent ancient lawyers of our own.

Andrew Horne, an eminent lawyer in Edward I's reign, in his *Mirror of Justices*, chap. 1, sect. 2, pp. 7–9, writes thus of the original institution of our English monarchs: 'after that God had abated the nobility of the Britons, who rather used force than right, he delivered it to the most humble and simple of all neighbour nations, the Saxons, who came from Germany to conquer it . . . [This] nation [had] . . . forty kings, all which held themselves to have companions. These princes called this land England (which was before named Greater Britain). These, after great wars, elected from among them a King to reign over them, to govern the people of God and to maintain and defend their persons and goods in peace, by the rules of law or right. And at the beginning they caused the King to swear that he will maintain the holy Christian faith to the utmost of his power and to guide his people by law without respect of any person, and . . . be obedient to suffer . . . the law as well as others of his people. And afterwards this realm was turned into an heritage according to the number of his companions, who divided the realm into thirty-eight Counties, and delivered each one a County to keep and defend from enemies . . . And although the King ought to have no peers in his land, yet because the King of his own wrong should offend against any of his people, neither he nor any of his commissaries [i.e. officers] can be both judge and party. [Therefore] of right it behoves that the King should have *companions* for to hear and determine in Parliaments all the writs and plaints of the wrongs of the King, the Queen and their children. Of those wrongs especially, [the people] could not otherwise have common right. These companions are now called counts, after the Latin, *comites* . . . .' Henry de Bracton, who writ in Henry III's reign, . . . resolves that 'the King is under the law, because the law makes him a King by giving him dominion and power'. Now how doth the law thus make him a King but by the Parliament, the King's Great Council, by whose counsel and advice alone all laws were first enacted, and yet are [themselves] under the law? A King is created and elected (by whom but his kingdom?) to this purpose: to do justice to all . . . [Bracton says], 'God, the law and his Court, to wit earls and barons' – in Parliament – 'are above the King and ought to bridle him, and are thence called *comites* because they are the King's companions'. *Fleta*, an ancient lawbook written in King Edward III's reign, useth the self-same words that Bracton doth, and concludes that 'the King hath a superior, to wit God, and the law by which he is made King, and his Court of earls and barons', to wit, Parliament.

## 8.3 THE POPULAR BASIS OF KINGLY POWER: II

From Henry Parker, *Observations upon some of his majesties late answers and expresses* (1642), 1–6, 11, 13–15, 21, 44–6: Wing P 423. The tract is reproduced in facsimile in Haller (1934, vol. II).

This extract is from Parker's most controverted tract, the first major work defending Parliament. The reader will notice the same mix as in Prynne: a scholastic theory of causes, an only partially separate discussion on the purposes of government, and a glossing of constitutional practices to yield a doctrine of government's being based on consent. Parker goes further and provides a theoretical history of the origins of government, one designed to admit what was to be found in Aristotle and in *Genesis* – that the first governments were expressions of domestic relations – and yet to show how the fact of original consent might not be denied. While Parker argues the origin of government to lie in popular consent, though, and its end to be the maintenance of popular safety, he does not allow the people a power to dissolve and reconstitute government (Franklin 1978); nor does he contemplate the possibility that the two Houses could be disobeyed, and thinks of their 'arbitrary power' as one to be exercised only in extreme emergency, the existence of which is to be determined by the two Houses and the nature of which would consist in a threat to the established law. His arguments clearly could, and did, lead in many directions. In later career he himself came to place more emphasis on the power of the Commons alone; but he opposed the leveller doctrine of an Agreement of the People's reforming the constitution to broaden its popular base and to reserve certain rights to the people. It is even possible that he was unhappy with the independents' revolution (Aylmer 1973) though in the event he supported the new regime and died in its service in Ireland. Tuck (1979) has shown how Parker was to be embarrassed by more radical theorists of individual natural rights who were to claim such rights were inalienable and *could* not be transferred to Parliament. Like Prynne's, his words had implications he did not intend.

In this contestation between regal and parliamentary power, for method's sake it is requisite to consider first of regal, then of parliamentary power, and in both, to consider the efficient and final causes and the means by which they are supported. The King attributeth the original of his royalty to God and the law, making no mention of the grant, consent, or trust of the people therein. But the truth is, God is no more the author of regal than of aristocratical power, nor of supreme than of subordinate command. Nay, that dominion which is usurped and not just, yet whiles it remains dominion and till it be legally again divested, refers to God as to its author and donor as much as that which is hereditary. And that law which the King mentioneth is not to be understood to be any special ordinance sent from heaven by the ministry of the angels or prophets (as amongst the Jews it sometimes was). It can be nothing else amongst christians but the pactions and agreements of such and such politic corporations. Power is originally inherent in the people, and it is nothing else but that might and vigour which such or such a society of men contains in itself; and when by such and such a law of common consent and agreement it is derived into such and such hands, God confirms that law. And so man is the free and voluntary author, the law is the instrument, and God is the establisher of both.

And we see, not that prince which is most potent *over* his subjects but that prince which is most potent *in* his subjects is indeed the most truly potent. For a King of one small city, if he be entrusted with a large prerogative, may be said to be more powerful over his subjects than a King with a great many regions whose prerogative is more limited. And yet in true reality of power, that King is the most great and glorious which hath the most and strongest subjects, and not he which tramples upon the most contemptible vassals . . . Thus we see that power is but secondary and derivative in princes. The fountain and efficient cause is the people. And from hence the inference is just: the King, though he be *singulis major* [greater than any single subject] yet he is *universis minor* [less than the whole society]. For if the people be the true efficient cause of power, it is a rule in nature, *quicquid efficit tale, est magis tale* [whatever causes a thing is greater than that thing]. And hence it appears that at the founding of authorities, when the consent of societies conveys rule into such and such hands, it may ordain what conditions and prefix what bounds it pleases, and that no dissolution ought to be thereof but by the same power by which it had its constitution.

As for the final cause of regal authority, I do not find anything in the King's papers denying that the same people is the final, which is the efficient cause of it. And indeed it were strange if the people, in subjecting itself to command, should aim at anything but its own good in the first and last place. . . . If Ship Money, if the Star Chamber, if the High Commission, if the votes of the popish lords and bishops in the Upper House be inconsistent with the welfare of the kingdom, not only honour but justice itself challenges that they should be abolished. The King ought not to account that a profit or a strength to him which is a loss and wasting to the people. The word 'grace' sounds better in the people's mouths than in his. His dignity was created to preserve the commonalty; the commonalty was not created for his service. And that which is the end is far more honourable and valuable in nature and policy than that which is the means. This directs us then to the transcendent αχμή [acme = highest point] of all politics – to the paramount law that shall give law to all human laws whatsoever, and that is *salus populi*. The law of prerogative itself, that is subservient to this law; and, were it not conducive thereunto, it were not necessary nor expedient. Neither can the right of conquest be pleaded to acquit princes of that which is due to the people as the authors, or ends, of all power; for mere force cannot alter the course of nature, or frustrate the tenor of law; and if it could, there were more reason why the people might justify force to regain due liberty than the prince might to subvert the same. . . .

I come now from the cause which conveys royalty and that for which it is conveyed, to the nature of the conveyance. The word 'trust' is frequent in the King's papers, and therefore I conceive the King does admit that his interest in the Crown is not absolute, or by mere donation of the people, but in part conditionate and fiduciary. And indeed all good princes, without any express contract betwixt them and their subjects, have acknowledged that there did lie a great and high trust upon them. . . . And we cannot imagine in the fury of war (when the laws have the least vigour) that any *generalissimo* can be so uncircumscribed in power, but that if he should turn his cannons upon his own soldiers, they were [not] *ipso facto* absolved of all obedience and of all oaths and ties of allegience whatsoever for that time and bound by a higher duty: to seek their own preservation by resistance and defence. Wherefore if there be such tacit trusts and reservations in all public commands (though of the most absolute nature that can be supposed) we cannot but admit that in all well-formed monarchies, where kingly prerogative has any limits set, this must needs be one necessary condition: that the subjects shall live both safe and free. The charter of nature entitles all subjects of all countries whatsoever to safety by its supreme law.

But freedom indeed has divers degrees of latitude, and all countries therein do not participate alike, but positive laws must everywhere assign those degrees. The Great Charter of England is not so strait in privileges to us, neither is the King's Oath of small strength to that Charter. . . . It confirms all laws and rightful customs, amongst which we most highly esteem parliamentary privileges. And as for the word *elegerit*, whether it be past or future, it skills not much. For if by this Oath, law, justice and discretion be executed among us in all judgement . . . . and if peace and godly agreement be entirely kept among us all, and if the King uphold our laws and customs, we need not fear but the King is bound to consent to new laws if they be necessary as well as defend old. . . . And if the word *elegerit* be in the perfect tense, yet [this would] show that the people's election had been the ground of ancient laws and customs – and why the people's election in Parliament should not be now of as great a moment as ever, I cannot discover.

That which results from hence is, if our King receive all royalty from the people and for the behoof of the people (and that by a special trust of safety and liberty expressly by the people limited and by their own grants and oaths ratified) then our Kings cannot be said to have so unconditionate and high a propriety in all our lives, liberties and possessions or in anything else to the Crown appertaining as we have in their dignity, or in ourselves. And indeed if they had, they were not born for the people but merely for themselves. . . .

But now of Parliaments. Parliaments have the same efficient causes as monarchies, if not higher; for in truth the whole kingdom is not so properly the author as the essence of itself in Parliaments (and by the former rule is *magis tale* because we see *ipsum quid quod efficit tale*). [It is *itself* that which makes or causes.] And it is, I think, beyond all controversy that God and the law operate as the same causes both in Kings and Parliaments, for God favours both and the law establishes both, and the act of all men still concurs in the sustenation of both. And, not to stay longer upon this, Parliaments have also the same final causes as monarchies if not greater, for indeed public safety and liberty could not be so effectually provided for by monarchs till Parliaments were constituted for the supplying of all defects in that government.

Two things are especially aimed at in Parliaments, not to be obtained by other means. First, that the interest of the people might be satisfied; secondly, that Kings might be better counselled. In the summons of Edward I we see the first end of Parliaments expressed: . . . . *quod omnes tangit ab omnibus approbari debet*, or *tr*[*a*]*ctari*. [That which concerns everyone ought to be approved (or treated on) by everyone.] And in the same writ . . . there is not a word . . . but it is observable [that] public approbation, consent or treaty is necessary in all public expedients. And this is not a mere usage in England, but a law. And this law is not subject to any doubt or dispute. There is 'nothing more known'. Neither is this known law extorted from Kings by the violence and injustice of the people. It is duly and formally established, and that upon a great deal of reason, not without 'the providence and circumspection of all the states'. . . . Now upon a due comparing of these passages with some of the King's late papers, let the world judge whether Parliaments have not been of late much lessened and injured. The King, in one of his late answers alleges that his writs 'may teach the Lords and Commons the extent of their commission and trust, which is to be councillors, not commanders; and that not in all things, but [only] in *quibusdam arduiis*' [i.e. such difficult matters which Kings choose to bring to their attention]. . . .

Little need to be said (I think every man's heart tells him) that in public consultations the many eyes of so many choice gentlemen out of all parts see more than fewer, and that the great interest the Parliament has in common justice and tranquillity and the few private ends they can have to deprave them, must needs render their counsel more faithful, impartial and religious than any other. That dislike which the court has ever conceived against Parliaments, without all dispute is the most pregnant proof of the integrity and salubrity of that public advice and is no disparagement thereof. For we have ever found enmity and antipathy betwixt the court and the country, but never any till now betwixt the representatives and the body of the kingdom represented. And were we not now those dregs of the human race upon which the unhappy ends of the world are fallen, calumny and envy herself would never have attempted to intrude upon us such impossible charges of treason and rebellion against our most sacred Council from the mouths of popish, prelatical and military courtiers. . . . We have had almost forty years' experience that the court way of preferment has been by doing ill offices, and we can nominate what dukes, what earls, what lords, what knights, have been made great and rich by base disservices to the state . . . What blame is it then in princes when they will pretend reluctance of conscience and reason in things behoveful for the people and will use their fiduciary power in denying just things? (as if they might lawfully do whatsoever they have power to do, when the contrary is the truth, and they have no power to do but what is lawful and fit to be done). So much for the ends of parliamentary power.

I come now to the true nature of it: public consent. We see consent as well as counsel is requisite and due in Parliament; and that [is] the proper foundation of power, for . . . we cannot imagine that public consent should be anywhere more vigorous or more orderly than it is in Parliament. Man, being depraved by the fall of Adam, grew so untame and uncivil a creature that the law of God written in his breast was not sufficient to restrain him from mischief or to make him sociable; and therefore without some magistracy to provide new orders and to judge of old and to execute according to justice, no society could be upheld. Without society men could not live; and without laws men could not be sociable; and without authority somewhere invested to judge according to law and execute according to judgement, law was a vain and void thing. It was soon therefore provided that laws agreeable to the dictates of reason should be ratified by common consent and that the execution and interpretation of those laws should be entrusted to some magistrate for the preventing of common injuries betwixt subject and subject. But when it after appeared that man was yet subject to unnatural destruction by the tyranny of entrusted magistrates (a mischief almost as fatal as to be without all magistracy), how to provide a wholesome remedy therefore was not so easy to be invented. 'Twas not difficult to invent laws for the limiting of supreme governors; but to invent how those laws should be executed and by whom interpreted was almost impossible. *Nam quis custodiat ipsos custodes?* [For who shall control those controllers?] To place a superior above a supreme was held unnatural. Yet what a lifeless, fond thing would law be without any judge to determine it or power to enforce it; and how could human society be preserved without some such law? Besides, if it be agreed upon that limits should be prefixed to princes, and judges appointed to decree according to those limits, yet another great difficulty will soon affront us. For we cannot restrain princes too far but we shall disable them from some good as well as inhibit them from some evil; and to be disabled from doing good in some things may be as mischievous as to be enabled for all evils at mere discretion.

Long it was ere the world could extricate itself out of all these extremities, or find out an orderly means whereby to avoid the danger of unbounded prerogative on this hand and [of] excessive liberty on the other; and scarce has long experience yet fully satisfied the minds of all men in it. In the infancy of the world, when man was not so artificial and obdurate in cruelty and oppression as now and when policy was more rude, most nations did choose rather to submit themselves to the mere discretion of their lords than to rely upon any limits, and to be ruled by arbitrary edicts [rather] than written statutes. But since, tyranny being grown more exquisite and policy more perfect (especially in countries where learning and religion flourish), few nations will endure a thralldom which uses to accompany unbounded and unconditionate royalty. Yet long it was ere the bounds and conditions of supreme lords were so wisely determined or quietly conserved as now they are. For at first when *ephori*, *tribuni*, *curatores*, etc. were erected to poise against the scale of sovereignty, much blood was shed about them . . . and in some places the remedy proved worse than the disease. In all great distresses, the body of the people was ever constrained to rise and by the force of the major party to put an end to all intestine strifes and to make a redress of all public grievances. But many times calamities grew to a strange height before so cumbersome a body could be raised; and when it was raised, the motions of it were so distracted and irregular that after much spoil and effusion of blood, sometimes only one tyranny was exchanged for another. Till some way was invented to regulate the motions of the people's molimenous [straining] body, I think arbitrary rule was most safe for the world. But now, since most countries have found out an art and peaceable order for public assemblies, whereby the people may assume its own power to do itself right without disburbance to itself or injury to princes, he will be very unjust that will oppose this art and order.

That princes may not now be beyond all limits and laws, nor yet left to be tried upon those limits and laws by any private parties, the whole community in its underived majesty shall convene to do justice. And that this convention may not be without intelligence, certain times and places and forms shall be appointed for its regiment . . . That the vastness of its own bulk may not breed confusion, by virtue of election and representation a few shall act for the many, the wise shall consent for the simple, the virtue of all shall redound to some and the prudence of some shall redound to all. And sure, as this admirably-composed Court which is now called a Parliament is more regularly and orderly formed than when it was called the Mickel Synod or Witenagemot or when this real body of people did throng together at it, so it is not yet perhaps without some defects which by art and policy might receive further amendment.

Some divisions have been sprung of late between both Houses and between the King and both Houses by reason of the uncertainty of their jurisdiction . . . Some lawyers doubt how far the Parliament is able to create new forms and precedents and [whether] it hath a jurisdiction over itself. But in the first place the true privileges of Parliament, not only belonging to the being and efficacy of it but to the honour also and compliment of it, [sh]ould be clearly declared. . . . The virtue of representation hath been denied to the Commons, and a severance hath been made betwixt the parties chosen and the parties choosing; and so that great privilege of all privileges, that unmovable bastion of all honour and power whereby the House of Commons claims the entire right of all the gentry and commonalty of England, has been attempted to be shaken and disturbed. Most of our late distempers and obstructions in Parliament have proceeded from this. . . .

That there is an arbitrary power somewhere, 'tis true; 'tis necessary, and no inconvenience follows upon it. Every man has an absolute power over himself, but because no man can hurt himself this power is not dangerous nor need[s] to be restrained. So every State has an arbitrary power over itself and there is no danger in it, for the same reason. If the State entrusts this to one man or a few there may be danger in it; but the Parliament is neither one nor a few; it is indeed the State itself....

There is in the interpretation of law upon the last appeal, the same supremacy of power requisite as in making it... Grant the King supreme interpreter and 'tis all one as if we granted him to be supreme maker of law... Grant him this and we grant him to be above all limits, and conditions, all human bonds whatsoever. In this intricacy therefore, where the King and Parliament disagree and judgement *must* be supreme, whether in the one or other, we must retire to ordinary justice. And there we see, if the King consent not with the ordinary Judge, the law thinks it fit that the King subscribe rather than the Judge. And if this satisfy not, we must retire to the principles of nature and there search whether the King or kingdom be looked upon as the efficient and final cause and as the proper subject of all power. Neither is the Oath of Supremacy endangered thereby, for he that ascribes more to the whole universality than to the King yet ascribes to the King a true supremacy of power and honour above all particulars. Nor is our allegiance temerated [moderated]. For when the Judge on the Bench delivers law contrary to the King's command, this is not the same thing as to proceed against the King's person upon any judgement given against him. The King in his own person is not to be forcibly repelled in any wrongdoing. Nor is he accountable for ill done. Law has only a directive but no coactive force upon his person. But in all irregular acts where no personal force is, Kings may be disobeyed, their unjust commands may be neglected, not only by communities but also by single men sometimes. Those men therefore that maintain that all Kings are in all things and commands... to be obeyed (as being like Gods, unlimitable) and as well in evil as in good unquestionable, are sordid flatterers. And those that will allow no limits but directive only, and those no other but divine and natural (and so make all princes as vast in power as the Turk, for he is subject to the directive force of God and nature's laws [alone]) and so allow subjects a dry right without all remedy, are almost as stupid as the former. And those, lastly, that allow human laws to oblige Kings more than directively in all cases where personal violence is absent, and yet allow no judges of those laws but the King himself, run into absurdities as great as the former....

I come now to those seven doctrines and positions which the King... lays upon as offensive. And they run thus:

1. 'That the Parliament has an absolute, indisputable power of declaring law, so that all the right of the King and people depends

upon their pleasure.' It has been answered that this power must rest in them, or in the King, or in some inferior Court (or else all suits must be endless). And it can nowhere rest more safely than in Parliament.

2. 'That parliaments are bound to no precedents.' Statutes are not binding to them, why then should precedents? Yet there is no obligation stronger than the justice and honour of a Parliament.

3. 'That they are Parliaments, and may judge of public necessity without the King, and dispose of anything.' They may not desert the King, but being deserted by the King when the kingdom is in distress, they may judge of that distress and relieve it, and are to be accounted by the virtue of representation as the whole body of the state.

4. 'That no member of Parliament ought to be troubled for treason, etc., without leave [of Parliament].' This is intended of suspicions only. And when leave may be seasonably had and when competent accusers appear not in the impeachment.

5. 'That the sovereign power resides in both Houses of Parliament, the King having no negative voice.' This power is not claimed as ordinary, nor to any purpose but to save the kingdom from ruin in case where the King is so seduced as that he prefers dangerous men and prosecutes his loyal subjects.

6. 'That levying forces against the personal commandments of the King (though accompanied by his presence) is not levying war against the King. But war against his authority, though not person, *is* war against the King.' If this were . . . so, the Parliament, seeing a seduced King ruining himself and the Kingdom, could not save both but must stand and look on.

7. 'That according to some Parliaments, they may depose the King.' 'Tis denied that any King was deposed by a free Parliament fairly elected.

## 8.4 PATRIARCHAL ORIGINS DENIED

From Herle, *An answer to Doctor Ferne's reply*, 16–17 (see headnote to [5.1]); [Palmer], *Scripture and reason*, 30.2 (see headnote to [5.2]).

It is disputable that patriarchalism is a historical fact; it is, moreover, possible to question the wisdom of seeing all social relations – even those entailing inequality of authority – as patriarchal. Nimrod, 'the mighty hunter' and tyrant, was traditionally a candidate for being the first King; and Aristotle had taught that there were different and distinct relations among men: political, domestic and economic, each having their 'proper' (i.e. separate and good) ends. In these extracts the patriarchalists are reminded of these considerations by Herle and Palmer. Locke's *Two treatises* were to do this much more fully (Schochet 1975) though still not quite to the extinction of the enemy (Daly 1979a). 'The Doctor' attacked in the extracts is Ferne.

### *8.4.1 Herle*

First: 'that monarchy was the first kind of government'... Whether true or no 'tis uncertain from what any way appears in the text he cites (*Genesis* x. 5.20). Nay, rather the contrary is thence probable, *viz.* that they were governed in an aristocratical way by the *heads or chiefs of their several families in their countries and nations*, as the words are. And therefore it is that Nimrod is singled out among all the rest, as a *mighty hunter* (or usurper) in the first beginning a kingdom (verse 10).

The second thing he infers is that, 'the first Kings were not by the choice of the people, yet... not by divine right or nature's law, and yet by divine example... and by nature's leading', whereas we see that the first King we ever read of, Nimrod, was flatly against both....

The sum of his third, fourth and fifth inferences is ... that, 'the government of Kings being a result from that of fathers over their families, their people have no more power of coercion over them than children have over their fathers'. Whereunto I answer that it hath already appeared that the first King we ever read of and his government, was far from paternal either in example or manner of rule. Next, that allegories are no good arguments; they only illustrate as far as the likeness holds. Because a King may in some respects be called the father, the head, the husband of his kingdom (as the Doctor insists) doth it therefore follow that because he should govern with the providence of a father he may therefore govern with the arbitrariness of a father, without the consent of his people to the laws or rules of his government, as a father doth without that of his children; or because he should govern with the wisdom of a head that therefore he may govern not only without the consent but without the counsel of the rest of the members, as the head doth; or because with the love of a husband, therefore with an absolute power of disposal of whatever the subject hath, as the husband hath towards the wife?

## *8.4.2 Palmer*

Our Doctor, though he occasionally mentioneth the people's good as an end upon which rulers ought to attend, yet he speaks so little of it as it had need be a little more remembered than it is – and God's glory also, which is the chiefest end of all. But indeed the thought and mention of those ends . . . would be too cross to his purpose . . . Therefore to the other side. I must make bold to tell him that though the physical end of things may be silenced in a discourse or definition, yet in normal things such as government, the end, at least the chief end, is a necessary ingredient of both definition and discourse, if a man will consider it as he ought, practically. Let me therefore add to his definition and description of the power of government, and then it will run thus: 'It is a sufficiency of authority for command and coercion in the governing of a people, for God's glory, and for the good of society.' And all lawful power hath this effect in part. Even heathen authority redounds to God's glory as the conservator of mankind, and effects also the civil good of the commonwealth.

Now the Doctor saith this power itself (not naming the end) is to be distinguished from the designing of the person to bear that power and the qualification [i.e. specific extent] of that power. This I grant him, and, accepting his grant of the two latter being from men after their consent, ratified by God's permissive approbation, I desire a little to examine how far that may be granted him which he earnestly contends for, that the power itself is from God, and what may be inferred from thence for him or us.

His meaning is that all men are . . . bound to set up and live under government, this being the ordinance and appointment of God unto men, as they are reasonable creatures. [I concur] if he mean this of parental government: that it is set up to their hands by God and nature as long as the parents and children live together, and bind[s] the children to live with their parents, and under them, till either necessity drives them away or their parents dismiss them. But if he means this of political government – of a people, of many families – as it is plain he doth . . . then I cannot absolutely grant it him. Neither will his text or reasons prove it.

My reasons of denial are: first, that all mankind whose parents are dead and were not by them while they lived subjected to a government are naturally free and so not bound to part with that freedom (as even a monarch doth part with much freedom when he takes the rule) unless they see a necessity or at least a great advantage for God's honour and their own and others' good, which is not always to be found in setting up a politic government. Wherein I am confirmed by a consideration of the three great patriarchs, Abraham, Isaac and Jacob, who, while they lived in Canaan were not within any government but only domestical, and neither did rule nor were ruled by the inhabitants of Canaan, nor joined with them in a common government. Though Abraham's family was very numerous for a family, yet it would be hard to call him a monarch; much less Isaac; and Jacob less, who, when he went down to Egypt, doth not seem to have had any servants, but only his sons and their wives and children. And to this may be added, that by all authors, it seems to be late before any settled government beyond parental, any of divers families in [continuous conjunction], came to be in the world. When the world was more empty, as in Abraham's time, a Godly man . . . might subsist without others joining in government with him. And he could not do them any remarkable good or gain glory to God by it, they being pagans.

So that it is not . . . absolutely true that men are bound universally, as by ordinance from God, to set up [and] live under government in the Doctor's sense. Marriage is God's institution and ordinance, and more originally than the government political, and necessary for increase. Yet are not all of mankind bound to marry, but for their own good and comfort, and so of others, and advancing God's glory in both. So it is with power, or government political, though new when the world is peopled. As there is less necessity of marriage than when the world was thinner (though still a necessity to many, even to most) so there is more necessity of being within government to secure onself and others' good and glorify God in all. And so far I grant God's ordinance to all.

But one thing more I must remember him and the readers of, namely that this power will not be proved absolutely to extend to the making of *any* human laws, but only to the observation of the laws of nature and of God, by his word and special revelation both of the First and Second Table, and to no other power of coercion than what the light of nature will argue necessary for the observation of the laws of nature . . . All further power belongs to the third particular which he calls the qualification of power, and depends upon man's consent – so it be not against God's law and word – which I call the 'extent' of power. Which, if it be true, it shall be seen anon what consequence may be drawn from it to the disadvantage of the Doctor's purpose. . . .

## 8.5 THE LOGIC OF MIXED GOVERNMENT: I

From Herle, *A fuller answer*, 2–6, 10–11, 14; Herle, *An answer to Doctor Ferne's reply*, 20–1, 28–9 (see headnote to [5.1]). For the sake of sequence I have had to run the selection thus: *FA*, 2–4; *A*, 28–9; *FA*, 5–6; *A*, 20–1; *FA*, 10–11, 14. The break points are indicated.

Here Herle (headnote to [5.1]) takes advantage of the King's *Answer to the nineteen propositions* [3.4] and develops a much-repeated parliametarian argument: that if 'supremacy' is mixed, and if one part of the mixture 'deserts its trust', the other parts may 'supply' the deficiency. The two Houses of Parliament therefore had the judicial power of 'final arbitration' in their quarrel with the King. Like Parker, he was basically happy with the constitution, and held that 'final arbitration' should be exercised only in extreme emergency; unlike Parker he did not see or would not say that 'final arbitration' entailed the right to legislate without the King. The practical difference between the two parliamentarians was nil – Parliament could after all, determine by 'final arbitration' that law-making by ordinance was already lawful – but the theoretical difference has been noted by those interested in the history of the idea of parliamentary sovereignty (Judson 1936, 1949). Herle's theory of what the 'fundamental law' is – the mixture itself as expressed in customary practice – and how it arose – by consent 'time out of mind' – will be noted.

Before we can judge of what a Parliament can do in England it will be needful to know what kind of government this in England is. We are therefore to know that England's is not simply subordinative and absolute, but a co-ordinative and mixed monarchy. This mixture or co-ordination is in the very supremacy of power itself, otherwise the monarchy were not mixed. All monarchies have a mixture or composition of subordinate and under-officers in them; but here the monarchy (or highest power) is itself compounded of three co-ordinate estates: a King, and two Houses of Parliament. Unto this mixed power no subordinate authority may, in any case, make resistance. The rule holds still: *subordinata non pugnant* (subordinates may not strive). But in this our mixed highest power, there is not subordination but a co-ordination. And here the other rule holds as true: *coordinata invicem supplent* (co-ordinates supply each other). This mixture, the King's Majesty himself is often pleased in his declarations to applaud as by a 'mutual counterpoise' to each other, sweetening and allaying whatever is harsh in either. [Ferne] himself doth no less, calling it, 'that excellent temper of the three estates in parliament', confessing them to be the 'fundamentals' of government . . . Fundamentals admit not of higher and lower. All foundations are principal alike. And I cannot but wonder that the position of [Henry Parker] – the King is *universis minor* – should be by [Ferne] and others so much exploded; for if the 'temper', as he speaks, of this government be of three estates, he needs not . . . the almanac he speaks of, to reckon . . . that one is less than three.

But you'll say: 'what, is not the Parliament subordinate to the King; are they not all subjects?' I answer: the Parliament cannot be said properly to be subject, because the King is a part, and so he should be subject to himself. No, nor are the two Houses without him subjects. Every member, . . . taken severally [i.e. separately] is a subject; but all, [taken collectively] in their Houses, are not. Nay Bracton, the great lawyer, is so bold as to say: 'The King has above him, besides God, the law whereby he is made King, likewise his Court of earls and barons, etc.' But we need not go so high. It will serve our turn if the Houses be in this mixture or temper of government, not subordinate or subject. Then if they do as co-ordinates should – supply each others' failings – no 'highest' power is resisted.

But you'll say: 'How can they which are every one apart subjects, not be subjects in their Houses; doth the King's writ unsubject them? No. It was the consent of both King and people, in the first constitution or coalition of the government, that makes them in their several Houses co-ordinate with His Majesty, not subordinate to him. How else were the monarchy mixed more than that of Turkey? 'But doth not the King's writ make them a Parliament?' It doth ordinarily, in *actu exercito*. But in *actu signato* it is the constitution of the government designs them to it, and accordingly provides for it in an annual (now triennial) vicissitude – here (note by the way) that whereas it is often urged that they are but his Council to be called by him, it is true that the office [of calling them] is ordinarily betrusted to him but they are by the first constitution not to be elected by him, but assigned to him . . . not only the King's but the kingdom's Council, elected by it not by him, and have the power not only of consulting but of consenting. The writ for the House of Commons is *ad faciendum et consentiendum*. However we know that they must consent before it can be a law, whereby it sufficiently appears they are a co-ordinative part in the monarchy, or the highest principle of power, in as much as they bear a consenting share in the highest office of it – the making of laws. . . .

[In *An answer*, Herle was to provide further arguments directed against the King's powers over Parliament]:

The original ground or foundation of this co-ordination, 'tis not other than the mutual consent of all three estates from the first beginning at least of [there] being such. The usual way of its continuance 'tis accordingly threefold: the King succeeds, the Lords created, the Commons elected; yet so as although the King be entrusted with the ordinary power of calling the other two (a thing the Doctor much insists on) yet we see he is neither at all entrusted with their power when called, nor absolutely with their call. Parliaments, as we have seen ... have in times of extraordinary exigence been called without Kings, and now by the late Act for a Triennial Parliament are ordinarily, if the King refuse, so to be. The which power if so inseparable to sovereignty as the Doctor would have it, no question His Majesty ... would never have so much prejudiced succession as to have parted with it. And for this power of dissolution of Parliaments at pleasure (which the Doctor likewise so much and so often makes use of) 'tis but a power of ordinary entrustment ... and limitable we see by that late Act, not to be exercised within fifty days. ... By the constitution, equity and purpose of Parliaments, and – as I have heard – by law too, no Parliament is to be dissolved while there is any petition or grievance of any subject unheard. ...

[The argument of *A fuller answer* is resumed]:

But you'll say: 'can there be more than one highest?' No. There is but one; but that one is a mixed one, else the monarchy were not mixed. But you'll say: 'how [else] doth it appear that the constitution of this government is such?' Fortescue is herein full and home. 'The King is to govern his people by no other than that kind of power which flows to him from their consent, and that is political, not regal, power.' Now he that knows anything of Greek knows that the word 'political' implies mixed principles, specially when opposed to regal ....

But you'll say: 'Tis hard to apprehend how the same men that are all subjects severally should in their Houses not be subject but co-ordinate with the King.' It may appear easily thus. A father and a son are by deed of enfeoffment jointly entrusted with certain lands to uses. The son is still subordinate to the father as son; but as feoffee in the trust, he is not subject but co-ordinate and joint with him. And therefore it is not a little to be wondered at, that so many, especially of the Lords who are *conciliarii nati* (born councillors to the state), in whom their shares both of trust and interest in this supremacy of power in Parliament the very constitution itself of the government hath invested their ... blood with, should be so much wanting to themselves, their posterities, and it, as upon a bare whistle to desert that trust and interest in the Government which their fathers with so much of their care conveyed upon them. . . . Their very style *comites* and *peers* imply in Parliament a co-ordinative society with His Majesty in the government. They are in Parliament his *comites*, his peers. . . .

Now the end or purpose of this mixture of the three estates in this government, 'tis the safety of its safety. As all government aims at safety, so this temper in it [aims] at making the safety more safe or sure. The common interest of the whole body of the kingdom, thus twisted with the King's, makes the cable of its anchor of safety stronger. So then the government, by law its rule, unto safety its end, is ordinarily entrusted to the King, wherein if he fail and refuse either to follow the rule, law, or its end, safety, his co-ordinates in this mixture of the supreme power must, according to their trust, supply. But you'll say: 'there is no written or fundamental law for this'. I answer. . . . If it be written it is superstructive and not fundamental. Written laws that were not laws before written are repealable and alterable even while the government remains the same. Fundamentals [are] not. A foundation must be stirred while the building stands. That of Magna Carta, where most of the fundamentals are at least implied, was law before 'twas written, and but there and then collected for easier conservation and use. But if we would know what is meant by those fundamental laws of this kingdom, so much jeered at in . . . pamphlets: it is that original frame of this co-ordinate government of the three estates in parliament, consented to and contrived by the people in its first constitution, and since in every reign confirmed both by mutual oaths between the King and people and constant custom 'time out . . . of mind', which with us amounts to a law – wherein the rule is . . . it cannot be disproved from taking place upon all occasions, therefore it is to be presumed to have continued from the beginning, even in the Parliament Summons of Edward I. This law is called *Lex stabilita et notissima* [established and known law], even before it was a record.

Now as this mixture . . . dies not ('tis not personal but incorporate, and corporations, the law says, die not) so that reason or wisdom of state that first contrived it dies not neither. It lives still in that which the law calls the 'reason of the kingdom', the votes and ordinances of Parliament, which – being the same in construction of law with that which first contrived the government – must needs have full power to apply this co-ordination of government to its end, safety, as well it had at first to introduce it. . . . Here in our present case, the necessity of applying this co-ordination or mixture of the government is immanency of danger, which . . . has [a] competent and entrusted judge, the two Houses, wherein the law makes the reason of the kingdom to reside. [They] have by vote concluded it.

[Herle's argument on 'supremacy' and 'casting resolution' draws the practical consequence]:

*Answer*, 20–1: Supremacy consists not in declaring law. For every Court hath in it this power, though not sufficiently as the Houses, yet sufficiently even to judge the King himself in his title, and to carry it against his will and judgement. 'Tis in the making of law supremacy especially consists . . . and therefore [I] cannot see . . . how they have not a share in the supremacy when we call the King the 'only supreme head and governor'. It is not to be understood that he is so in his single person or natural capacity – for then he should govern by his own personal will as the supreme rule – but in his politic or mixed capacity, which takes in law and Parliament. . . . .

*Fuller Answer*, 10–11, 14. A power of consenting is of all hands agreed to be in the two Houses. The faculty of *legem dare* [making law] is not in difference. The question is about the declarative, that of *legem dicere*. The law is the rule, and cannot be framed without the three estates. But who must apply this rule by giving it the final and casting resolution of its sense? . . . Such a power or faculty there must be in every legal government, after all debatement to give laws their sense beyond all further debatement. Otherwise there would be a *processus in infinitum*, debatement still upon debatement . . . and it were a defect of no less than infinite inconvenience to the end of law, were [it] not resident in the government . . . And where should this faculty reside but in the two Houses? . . . .

This last and casting resolution we see resides in the two Houses of Parliament. . . . But how resides it in them? Infallibly? . . . . No. They are not in themselves infallible, but to us inevitable. Our judgements are not enthralled, 'tis our interests are entrusted to and so subjected to their decision. Our judgements are not infallibly guided . . . . but bound up in and superseded by theirs from gainsaying or resistance. . . . We ascribe to a rightly constituted General Council [of the church] a power of binding all under it from all manner of disturbance to its decisions. And why should a civil general council of England have less power in it? Yea, why should we not, as we have bound ourselves by our choice and trust externally to submit to their determinations, be induced to believe their joint judgements better than our single opinions? Their intelligence and assistance is in all likelihood better. . . .

Well then, we see what power the law, through our trust, gives the two Houses, and all in order to the safety of the King, law and state. They judge by the reason of this state and the rule of this law – both residing in them – that all three . . . are not only imminently endangered but actually invaded by an army . . . There remains no way in the highest result of the state's reason to preserve these . . . but an army to withstand this other army ready to advance . . . before in any parliamentary army there was so much as [a] man listed (before were but musters, and manning of forts for the kingdom's better defence against foreign dangers). . . .

It is natural all the faculties and members in the natural body are to the defence of the whole commanded to their offices by the understanding's last result or dictate. [In politics] prevention is the right eye of policy; recovery is but the left, the after-game. What other authority hath a Sheriff or executioner to put a malefactor to death? But you'll say: 'conscience must have some higher footing. 'Tis God's accountant and must have his warrant.' And it has that fully too. First a warrant of charity in the sixth commandment, which not only forbids murder but commands the preservation of our own and our neighbours' lives. Secondly of justice ('render to all what is due'); and we have seen that in the case of the King's refusal, already voted by the kingdom's reason, the command of the kingdom's power in order to its safety 'tis its Council's due. Lastly of obedience: *Submit yourselves to every ordinance of man, and that for the Lord's sake*, says St Peter. We have seen that it was the ordinance of man, the first men that introduced the government of this state, and now of the men that are ordained to administer that government . . . We have seen the co-ordination of this highest power in this kingdom for its better safety, and therein the entireness still of its efficacy to its end, though one part withdraw. . . .

## 8.6 THE LOGIC OF MIXED GOVERNMENT: II

From Philip Hunton, *A treatise of monarchie* (1643), 26–9, 68–73: Wing H 3781; Hunton, *A vindication of the treatise of monarchy* (1644), 49–50: Wing H 3784.

Philip Hunton (1604–82) was a Wiltshire man, a schoolmaster and nonconformist clergyman, who rose to be Master and Provost at the first foundation of the University of Durham by Cromwell. The courage, moderation and power of his constitutional thought has been appreciated for the last half-century (McIlwain 1935 to Franklin 1978); he was reprinted in 1651 and during the 1680s, and had the distinction of having his works burned by a notorious decree of the University of Oxford in 1683. Hunton took seriously the notion of mixed supremacy, refused to give weight to any distinction between adjudication and legislation in conditions where the right to either was in question, and concluded that where the constituent parts of a 'mixed supreme' could not co-operate there could be no authority to command obedience. Each subject would be a masterless man. Filmer correctly called this theory anarchical [7.8]; but at least Hunton's man of conscience does not quite inhabit an existentialist hell in which he has the right, and is indeed required, to construct all anew; his conscience has rules to go by and ends which it must attain by a probabilistic analysis of the options open to it. Conscience is to seek to preserve the 'fundamental law'. Still, Hunton has reached the awkward point of contemplating a void in place of authority; he comes perilously close to asserting that God must judge men's 'appeal to the sword' (Pocock 1973a, 1973b, 1975, 1980). Hunton's analysis of the problem seems the perfect expression of where a principled moderate would have to end up.

The supreme power being either legislative or gubernative, in a mixed monarchy sometimes the mixture [is seated] in the legislative power (which is the chief of the two), the power of constituting officers being left to the monarch; or else the primacy of both these powers is jointly in all three. (For if the legislative power be in one, then the monarchy is not mixed but simple, for that is the superior. If that be in one, all else needs be too.) By legislative, I mean the power of making new laws if any new be needful to be added to the foundation, and the authentic power of interpreting the old (for I take it this is a branch of the legislative and is as great and in effect the same power).

Every mixed monarchy is limited, but it is not necessary that every limited [monarchy] should be mixed. For the prince in a mixed monarchy, were there no definement of him to a law but only this: that his legislative acts have no validity without the allowance and joint authority of the other, this is enough to denominate it exactly a limited monarchy. And so much it must have if it be mixed. On the other side, if in the foundations of his government he be restrained to any law besides his own will, he is a limited monarch though that both the legislative and gubernative power (provided he exceed not those laws) be left in his own hands. But then the government is not mixed.

Now concerning the extent of the prince's power and the subject's duty in a mixed monarchy . . . It is a general rule in this matter [that] such as the constitution of government is, such is the ordinance of God; such as the ordinance is, such must our duty of subjection be. No power can challenge an obedience beyond its own measure, for if it might we should destroy all rules and differences of government and make all absolute and at pleasure. In every mixed principality:

First, look to what power is solely entrusted and committed to the prince by the fundamental constitution of the state. In the due execution thereof all owe full subjection to him – even the other estates, being but societies of his subjects bound to him by Oath of Allegiance as to their liege Lord.

Secondly, [look to] those acts belonging to the power which is estated in a mixed principle. If either part of that principle, or two of the three undertake to do them, it is invalid. It is no binding act. For in this case all three have a free negative voice; and take away the privilege of a negative voice – so that in case of refusal the rest have the power to do it without the third – then you destroy that third and make him but a looker-on. So that in every mixed government, I take it, there must be a necessity of concurrence of all three estates in the production of acts belonging to that power which is committed in common to them (else, suppose those acts valid which are done by any major part, i.e., any two of the three, then you put it into the power of any two by a confederacy at pleasure to disannul the third or suspend all its acts and make it a bare cipher in government).

Thirdly, in such a composed state, if the monarch invade the power of the other two or run into any course tending to the dissolving of the constituted frame, they ought to employ their power in this case to preserve the state from ruin. Yea, that is the very end and fundamental aim in constituting all mixed polities. Not that they by crossing and jarring should hinder the public good, but that if one exorbitate, the power of restraint and providing for the public safety should be in the rest. And the power is put into divers hands that one should counterpoise and keep even the other. So that for such other estates it is not only lawful to deny obedience and submission to illegal proceedings (as private men may) but it is their duty and by the foundations of the government they are bound to prevent dissolution of the established frame.

Fourthly, the person of the monarch, even in mixed forms . . . ought to be above the reach of violence in his utmost exorbitances . . . For when a people have sworn allegiance and invested a person or line with supremacy they have made it sacred, and no abuse can divest him of that power irrevocably communicated. And while he hath power in a mixed monarchy he is the universal sovereign even of the other limiting estates; so that being above them he is *de jure* exempt from any penal hand.

Fifthly, [there is] . . . one inconvenience must necessarily be in all mixed governments, which I showed [before] to be in limited governments. There can be no constituted, legal, authoritative judge of the fundamental controversies arising betwixt the three estates. If such do arise it is the fatal disease of these governments for which no salve can be prescribed, for the established being of such [an] authority would *ipso facto* overthrow the frame and turn it into absoluteness. So that if one of these (or two) say their power is invaded and the government assaulted by the other, the accused denying it, it doth become a controversy. Of this question there is no legal judge. It is a case beyond the provision of such a government. The accusing side must make it evident to every man's conscience. In this case, which is beyond government, the appeal must be to the community as if there were no government. And, as the evidences of men's consciences are convinced, they are bound to give their utmost assistance. For the intention of the frame in such states justifies the exercise of any power conducing to the safety of the universality and government established. . . .

It may be alleged by one or two of the estates against the other, that, not content with the powers allowed to it by the laws of the government, it seeks to swallow up or entrench on the privileges of the other, either by immediate endeavours or else by protecting and interesting itself in the subversive plots of other men . . . In this case we must . . . distinguish betwixt, first: authority of raising forces for defence against such subversion, *being known and evident*, and secondly: authority of judging and final determining that the accused estate is guilty of such design and endeavour of subversion *when it is denied and protested against*. This last is the particular in this question to be considered: not whether the people are bound to obey the authority of two (or one) of the legislative estates in resisting the subversive assays of the other, being apparent and self-evident . . . but, when such plea of subversion is more obscure and questionable, which of the three estates hath the power of *ultime* and supreme judicature by vote or sentence to determine it against the other so that the people are bound to rest in that determination and accordingly to give their assistance, *eo nomine*, because it is by such a power noted and declared.

For my part . . . I will prescribe to the very question, for it includes a solecism in government of a mixed temperature. To demand which estate may challenge this power of final determination of fundamental controversy arising betwixt them is to demand which of them shall be absolute . . . This final, utmost controversy arising betwixt the three legislative estates can have no legal, constituted judge in a mixed government. For in such a difference, he who affirms that the people are bound to follow the judgement of the King against that of the Parliament destroys the mixture into absoluteness; and he who affirms that they are bound to cleave to the judgement of the two Houses resolves the monarchy into an aristocracy or democracy according as he places this final judgement; whereas I take it to be an evident truth that in a mixed government no power is to be attributed to either estate which directly or by necessary consequence destroys the liberty of the other.

Yet it is strange to see how in this epidemical division of the kingdom the abettors of both parts claim this unconcessible judgement . . . Dr Ferne lays down two reasons why this final judgement should belong to the King. (1) Monarchy, says he, settles the chief power and final judgement in one. This position of his can be absolutely true nowhere but in absolute monarchies. And in effect his book knows no other than absolute government. (2) Seeing someone must be trusted in every state, 'It is reason', says he, 'the highest and final trust should be in the higher and supreme power.' I presume by 'final trust' he means the trust of determining these supreme and final disagreements and accordingly I answer: it is *not* necessary that anyone be trusted with a binding power of judicature in these cases, for by the foundation of this government, none is, yea none can be, trusted with it. For to intend a mixed government and yet to settle the last resolution of all government in one is to contradict their very intention. . . .

On the contrary [Charles Herle, in his] *Fuller answer*, . . . hath two main assertions placing this judgement in the two Houses. (1) The final and casting result in this state's judgement concerning what these laws, dangers and means of prevention are, resides in the two Houses of Parliament . . . (2) In this final resolution of state's judgement the people are to rest . . . Good Lord! What extreme opposition between these two sorts of men. If the maintenance of these extremes be the ground of this war, then our kingdom is miserable and our government is lost whichever side soever overcome . . . I am rather persuaded that these officious propugners overdo their work and give more to them whose cause they plead than they ever intended to assume. Nay, rather give to everyone their due. Give no power to one of these three to crush and undo the other at pleasure. But why doth this *Answer* give all that to the two Houses which erewhile they would not suffer when the Judges in the Case of Ship Money had given it to the King? Sure, when they denied it to him, they did not intend it to themselves.

[Herle] tells us: 'In them resides the reason of state', and that [this is], 'the same reason and judgement of the state which first gave this government its being and constitution; therefore all the people are to be led by it and submit to it as their public reason and judgement.' I answer: If by 'state' he mean the whole kingdom, I say the reason of the two Houses divided from the King is not the reason of the kingdom, for it is not the King's reason, who is the head and chief of the kingdom. If by 'state' is meant the people, then it must be granted that as far forth as they represent them, their reason is to be accounted the reason of the kingdom and doth bind so far forth as the public reason of the kingdom can bind after they have restrained their reason and will to a condition of subjection. So that put the case it be the reason of state, yet not the same which first gave this government its being . . . Then, it was the reason of a state yet free . . . to use their reason and judgement in ordaining a government, and not at liberty to resolve again or to assume a supreme power of judging destructive to the frame of government they have established and restrained themselves unto. Their reason is ours so far as they are an ordained representative body. But . . . in this frame the Houses could not be ordained a legal tribunal to pass judgement in this last case, for then the architects by giving them that judicature had subordinated the King to them, and so had constituted no monarchy.

[Herle] argues [that] the Parliament, being the Court of supreme judicature and the King's Great (and highest) Council, therefore that is not to be denied to it which inferior Courts ordinarily have the power to do, *viz.* to judge matters between the King and subject, yea, in the highest case of all. [He notes, e.g., that] the King's power to tax the subject in case of danger and his being sole judge of that danger was brought to cognisance and passed by the Judges in the Exchequer. I answer: (1) There is not the same reason betwixt the Parliament and other Courts. In th[o]se the King is Judge (the Judges being deputed by him and judging by his authority), so that if any of his rights be tried before them, it is his own judgement and he judges himself, and therefore it is fit he should be bound by his own sentence. But in Parliament, the King *and* people are judges, and that not by an authority derived from him but originally invested in themselves. So that when the two estates judge without him in any case not prejudged by him, it cannot be called his judgement as that of the other Courts [can], being done by his authority. And if he be bound by any judgement of the two estates without him he is bound by an external power which is not his own, i.e., he is subordinated to another power in the state where he is supreme – which is contradictory. (2) In other Courts, if any case of right be judged 'twixt him and the subject, they are cases of particular rights which diminish not royalty if determined against him. Or if they pass cases of general right (as they did in that of Ship Money) it is but declaratively to show what is by law due to one and the other. Yet their judgement is revocable and liable to a repeal by a superior Court (as that was by Parliament). But if the King's prerogatives should be subjected to the judgement of the two estates (the King dissenting) then he should be subject to a sentence in the highest Court, and so irremediable. A judicatory should be set up to determine of his highest rights without him from which he could have no remedy.

Thus main causes may be alleged why, though other Courts do judge his rights, yet the two estates in Parliament, without him, cannot. And it is from no defect in their power but rather from the eminency of it that they cannot. If one, deputed by common consent of three, doth by the power they have given them determine controversies between those three, it is not for [any] of them to challenge right to judge those cases because one who is inferior to them doth it. Indeed if the power of the two Houses were a deputed power as the power of other Courts is, this argument were of good strength. But they, being concurrents in a supreme Court by power originally their own, I conceive it hard to put the power of final judgement in all controversies 'twixt him and them exclusively into their hands.

If it be demanded then how this cause can be decided and which way the [people must] turn in such a contention, I answer: If the non-decision be tolerable it must remain undecided whiles the principal of legal decision is thus divided and by that division each suspends the others' power. If it be such as is destructive and necessitates a determination on, this must be made evident. And then every person must aid that part which in his best reason and judgement stands for the public good against the destructive. And the laws and government which he stands for and is sworn to justifies and bears him out in it, yea binds him to it. If any wonder I should justify a power in the two Houses to resist and command aid against any agents of destructive commands of the King and yet not allow them power of judging when those agents or commands are destructive, I answer: I do not simply deny them power of judging and declaring this but I [do] deny them to be a legal Court ordained to judge of this case authoritatively so as to bind all people to receive and rest in their judgements for conscience of its authority and because they have voted it. 'Tis the evidence, not the power or their votes, must bind our reason and practice in this case. We ought to conceive their votes the discoveries made by the best eyes of the kingdom and which in likelihood should see most. But when they vote a thing against the proceedings of the third and supreme estate, our consciences must have evidence of truth to guide them and not the sole authority of votes. . . .

*Vindication*

*[Ferne]* much mislikes when I say 'the fundamental laws must judge in every man's conscience'. 'This is', says he, 'a ready way to anarchy and confusion.' I refer not this case to the consciences of men as to an authoritative judge but [as to] a moral principle of discerning right. And who can deny unto man such a liberty to conceive of right according to the light he hath from the fundamentals of the state? Let the judicious read what I have said here (about p. 67 of a *Treatise of Monarchy*) and let him then tell how that question can be otherwise determined. . . . So when I say 'the wronged side must make it evident to every man's conscience'; also, 'the appeal must be to the community as if there were no government, and as every man is convinced in conscience he is bound to give assistance' (p. 29), he calls this 'good stuff'. Why? . . . I say not simply that people are at liberty as if there were no government, but *in this particular question*. [They] are bound still, in all besides. He takes me as if by 'community'; I meant only the Commons, when I expressed it by *genus humanum*, especially of that kingdom. He censures the 'reason of mankind' of partiality towards their representatives. Not so; for in so great a question wise men cannot be blinded. Honest men will go according to their conscience and reasonable men according to evidence, and will see it concerns them as well to avoid anarchy by aiding a wronged monarch as tyranny by aiding an oppressed state. But sith [Ferne] is so bitter an inveigher against an appeal *ad conscientiam generis humani*, in this last case so uncapable of an authoritative decision, let him: (1) consider on what foundation God hath built monarchy and all other

powers but the consciences of men (*Romans* xiii. 2), let him (2) weigh whether, when he hath said all he can say, such an appeal be avoidable ... Suppose the Doctor and I should agree in this, that the King is the *ultime* judge of controversies. Yet it is very like those states with whom the contention is will not yield him so to judge against them in his own cause. But suppose they do not submit to his determination. He will say they sin, and rebel against him. Well let it be granted, yet submit they do not. I demand in this case what course the King hath to make effectual his sentence. It must be by force of arms, by the sword. But of whom? Either the people's whose representatives [the estates] are, or other men's. But what shall bind them to afford their force to make good his sentence? It must be their conscience of his right. Thus when all is said and done, to the consciences of men *must* his appeal be, and to them *must* he make evident his right, in this extreme contention.

## 8.7 THE INTERESTS OF PARLIAMENT AND THE KINGDOM

From [Henry Parker], *Some few observations*, 5–6 (see headnote to [8.1]); Herle, *A fuller answer* 12–13; [William Strafford], *The question disputed* (1645), 9–15: Wing S 5151.

Royalists continually claimed that Parliament's supporters – even some of the Parliamentmen – were 'low men', intent on bettering themselves at the kingdom's expense, even on destroying the kingdom. Some fine historians have used such remarks as evidence of the social composition of the opposing sides and of the intentions of Parliament's supporters (e.g. Hill 1972; Manning 1976). Here these parliamentarians reply to the accusations as if they were simply propaganda. Gunn (1969) has noted a growth in argument from 'interest' rather than principle over the civil war years, and it is clear that such 'Machiavellian' calculation was to find a considerable place in interregnum thought (Raab 1964). The pieces here confidently argue that there is in fact no difference between acting rightly and acting according to the dictates of interest; Parliament's interest must be the good of the kingdom. Their claims are as plausible as those of the royalists.

### *8.7.1 Parker*

[The members of the Lords and Commons] can have no private interest to deprave them. Nothing can square with the Common Council but the common good. And if five hundred of the nobility and gentry should aim at oppression they could never compass their ends. It were folly in them. Some such objections have been made against this Parliament, but, finding little credit, at last some *few* of the Parliament are pitched upon, as if it were credible that all the kingdom, in whose hands all real power consists, would enslave themselves to five hundred, or those five hundred voluntarily become the slaves of five men.

### *8.7.2 Herle*

If this last casting principle be so necessary, and cannot be a divided one, why not the King . . . rather than the Parliament? Why may there not be a factious, packed or enslaved Parliament, as well as a wilful, flattered, abused King? . . . . Now experience shows that most men's actions are swayed . . . by their ends and interests. Those of Kings . . . (as absoluteness of rule, enlargement of revenue by monopolies, patents, etc.) are altogether incompatible and cross-centered to those of subjects (as property, privilege, etc.) with which the Parliaments' either ends or interests cannot thus dash and interfere. The Members are subjects themselves, not only entrusted with but self-interested in those very privileges and properties. Besides they are many, and so they not only see more but are less swayable, as not easily reducible to one head of private interest. But 'by a near equality of votes', you'll say, 'in Parliament, it may come to an odd man to cast by; and then the whole trust and interest lies in him wholly'. I answer: no such matter . . . The last odd sand doth not make the hourglass empty more than any of the rest; it doth but tell us when 'tis empty. Suppose two hundred and one. The odd one tells us 'tis the major part, but 'tis all the rest that make it so. So that we have . . . the judgement, trust and interest of two hundred and one chosen men engaged in the equity and fitness of the vote. . . .

But yet . . . if ability and fidelity make up the competency of a faculty to give law, why not then the Judges in Exchequer Chamber rather than the Members in Parliament? They for matters of ability are skilled, and for matter of fidelity sworn, have more dexterity to judge and less liberty to err. I answer: for their skills and oath, the Houses may make use of both if they please. It was the wisdom of this government, considering men's aptness rather to warp after their interests and ends than to be kept upright by their skills and oaths, to trust it rather to many independent men's interests than to a few dependent men's oaths. Every day's experience tells us that interests are better state security than oaths.

### *8.7.3 The question disputed*

Others, wishing well to the King's party, of the like dividing spirit, contend . . . to have the nobility and gentry of this kingdom think that the yeomanry and commonalty frame hopes to themselves of making the gentry in an equal rank. These sinister contemplations of some disaffected and discontented persons are invented on purpose to sever and divide the mutal concurrence of the gentry and commonalty in a proportionate aiding one another. How frivolous it is all men may guess whenas the Parliament Members of both Houses are lords and gentry, themselves a bulwark strong enough to retard and provide against any such encroaching thought of parity – if any such there be in the commonalty. And there needs no other argument to envince such sinister superstitions. . . .

*Part nine*
# THE VOICE OF A MODERATE

## 9.1 THE KINGDOM'S INTEREST IN PEACE

From Thomas Povey, *The moderator expecting sudden peace, or a certain ruin* (1643): Wing P 3042.

Not much is known about Povey (*c.* 1614–84 and more). He trained as a lawyer before the war and was ultimately to co-operate with the interregnum regimes, though there seems to have been a warrant out for his arrest in 1650. He was 'favoured at court' at the Restoration and continued a career as a civil servant. It is hard not to detect an element of cant in Povey's professions of moderation; his *Moderator* was correctly attacked as being crypto-royalist; but the piece does give lengthy expression to sentiments of desolation often voiced by others, but given less weight as arguments regarding what should be done (Lamont and Oldfield 1975). Povey argues the counter-productivity of appealing to principles to resolve the crisis. There must be a trade-off, for what really matters is the 'interest' of all, and that lies in a peace which can be obtained only through compromise. The *Moderator* is perhaps to be seen as part of a royalist–defeatist genre, best represented by Marchamont Nedham's *The case of the kingdom stated* (1647) and some minor royalist tracts of 1648–49. They appeal to the great political interests – the Army, the presbyterians, the independents, the Scots, the royalists and the city – to reach an accommodation for the mutual benefit. The basic notion is that private and public interest coincide – a far cry from normal partisan rhetoric which identified the enemy as a self-seeking faction – and one the implications of which were later to be worked out during the interregnum by the 'classical republicans': Nedham himself (who changed sides) and the influential James Harrington, author of *Oceana*, prominent among them (Raab 1964; Gunn 1969; Pocock 1977).

The best part of a year hath been made unhappy . . . and after all this, how much farther off are we from the peace, or from the ends we seemed to aim at? The quarrel by all this is but inflamed.

Jealousies grow higher; malice grows stronger; poverty comes upon us like an armed man. Humanity is almost turned to cruelty, and nature and friendship are not able to restrain our inconsiderate fury. The sword must hereafter become Chief Justice, and will dispense with and control all law . . . The opposing ourselves against the chief fort and strength of the subject, the Great Council of Parliament, must be called 'allegiance' and 'duty'; disobedience to the commands of our Prince must be called 'loyalty'. And in brief, such is the tyranny of war, we must see an inversion of all order, confusion in all our services to heaven and earth, and chaos instead of that admirable composure which many years of peace had ere now fixed this state in, if those that have of late times been over us had done their parts. . . .

When [reason] shall tell me how requisite the prosecution of this war is and how it may advantage the state, I shall be convinced. But until then I shall be obstinate in this opinion (hoping that it will not fall out to be against the sense of Parliament): that a peace warily concluded by an accommodation must be the happiest issue that can be given to these differences. . . .

We shall not therefore examine . . . whether the prerogative commenced it to protect itself . . . (as some would have it) or to perfect the design of many years before to be absolute master of the people (as others conceive); or whether the Parliament begun it to secure themselves and fetch in delinquents (as we are bid believe) or to confirm by the sword [that] which no other assurances could ever make good unto them, and so bring in a government somewhat near to an aristocracy (as some have suggested). [N]or whether indeed the reason of war be a miscellany of all these . . . How justifiable, how necessary, and on which side this war was defensive or offensive, I shall not attempt to debate or determine. These are dangerous mysteries not to be pried into. It will be enough for us to enquire how far it tends to the general good. . . . And it is confessed (though not agreed on) by both armies, that our religion, laws and liberties and whatsoever is or should be dear to us lies at stake and that they wear their swords only to defend these . . . Thus our cause is much like a riddle. It were surely better for us to have it understood by the deliberation and wisdom of a parley than by . . . the violence of the sword. . . .

But, it will be told me, when Parliament's army hath gotten the victory, and all oppositions shall be removed so that they may without interruption reach their ends, such a reformation will be effected as shall recompense the disturbance in the gaining of it . . .

We will suppose them conquerors. . . . Then it is likely neither root nor branch of our old church order shall be left, nor any sign where it grew. And though perhaps themselves could be contented with a more even and moderate reformation, it may be feared that the loud people, delighting in change and grown insolent with their success, will call for a mutation of every circumstance, and when they have found their strength will think nothing enough if they have not all that their wild and unlimited zeal approves of. And so that upon this enquiry, it is hard to be satisfied how our religion, laws or liberties shall be improved by such a war as we are engaged in. . . .

As yet the soldier has not yet devoured the husbandman's store, but without much trouble finds bread for himself and provender for his horse. But where will he seek it when he hath spoiled the springing grass and trampled down, or eaten up, the growing corn? The husbandman will be afraid to venture his seed in the ground not knowing who shall reap it, or, if he should be so hardy perhaps, he wants [i.e. lacks] his horses to plough or his hinds [i.e. labourers] to help him. . . . A famine never comes without sad companions, as the plague, smallpox, flux, and many more such servants of death. Thus provision, the chief support of this populous kingdom, will be suddenly wasted; and thus those whom the war spares, want or violent diseases will devour; and so we see shall many . . . perish without the sword, yet by it. It is to no purpose to demonstrate how the treasure of the land, heaped up by a long-lived peace, will be suddenly poured out, and be seen no more. . . .

The question hereafter will be not so much, 'where is the right'? but, 'where is the power'? For the right of power must carry the business. And then it will be beyond probability that this kingdom will ever recover the purity of its religion, its laws, its customs, its government, which have been settling about five hundred years . . . And it hath in all ages been observed that designs in war change like scenes in a masque, where we see new apparitions ere we are aware of them; and the events of one year may beyond all expectation vary or heighten the quarrel. . . . We will not undertake to define the quarrel as it now stands largely or saucily. We will conceive it thus: 'A working jealousy, fixed in a divided kingdom, both sides choosing rather to die than to trust one another.' From this root must necessarily spring these inconveniences.

The most uncharitable mischief that a commonwealth can be engaged in is that we must execute the designs of our enemies upon ourselves; that the King may receive his death from the hand of a subject while it is reached forth – if you will believe his vows – for his good and safety; that the father sending his bullet at a venture may kill his son, or the son his father, this is probable enough. But it is impossible that brothers, kindred and friends should not mingle in one anothers' blood . . . we see such an eager division in all families. And it is so universal, that no county, scarce any city or corporation is so unanimous, but they have division enough to undo themselves. . . .

The ground of such a war as this is the affections of the people, and upon this both armies are built and kept up. We will therefore guess which of them hath the surest foundation. It hath been observed the Parliament hath made little difference – or not the right [one] – between the gentry and yeomanry, rather complying and winning upon the latter than regarding or applying themselves at all to the former. And they may be thus excused: they did not think it justice to look upon any man according to his quality, but as he was a subject. I hope this was all the reason. But however, it appears not that they yet have or are likely to gain by this policy. The common people, could they be fixed, were only worth courting at such a time. But they are almost always heady and violent, seldom lasting and constant in their opinions. They that are to humour them must serve many masters who though they seem, and are, their inferiors, yet grow imperious upon many occasions. Many actions of merit, how eminent soever, shall not prevail with them to excuse one mistake. Want of success, though that be all the crime, makes them angry, murmuring and jealous, whereas a gentleman is better spirited and more resolute, and though he suffereth by it, had rather stick to that power that will countenance him than to that which makes no difference betwixt him and a peasant. The gentleman follows his resolution close and wins his silly neighbours many times, either by his power, his example, or his discourse; whenas they have an easy faith, quickly wrought upon, and upon the next turn will fall off in shoals. They are a body of great consequence when they are headed and ribbed by the gentry, but they have a craven or an unruly courage – which at best may be called obstinacy than resolution – and are far less considerable when the most part of the gentry or chief citizens divide themselves from them . . .

The people – not being able to see far into the secret consequences of war and peace – will begin to look upon those as their enemies whom they shall find most adverse to peace. And therefore though a treaty may bring many weighty inconveniences to one side more than the other, yet the humouring of the people is of so much consequence that it is too great an advantage to let it be often pressed and not received with the same seeming eagerness. . . .

And whilst we are to consider our own interests, let us lay aside partiality and those passions and conceits which will not give us leave to seek peace the nearest and the best way. Let us own reason on which side soever we shall find it. It is worth a man's wonder to see on both sides men that have been always reckoned (and deservedly) amongst the most wise and sober, [and] to see these bent to such extremes that they will justify their party in every circumstance, and so fix their opinions to one side, as if infallibility were inherent to it and as if they were not at all concerned in the actions of the other party . . . I shall be of their form that have indifferent wits and middle judgements . . . The true character of a moderate man I conceive to be this. He is one that loves his country so well that he grieves to see it destroyed out of a saving policy. One that is not a friend to this war not because he is afraid to die but because he would hereafter live in an even and well-poised temper. One that could never be so well satisfied of the necessity why this war began as he is now why it should see an end, which though he longs for, yet knows not how to pray for a victory. One that in earnest loves the King, and thinks him essential to the being of a Parliament; and the life of this [Parliament essential] to the well-being of all hereafter. One that honours, not adores, the Parliament, because he sees they are also but men, and rather wishes them safe and what they should be, than omnipotent. One that would have his religion nor gaudy nor stripped stark naked. One that loves the law and the gospel and would gladly have those that meddle with either to hold themselves closer to their text. One that is equally as much afraid of the meddling, severe clergy of New England as of the ambitious, pragmatic clergy of old England. One that is sorry to see it more seasonable than safe to speak truth. One that would have peace, not as an effect of war but of an accommodation. . . .

Suppose the lengthening of this war so to shake the estates of the nobility and the gentry about the King as that there will be little to maintain them like themselves when the war is ended: who do we think is, as it were, bound to repair their fortunes? And whether will not they, reduced to such necessities, be contented to enlarge that power, that may be so enabled to revenge and requite them, making the public interest to bend a little to theirs? And that among these there will not be some chiefs, some that unseen and closely will wind up the prerogative to make themselves greater? And do we believe that the nature and disposition of the people will not be altered, who being tired and worn out with the contentions of King and Parliament, will more easily undergo such things as they would heretofore have called slavery? And although the Prince have no aim at it, yet before he shall be aware he shall find himself engaged (by the concurrencies of so many circumstances that conduce to it) in a higher and more absolute government, so that the constitution of this state will become a little unlike itself. And then we must know that princes and all as such have the government of a commonwealth are compelled sometimes by a kind of necessity to dispense with the settled rules of law for reasons of state; and it cannot be expected that a prince, if he be wise as well as pious, shall be so superstitious to the strict sense of his protestations as to neglect his interest and the present condition of his state – which may, as it may happen, suffer very much whilst he makes a conscience to do things fit and requisite. And there will not then want men of both gowns [i.e. lawyers and clergy] that will prove that conveniency and necessity shall excuse the conscience in such a case. Would we avoid these inconveniences? Let us not run the hazard of them. Let us prevent a delayed victory by a sudden agreement. . . .

It is likely the Nineteen Propositions will be very reasonable things then. It will seem requisite that monarchy, or that which is called the prerogative, should be circumscribed within more popular limits – that some wiser, some honester, some more pious men, some that are unbiased with private respects or opinions . . . should be supervisors of the state and settle it in such an order as should please and benefit the people . . . It may perhaps fall out that some other politic security – not to be guessed at – may seem necessary to be innovated, which this state hath wanted, yet perhaps not needed, for many hundred years. And innovations come not alone. Rules of government are like links in a chain; they hang by one another and require proportion and evenness. If a new one be added it must be warily fitted to the rest, or the rest reduced as near as can be to the resemblance of the other. And what do we believe will satisfy the numerous victors, the people? Will not their ends and desires be as various as their humours are now? Will they submit their opinions to that which the judgements of those in the Parliament – as many as the war and the consequences of it will leave – shall agree upon? Or will it lie in the power of the Parliament, when the state shall be in such a general confusion as an expiring war must leave it in, to order the government so that the King may rule, and the people obey, as beseems them? . . .

Our next government must have a tincture at the least of the humours of those that shall become masters of the field, which may perhaps be of our own nation, or of another, so uncertain are the issues of war.

*Part ten*
# VARIETIES OF RADICALISM, 1645–1649

## 10.1 A LEVELLER ADAPTS PARLIAMENTARIAN ARGUMENT

From [John Lilburne], *Englands birth-right justified* (1645), 1–4: Wing L 2102. Haller (1934, vol. III), discusses the authorship and reprints the tract in facsimile.

John Lilburne (1615–57) was the most prolific of the 'leveller' writers, tirelessly detailing the injustices done him by Star Chamber, by royalists, by the House of Lords, the Commons, the London oligarchy, the Army 'grandees' and the Rump (Gregg 1961). More than that though, he was an absolute master at identifying his own grievances with those of every 'free-born' Englishman; and he was capable of a marvellous eclecticism of argument, ranging from the millenarian anti-Arminian tract of 1637, *A work of the beast*, through a radical natural right populism, to the baroque legalism which made him more of a royalist than anything else in 1649. He always claimed gentility, and with the exception of William Walwyn was the most respectable of the leveller leaders; however, there is no question but he was not of the class of any other pamphleteer printed here so far; he was not graced with education at a university or Inn of Court, but came to London at fourteen, apprenticed to a cloth trader. He led a movement of soldiers and civilians composed mostly of urban artisans (Aylmer 1974). In this extract, disillusioned with Parliament, he begins to turn parliamentarian propaganda against the institution it was designed to justify. *The question answered*, an anonymous broadsheet which he quotes, had a chequered history. It was published during the Militia debates for an obvious purpose; the King then apparently saw the propaganda value of publishing it, together with a request for the Lords to prosecute the author of such dangerous material; Parker blandly used its argument – perhaps he wrote the original – in 1642 [8.3]; and the doctrine that soldiers might replace a General who turned his cannons on his soldiers – the one Parker had adopted to justify the two Houses – was to be used to various effects thereafter [10.6.2; 11.1; 11.4]. The words of the broadsheet were the instruments of very different intentions throughout the period. Here Lilburne uses them to express a vehement commitment to both the letter and the equity of the law. The penalties he envisages for erring magistrates are, however, far worse than those thought of by the original pamphleteer.

In the 150th page of the book called *An exact collection of the Parliament's remonstrances, declarations, etc*, published by special order of the House of Commons, 24 March 164[3], we find there a question answered fit for all men to take notice of in these sad times . . . '*Ques*. Now in our extreme distractions, when foreign forces threaten, and probably are invited, and a malignant and a popish party at home offend, the devil hath cast a bone and raised a contention between the King and Parliament touching the Militia. His Majesty claims the disposing of it to be in him by the right of the law; the Parliament saith . . . . the ordering of it is in them.

'Which question receives a solution by this distinction: that there is in laws an equitable and a literal sense. His Majesty (let it be granted) is entrusted by law with the Militia: but it is for the good and preservation of the republic against foreign invasions or domestic rebellions – for it cannot be supposed that the Parliament would ever by law entrust the King with the Militia against themselves or the commonwealth that entrusts them to provide for their weal and not for their woe. So that when there is a certain appearance of grounded suspicion that the letter of the law shall be improved against the equity of it (i.e. the public good, whether of the body real or representative) then the commander, going against its equity gives the commanded liberty to refuse obedience to the letter. For the law, taken abstract from its original reason and end, is made a shell without a kernel, a shadow without a substance and a body without a soul. It is the execution of laws according to their equity and reason which, as I may say, is the spirit that gives life to authority. The letter kills.

'Nor need this equity be expressed in the law, being so naturally implied and supposed in all laws that are not merely imperial from that analogy which all bodies politic hold with natural [bodies], whence all government and governors borrow a proportional respect. And therefore when the militia of an army is committed to the General it is not with any express condition that he shall not turn the mouths of his cannons against his own soldiers – for that is so naturally and necessarily implied that it is needless to be expressed, inasmuch as if he did attempt or command such a thing against the nature of his trust and place, it did *ipso facto* estate the army in a right of disobedience, except we think that obedience binds men to cut their own throats (or at least their companions').

'And indeed if this distinction be not allowed then the "legal" and "mixed" monarchy is the greatest tyranny. For if laws invest the King in an absolute power, and the letter be not controlled by the equity, then whereas other Kings that are absolute monarchs and rule by will and not by law are tyrants perforce, those that rule by law and not by will have hereby a tyranny conferred upon them legally; and so the very end of the laws (which is to give bounds and limits to the exorbitant wills of princes) is by the laws themselves disappointed. For they thereby give corroboration and much more justification to an arbitrary tyranny by making it legal, not assumed (which laws are ordained to cross, not countenance). And therefore is the letter, where it seems absolute, always to receive qualification from the equity, else the aforesaid aburdity must follow.'

*So far the Parliament's own words.*

It is confessed by all rational men that the Parliament hath a power to annul a law, and to make a new law, and to declare a law; but known laws in force and unrepealed by them are a rule, so long as they so remain, for all the commons of England whereby to walk; and upon rational grounds [the known laws are] conceived to be binding to the very Parliament themselves as well as others. And though by their legislative power they have authority to make new laws, yet no free man of England is to take notice (nor can he) of what they intend till they declare it. Neither can they (as is conceived) justly punish any man for walking closely to the known and declared law, though it cross some pretended privilege of theirs remaining only in their own breasts. For where there is no law declared there can be no transgression. Therefore it is very requisite that the Parliament would declare their privileges to the whole commons of England that so no m[e]n may through ignorance (by the Parliament's default) run causelessly into the hazard of the loss of their lives, liberties or estates. For here [in the piece quoted above] it is acknowledged by themselves that their power is limited by those that betrust them and that they are not to do what they list but what they ought, namely to provide for the people's weal and not for their woe. So that unknown privileges are as dangerous as unlimited prerogatives, being both of them secret snares, especially for the best affected people.

It is the greatest hazard and danger that can be run unto to desert the only known and declared rule, the laying aside whereof brings in nothing but will and power, lust and strength. And so the strongest carry all away. For it is the known, established, declared and unrepealed law that tells the freemen of England that the Knights and Burgesses chosen according to law and sent to make up the Parliament are those that all the commons of England (who send and choose them) are to obey. But take away this declared law, and where will you find the rule of obedience? And if there be no rule of obedience then it must necessarily follow that if the greater and stronger number come to a Parliament sitting, and tell them that they are more and stronger than themselves and therefore they shall not make laws for them, must they not needs give place? Undoubtedly they must.

Yea, take away the declared, unrepealed law, and where is *meum* and *tuum*, and liberty and property? 'But', you will say, 'The law declared binds the people but is no rule for Parliament sitting, who are not to walk by a known law.' It is answered: 'It cannot be imagined that ever the people should be so sottish as to give such a power to those whom they choose for their servants.' For this were to give them a power to provide for their woe but not for their weal, which is contrary to their own foregoing maxim.

Therefore doubtless, that man is upon the most solid and firm ground that hath both the letter and equity of a known, declared and unrepealed law on his side, though his practice do cross some pretended privilege of Parliament.

## 10.2 THE LAW CONVICTS AND CONDEMNS THE EXORBITANT MAGISTRATE

From John Lilburne, *For every individuall member of the House of Commons* [1647], [1]–[4]: Wing L 2109

Here Lilburne, appealing to the Commons against the Lords, exploits a combination of legalist and populist argument which is typical of him. The instability of the mix is hinted at in the doctrine that Parliamentmen are merely the 'trustees' of the people; he does not accept the legalist doctrine that 'representing' them, they could, *ipso facto*, bind the people to obedience – or even continue to rule – if they break the law. Prynne called Lilburne a 'monstrous upstart lawyer' in 1645, horrified at Lilburne's readings from Sir Edward Coke. And if Lilburne drew radical inferences from that parliamentarian legal source, he was also often and rightly to point out that he found his populism in Prynne and Parker, not to mention Parliament's 'own Declarations'.

The law of England having always been esteemed by me the visible state-security of my life, liberty and propriety, for the preservation of which I have in the field with my sword in my hand often run the hazard of death; and being oppressed contrary thereunto by the present House of Lords in June 1646, I could do no more for my preservation and the preservation of the liberties and freedoms of my native country, than to fly by way of appeal to the authority and jurisdiction of your House (my legal peers and equals) who by the commons of England are chosen and betrusted to be the great patrons and guardians of their liberties and freedoms, and ought not to suffer them to be trodden underfoot by all the lords in England....

The book called my *Plea to Judge Reeves*, for writing of which I was summoned to the Lords' bar, is an honest and just book, free from scandals and falsehoods.... and therefore neither punishable by the House of Lords nor any Court of Justice in England. But, admit it were full of notorious scandals in the highest nature, the main question will be thus: Whether the House of Lords, by the law of England, have any original jurisdiction ... to summon me, a commoner of England, to their bar to answer a charge for writing the aforesaid book (or any other book) though never so scandalous in itself? Which I positively deny [with] seven strong reasons or arguments I made before and gave unto [a committee of the House of Commons] which you may read in my *Grand Plea*, the heads of which briefly are:

First, that the Lords sit not in their House by any power or authority derived from the people's free election and choice, but are merely and altogether the creatures of the King, made by his prerogative (sometimes of the basest and corruptest of the people, being the mere issues of his will) who himself is limited and bounded by the law, and who by his writ that summons them to sit in Parliament only empowers them to confer and treat with him, or afford their counsel of certain hard and urgent affairs concerning himself, the State, and the defence of the kingdom of England and the church thereof. But my pretended offence toucheth none of these things. And besides the Lords had no conference nor treaty with the King, their prerogative fountain....

Secondly, I was.... summoned to the Lords' bar to answer such things as I stood charged with before their lordships ... which did not in the least belong to the jurisdiction of their Court, but at the most is merely an action triable at the common law and nowhere else (see Coke's *5th part of the Reports: de libellis famosis; and* 13 Hen. 7; Keilway; *and* 11 Eliz: Diver ... [etc.etc.]). And being so, they ought not to have meddled with it, it being a known maxim of law that when an ordinary remedy may be had, an extraordinary is not to be made use of.

Thirdly, no man is to be imprisoned nor judged, but by the known established and declared laws of the land, see the *Petition of Right*. But there is no established law of the land for the judgement of the Lords in anything where the King, their creator, is not concurrent – [cf.]14 Edw. III, c. 5, which Statute plainly shows that in delays of justice or error of judgement in inferior Courts (which is all the causes they have jurisdiction of by law, which binds them as well as any other Court. . . .) there ought to be a petition to the King, and a commission from him to them, to give them cognisance of it. But none of this was in my case. . . .

Fourthly, by Magna Carta, and 3 Edw. I, and the *Petition of Right*, no man is to be judged but by his peers or equals (that is men of his own condition), and by due process: by indictment, presentment, or original writ, by a jury of his equals, of good and lawful people of the same neighbourhood, according to the old law of the land. But the Lords are none of my peers (see Clarke's Case, 5th part Coke's *Reports*, and his *2 Part of the Institutes* . . . and Sir Simon de Beresford's Case . . .). Neither had I any one particular legal proceeding, being summoned before any charge was filed against me. . . .

Fifthly. By the laws of this land, no man is to be judge in his own case. . . . But the Lords were, with me, complainants, prosecutors, witnesses, jury and judges. . . .

Sixthly. If the Lords' judgement originally were binding against me, then a few Lords would bind not only me, but all the commons of England, who one by one may be served by them as I am – and that without any hope of redress, they being judges still in the appeal – . . . . and so by this means the weal and safety of the people (called by you the 'supreme law', 2 part *Book of Declarations*, p. 879) is totally destroyed, and we the commons of England made the perfectest slaves in the world, by having our fundamental laws destroyed and made ciphers, and the power of the representatives destroyed and made ciphers, which is an act of higher treason than ever was committed by Strafford. . . .

Seventhly, the Lords [are] mere creatures of the King, made by his will and pleasure, and sit there as prerogative persons only; and yet in law and by their own principles (as Lords without the King) they have no prerogative, and yet . . . have acted upon me . . . without the King or his particular commission, which makes all they have done unto me to be made null and void both in law and reason, and renders them in my apprehension . . . . to have forfeited their power and honour, and never ought any more by you, the trustees of the people (and who should be the careful and watchful guardians of their laws and liberties), to be owned or acknowledged to be a House of Peers, but a company of apostates fallen from their first institution, and absolutely degenerated into a pack of tyrants, and therefore in equity, reason and justice, ought as well as the Star Chamber, to be plucked up by the roots (and transcendentally fined besides).

### 10.3 THE RELIGIOUS BASIS OF THE RIGHTS OF MAN

From Richard Overton, *An arrow against all tyrants* (1646), 3–6: Wing O 622. The tract has been reprinted in facsimile by the Rota (1976).

Richard Overton was of much more obscure origins than Lilburne: it is not even known when he was born and when he died. 'Young Martin Mar-Priest', as he sometimes signed himself, is usually depicted as a rationalist, and anticlerical to the core, the product of the more shadowy reaches of the publishing trade, or perhaps even of the popular theatre (Heinemann 1978). But like Lilburne, whom he joined in 1645 as a leader of the emerging leveller party when Lilburne fell foul of the House of Lords, he was a 'darling of the sectaries'; and it is in his writings more than those of any other leveller that the doctrine of the inalienable rights of individuals is to be found, not just stated as an axiom, but justified. The justification is a religious one, and appeals to the notion that men do not own themselves but are 'stewards' of themselves for God, their creator and master. (Davis 1973). This passage from *An arrow against all tyrants*, 'shot from the Prison of Newgate', may well bring to the reader's mind the similar doctrine in Locke's *Second Treatise*, sect. 6 (cf. Dunn 1969). These 'inalienable rights' are peculiar ones: like most rights they can be claimed against others, and it is wrong not to allow their exercise; unlike most rights, however, the right-bearer is not free to exercise them or not, he is obliged to; their possession imposes a duty on the right-bearer, yet the duty is – unlike many duties and like most rights – to the advantage of he who owes it. Thus the levellers are doing more than asserting their human rights. They are attempting to discharge their duty to God.

Sir,

To every individual in nature is given an individual property by nature not to be invaded or usurped by any. For everyone, as he is himself, so he hath a self-propriety else could he not be himself; and on this, no second may presume to deprive any of without man ifest violation and affront to the very principles of nature and of the rules of equity and justice between man and man. 'Mine' and 'thine' cannot be except this be. No man hath power over my rights and liberties, and I over no man's. I may be but an individual, enjoy myself and my self-propriety and may write [right?] myself no more than myself or presume any further. If I do I am an encroacher and an invader upon another man's right to which I have no right. For by natural birth all men are equally and alike born to like propriety, liberty and freedom; and as we are delivered of God by the hand of nature into this world, everyone with a natural, innate freedom and propriety (as it were writ in the table of every man's heart, never to be obliterated) even so are we to live: everyone equally and alike to enjoy his birthright and privilege, even all whereof God by nature hath made him free.

And this by nature everyone desires, aims at and requires. For no man naturally would be befooled of his liberty by his neighbour's craft or enslaved by his neighbour's might; for it is nature's instinct to preserve itself from all things hurtful and obnoxious. And this in nature is granted of all to be most reasonable, equal and just, not to be rooted out of the kind, even of equal duration with the creature. And from this fountain or root all just human powers take their original, not immediately from God (as Kings usually plead their prerogative), but mediately by the hand of nature, as from the represented to the representors. For originally God hath implanted them in the creature and from the creature those powers immediately proceed, and no further and no more may be communicated than stands for the better being, weal or safety thereof. And this is man's prerogative and no further. So much and no more may be given or received thereof, even so much as is conducent to a better being, more safety and freedom and no more. He that gives more sins against his own self, and he that takes more is a thief and robber to his own kind. Every man by nature [is] a King, priest and prophet in his own natural circuit and compass, whereof no second may partake but by deputation, commission and free consent from him whose natural right and freedom it is.

And thus Sir, and no otherwise, are you instated into your sovereign capacity for the free people of this nation. For their better being, discipline, government, propriety and safety, have each of them communicated so much unto you (their chosen ones) of their natural rights and powers that you might thereby become their absolute commissioners and lawful deputies but no more... (that by contraction of those their several individual communications conferred upon and united in you, you alone might become their own natural, proper, sovereign power therewith singly and only empowered for their several weales, safeties and freedoms and no otherwise). For as by nature no man may abuse, beat, torment or afflict himself, so by nature no man may give that power to another seeing he may not do it himself, for no more can be communicated from the general than is included in the particulars whereof the general is compounded. So that such, so deputed, are to the general no otherwise than as a school-master to a particular (to this or that man's family). For as such a one's mastership, ordering and regulating power is but by deputation and that *ad bene placitum* and may be removed at the parents' or headmaster's pleasure upon neglect or abuse thereof and be conferred upon another (no parent ever giving such an absolute unlimited power to such over their children as to do to them as they list, and not to be retracted, controlled or restrained in their exorbitances) even so and no otherwise is it with you, our deputies, in respect of the general. It is in vain for you to think you have power over us to save us or destroy us at your pleasure, to do with us as you list, be it for our weal or be it for our woe, and not to be enjoined in mercy to the one or questioned in justice for the other. . . . The edge of your own arguments against the King in this kind may be turned upon yourselves; for if for the safety of the people he might in equity be opposed by you in his tyrannies, oppressions and cruelties, even so may you by the same rule of right reason be opposed by the people in general in the like cases of destruction and ruin by you upon them. For the safety of the people is the sovereign law to which all must become subject and for the which all powers human are ordained by them; for [all] tyranny, oppression and cruelty whatsoever and in whomsoever is in itself unnatural, illegal, yea, absolutely anti-magisterial, for it is even destructive to all human civil society and therefore resistable.

Now, Sir, the commons of this nation, having empowered their body representative (whereof you are one) with their own absolute sovereignty, thereby authoritatively and legally to remove from amongst them all oppressions and tyrannies, oppressors and tyrants (how great soever in name, place or dignity) and to protect, safeguard and defend them from all such unnatural monsters, vipers and pests bred of corruption. . . . And to that end you have been assisted with our lives and fortunes most liberally and freely with most victorious and happy success, whereby your arms are strengthened with our might that now you may make us all happy within the confines of this nation if you please. And therefore Sir, in reason, equity and justice we deserve no less at your hands.

And Sir, let it not seem strange unto you that we are thus bold with you for our own. For by nature we are the sons of Adam, and from him have legitimately derived a natural propriety, right and freedom which only we require. And how in equity you can deny us we cannot see. It is but the just rights and prerogative of mankind (whereunto the people of England are heirs apparent as well as other nations) which we desire. And sure you will not deny us that we may be men and live like men? If you do, it will be as little safe for yourselves and posterity as for us and our posterity. For Sir, . . . what bondage, thraldom or tyranny soever you settle upon us, you certainly, or your posterity, will taste of the dregs. If by your present policy and abused might you chance to ward it from yourselves in particular, yet your posterity (do what you can) will be liable to the hazard thereof.

And therefore, Sir, we desire your help for your own sakes as well as for ourselves: chiefly for the removal of two most insufferable evils daily encroaching and increasing upon us, portending and threatening inevitable destruction and confusion of yourselves, of us, and of all our posterities, namely, the encroachments and usurpations of the House of Lords over the commons' liberties and freedoms, together with the barbarous and inhuman bloodthirsty desires and endeavours of the Presbyterian clergy.

## 10.4 THE RECOVERY OF LOST RIGHTS

From [Richard Overton and William Walwyn] *A remonstrance of many thousand citizens . . . to their House of Commons* (1646), 3–7, 11–15, 19: Wing R 993. Reprinted in Haller (1934, vol., III), and in Wolfe (1944).

This manifesto was one of many leveller petitions to Parliament, and as such was part of a five-year campaign for reform begun in 1645. It is more, however: it foreshadows the mechanism of an Agreement of the People by which the levellers were to continue their campaign into 1649. The idea was that an Agreement would be a constitutive document, discussed and agreed to by the populace. It would specify the powers of government and its limits; it would bind the governors and the governed because it was both reasonable (it had been discussed) and because all had sworn or 'covenanted' to stand by it. The precise details of the Agreements varied, but usually made claims for regular (annual or biennial) Parliaments or 'Representatives of the people', an extended franchise, and the diminution, perhaps extinction, of the powers of King and Lords. The 'Representative' would be 'entrusted' with 'supreme power' but that power would be subject to certain limitations imposed by the rights of the people, rights in particular to the free exercise of conscience and free trade (Gough 1931; Wolfe 1944). Natural rights can be talked of synchronically: time – and the events it brings with it – is irrelevant to their existence. This is the view Overton developed in the *Arrow*. In *A remonstrance of many thousand citizens*, however, he elaborated the anti-Normanist account of English history, in which it is held that 'birthrights', once held, and always valid, have been denied. Royalist historiography is turned on its head – he speaks, as Pocock (in King and Parekh, 1968) would have it, diachronically; Pocock also holds that in speaking the language of history, Overton is saying the same thing as he is saying in the language of reason. However, Tuck (1979) thinks Overton turns to history because he believed that men *could* agree to waive their rights and was anxious to show that they had not. Rights were not inalienable. The reader may like to judge this scholarly disagreement in the light of the two pieces. Thomas incidentally (1972) suggests that the English really may have lost historic rights to the franchise, and that the levellers may have meant 'customary right' by 'birthright' (cf. Hirst 1975).

. . . The cause of our choosing you to be Parliamentmen was to deliver us from all kind of bondage and to preserve the commonwealth in peace and happiness. For effecting whereof we possessed you with the same power that was in ourselves to have done the same (for we might justly have done it ourselves without you if we had thought it convenient), choosing you as persons we thought fitly qualified and faithful, for avoiding some inconveniences.

But ye are to remember this was only of us but a power of trust (which is ever revokable and cannot be otherwise) and to be employed for no other end than our own well-being. Nor did we choose you to continue our trusts longer than the known, established constitution of this commonwealth will justly permit, and that could be but for one year at the most. For by our law, a Parliament is to be called once every year, and oftener if need be, as ye well know. We are your principals, and you our agents. It is a truth which you cannot but acknowledge. For if you or any other shall assume or exercise any power that is not derived from our trust and choice thereunto, that power is no less than usurpation and an oppression from which we expect to be freed, in whomsoever we find it; it being altogether inconsistent with the nature of just freedom – which ye also very well understand.

The history of our forefathers since they were conquered by the Normans doth manifest that this nation hath been held in bondage, all along ever since, by the policies and force of the officers of trust in the commonwealth, amongst whom we always esteemed Kings the chiefest. And what in much of the former time was done by war and by impoverishing of the people – to make them slaves and to hold them in bondage – our latter princes have endeavoured to effect by giving ease and wealth unto the people, but withall, corrupting their understanding by infusing false principles concerning Kings, and government, and Parliaments, and freedoms; and also using all means to corrupt and vitiate the manners of the youth, and the strongest prop and support of the people, the gentry.... They choose rather to trust unto their policies and court arts, to King-waste and delusion than to justice and plain-dealing, and did effect many things tending to our enslaving (as in your [*Grand Remonstrance*] you show skill enough to manifest the same to all the world). And this nation, having been by their delusive arts and long-continued peace much softened and debased in judgement and spirit, did bear far beyond its usual temper or any example of our forefathers...

But, in conclusion, longer they would not bear; and then ye were chosen to work our deliverance and to estate us in natural and just liberty agreeable to reason and common equity. For whatever our forefathers were, or whatever they did or suffered or were enforced to yield unto, we are men of the present age and ought to be free from all kind of exorbitancies, molestations or arbitrary power; and you we choose to free us from all, without exception or limitation either in respect of persons, officers, degrees or things....

But how ye have dealt with us we shall now let you know... The continual oppressors of the nation have been Kings, which is so evident that you cannot deny it; and ye yourselves have told the King – whom yet you own – 'that his whole sixteen years' reign was one continued act of the breach of the law'.... And yet, as if you were of counsel with him and were resolved to hold up his reputation, thereby to enable him to go on in mischief, you maintain that 'the King can do no wrong' and apply all his oppressions to 'evil counsellors', begging and entreating him in such submissive language to return to his kingly office and Parliament, as if you were resolved to make us believe he were a God, without whose presence all must fall to ruin, or as if it were impossible for any nation to be happy without a King. You cannot fight for our liberties, but it must be in the name of King and Parliament; he that speaks of his cruelties must be thrust out of your House and society; your preachers must pray for him as if he had not deserved to be excommunicated all christian society, or as if ye or they thought God were a respecter of the persons of Kings in judgement.

By this and other your like dealings – your frequent treating and tampering to maintain his honour – we that have trusted you to deliver us from his oppressions and to preserve us from his cruelties, are wasted and consumed in multitudes to manifold miseries, whilst you lie ready with open arms to receive him. . . .

Ye must also deal better with us concerning the Lords than you have done. Ye only are chosen by us the people; and therefore in you only is the power of binding the whole nation by making, altering, or abolishing of laws. Ye have therefore prejudiced us, in acting so as if ye could not make a law without both the royal assent of the King . . . and the assent of the Lords. Yet when either King or Lords assent not to what you approve, ye have so much sense of your own power as to assent to what ye think good by an order of your own House. . . .

Nor is there any reason why [the Lords] should in any measure be less liable to any law than the gentry are. Why should any of them assault, strike or beat any, and not be liable to the law as other men are, Why should they not be as liable for their debts as other men? There is no reason. Yet have ye stood still and seen many of us, and some of yourselves, violently abused without reparation. . . .

We must deal plainly with you. Ye have long time acted more like the House of Peers than the House of Commons. We can scarcely approach your door with a request or motion, though by way of petition, but ye hold long debates whether we break not your privileges. The King's or the Lords' prerogatives never made a greater noise, nor was made more dreadful than the name of the privileges of the House of Commons. Your members, in all impositions, must not be taxed in the places where they live, like other men; your servants have their privileges too; to accuse or prosecute any of you is become dangerous to the prosecutors; ye have imprisonments as frequent for either witnesses or prosecutors as ever the Star Chamber had; and ye are furnished with new-devised arguments to prove that ye only may justly do these gross injustices, which the Star Chamber, High Commission and Council Board might not do. . . .

Ye vex and molest honest men for matters of religion and difference with you and your Synod in judgement, and take upon you to determine of doctrine and discipline: approving this, and reproaching that, just like unto former ignorant politic and superstitious Parliaments and convocations, and thereby have divided the honest people amongst themselves by countenancing only those of the presbytery and discountenancing all separation – anabaptists and independents. . . . Ye countenance only one, open the printing press only unto one, and suffer them to rail and abuse and domineer over all the rest, as if ye . . . had discovered and digested that without a powerful compulsory presbytery in the church, a compulsive mastership or aristocratical government over the people in the State could never long be maintained. Whereas truly, we are well assured, neither you nor none else can have any power at all to conclude the people in matters that concern the worship of God; for therein, every one of us ought to be fully assured in our own minds, and to be sure to worship Him according to our consciences. Ye may propose what form ye conceive best and most available for the information and well-being of the nation, and may persuade and invite thereunto; but compel, ye cannot justly. For ye have no power from us so to do; nor could you have; for we could not confer a power that was not in ourselves – there being none of us that can, without wilful sin, bind ourselves to worship God after any other way than what, to a tittle, in our own particular understandings, we approve to be just. And therefore we could not refer ourselves to you in things of this nature; and surely if we could not confer this power upon you, ye cannot have it, and so not exercise it justly. . . . How is it possible you should try all things? It is not for you to assume a power to control and force religion or a way of church government upon the people because former governments have so done. Ye are first to prove that ye could have such a power justly entrusted to you by the people that trusted you (which you see you have not). We may haply be answered that the King's writ that summons a Parliament and directs the people to choose Knights and Burgesses, implies the establishment of religion. To which we answer that if Kings would prove themselves lawful magistrates, they must prove themselves to be so by a lawful derivation of their authority, which must be from the voluntary trust of the people; and then the case is the same with them as between the people and you, they (as you) being possessed of no more power than what is in the people justly to entrust. And then all implications in the writs of the establishment of religion, showeth in that particular – as many other – we remain under the Norman yoke of an unlawful power from which we ought to free ourselves, and which ye ought not to maintain upon us but to abrogate . . .

Ye know the laws of this nation are unworthy of free people, and deserve, from first to last, to be considered and seriously debated and reduced to an agreement with common equity and right reason, which ought to be the form and life of every government. (Magna Carta itself being but a beggarly thing, containing many marks of intolerable bondage, and the laws that have been made since by Parliaments have in very many particulars made our government much more oppressive and intolerable). . . .

[The *Remonstrance* then attacks the legal profession, imprisonment for debt, impressment, customs dues, and the revenue-raising activities of Parliament's committees. It had already complained of the Common Council of London and the monopolies enjoyed by trading companies.]

We cannot but expect to be delivered from the Norman bondage, whereof we now as well as our predecessors have felt the smart (by these bloody wars) and from all unreasonable laws made ever since that unhappy conquest. As we have encouragement, we shall inform you further, and guide you as we observe your doings. The work, ye must note, is ours and not your own – though ye are to be partakers with us in the well or ill doing thereof. And therefore ye must expect to hear more frequently from us than ye have done; nor will it be your wisdom to take these admonitions and cautions in evil part.

## 10.5 THE COMMONS CONDEMNED AND THE COMMONALTY CHASTISED

From Lawrence Clarkson, *A general charge, or impeachment of high-treason . . . against the communality of England* (1647), 1–3, 11–12: Wing C 4578A.

Lawrence Clarkson (1615–67) was the author of the amazing *Lost sheep found* (1660: Rota, 1974). In this autobiography he describes his spiritual pilgrimage out of his early bondage to the Anglican Church, through Presbyterianism, independency, and antinomianism. He then, in 1644, became a Baptist; in 1645, under the influence of William Erbury – an Army chaplain – a Seeker; in 1658 he turned Ranter; and from 1658 he was a sometimes-erring Muggletonian (Morton 1970). *A general charge* (1647) is in many respects a leveller tract: it is suspicious of Parliament's dealings with the King; it espouses soldiers' rights; it attacks lawyers, law officers, county committees, and the illegal imprisonment of subjects; it condemns tithes as the instrument of State tyranny in religion, the excise as an encroachment on free trade, and the control of the press as an attempt to muzzle principled opposition to the regime. There are differences, however. Firstly, the levellers never envisaged that participation in politics should depend on true religious belief: royalists might be excluded from the franchise and from holding political office, but not permanently; nor did the levellers lay down any substantive rules for virtuous political living – it was enough that a constitution should provide a framework within which people might act as they chose. Clarkson, on the other hand, speaks the language of the 'Saints': 'self-denying men, and hating covetousness' should rule, and true belief among the people should be accompanied by actions of Christian virtue. That the 'Saints' should rule was a doctrine preached by the Army chaplains like Erbury (Solt 1959; [10.7]); it was one indeed made concrete in the words and actions of the New Model as it swept all before it (Lamont 1969); it was a belief common among the politically ineffective millenarian sects as the civil wars came to a close (Capp 1972); John Milton believed it (Barker 1942); and it was the political formula under which Barebone's Parliament sat in 1653, though the tendency to seek for 'Godly rule' was exhausting itself by then. Secondly, it should be noted here that Clarkson's systematic exposition of the reality of class conflict is not common among levellers, though it is to be found elsewhere among those who had less political impact (Petegorsky 1940; Hill 1972; [10.8; 10.9]).

First, know that which giveth being to a thing is greater than the thing being. That which giveth power is greater than to whom the power is given; so that the party infusing is above the party infused, as the sun above the beam and the fountain above the stream.

This is the case with you, yea you the commonalty of England, . . . from and by whom had the Parliament their power and being, etc. (From themselves it could not be, in that they cannot choose themselves nor enable themselves to be so chosen to execute the pleasure of their wills over or against any but themselves.) Therefore from you, yea you the commonalty of England, had the Parliament their rise and original. By you it was they were chosen and enabled to sit as a Parliament; so that from you they have the power to prosecute not against, but for, you, not to destroy you but to preserve you (in that they are not your masters but your servants, for to that end you have chosen and employed them – to finish and perfect what you order and appoint them).

Therefore if that Parliament you have chosen and employed do not act according to the nature of your choice, do not work consonant to your proposals produced, know this from Experienced Reason: that as the father is above the child, the master above the servant, so are you the commonalty of England above the Parliament, and in every degree as able to command them and require them as the father the child, the master the servant. Therefore unto you they must empty that authority, that, as without you they could have had no power, so at your demand they must give up that power. This is your prerogative, this is your privilege for the meanest subject of your kingdom, yea the whole commonalty of England.

Then consider: what oppressions, what cruelty soever is acted by the Parliament is acted by you, yea you the commonalty of England. For by your power invested on them they authorise others under them, to wit Judges, Sheriffs, Committees, Justices of the Peace and [all] Ministers whatsoever; so that what tyranny and cruelty these exercise upon you, the commonalty, is countenanced by that Parliament, by that power that you the commonalty have given them. Therefore what oppression, cruelty or treasonable acts soever are exercised by the Parliament or others in authority under them is to be imputed to you, and not to them.

For if you, the commonalty of England, that hath armed the Parliament, would disarm them; that hath strengthened them, would weaken them; that hath made them to be what they are, would make them to be what they were; that hath made them your Judges, would have them by you judged, and in exchange thereof choose *self-denying men, hating covetouseness*, such as seek not themselves but you, men that are your fellow-sufferers in all your oppressions (these and only these you must employ for the regaining of the law of equity), then would oppression cease; yea and bondage and cruelty would leave your nation, and every one of your brethren that is in oppression would be at ease and liberty. But here is your blindness . . . in accusing the child for the father's guilt, in rebuking the servant for the master's offence, viz. in blaming the Parliament when you should blame yourselves. . . .

Whereas you plead that had it not been for oppressions and divisions you had not chosen a Parliament . . . Experience with Reason can make it appear that your oppressions and divisions came by those that you have chosen to ease you . . . Consider how unprofitable it is for those that oppress you to ease and free you from oppressions. For who are the oppressors but the nobility and gentry? And who are oppressed? Is not the yeoman, the farmer, the tradesman, the labourer? Then consider: have you not chosen oppressors to relieve you from oppression? So that your oppression is just, in not choosing *self-denying men hating covetouseness*, yea-such as are your equals . . . in estates, in love and humility, such that were your companions in oppressions and sufferings. These are the men worthy that place. Yea, none but these are able to quell the oppressors and ease the oppressed. For reason affirmeth [that] so long as you choose such as you say are your lords, your patrons and impropriators, injustice will continue, oppression will reign. For experience may teach you that it is naturally inbred in the major part of the nobility and gentry to oppress the persons of such that are not as rich and honourable as themselves, to judge the poor but fools and themselves wise. And therefore it comes, when you the commonalty calleth a Parliament, they are confident such must be chosen that are the noblest and richest in the County, not questioning but they are the wisest and ablest for that place, when reason affirmeth . . . these are not your equals, neither are these sensible of the burden that lieth upon you (for indeed how can they [be] whereas you, the commonalty, is oppressed?). It is they that oppress you, insomuch as that your slavery is their liberty, your poverty is their prosperity. Yea, in brief, your honouring of them dishonoureth the commonalty; [and it is] no marvel but when you oppose them they oppress you . . . You have armed them with your armour, so that if they destroy you it is by your own weapon. For from whom have they what they have, or by whom are they what they are, but from and by you, the commonalty? Therefore it is your prerogative, if you see cause to unlord those that are lorded by you, to unoffice those that are made officers by you. . . .

And whereas Justice-Equity is informed that, of the commonalty, none may have their vote in the choice of the Knight of the Shire or Burgess of a town, but such as are Freeholders or Freemen of the said cities or towns wherein those said Knights and Burgesses are to be chose, the said Justice-Equity affirmeth that if those who are not Freeholders, or Freemen of the said cities or towns of which the Knight or Burgess is to be chosen may not be admitted to vote in the choice thereof, the law of equity affirmeth that such, in reason, are not bound to obey the votes or ordinances of the said Members so chosen; neither are they to be at the pleasure of any of them whatsoever, only governed by the law of Justice-Equity held forth to them by Experienced-Reason.

## 10.6 SOLDIERS' RIGHTS DECLARED

From *A second apologie of all the private souldiers in his excellencies Sir Thomas Fairfax his Army to their commission officers* (1647) and *A declaration or representation from his excellency Sir Thomas Fairfax, and the Army under his command: humbly tendred to the Parliament* (1647). Extracted from the 'Army book of declarations', *A declaration of the engagements* (1647), [9]–[11], 38–40: Wing D 664

When the first war ended, Parliament not unnaturally sought to redeploy part of its military force (in Ireland especially) and to disband the rest. In the spring of 1647 the soldiers, penetrated by the leveller organisation, proceeded to make demands for military, and then for political, justice. They elected 'agitators' – the word derives from this period – to put pressure on their officers (Firth 1902; Woodhouse 1951; Kishlansky 1979b). *A second apologie* is one of their attempts to do this. The officers were tempted. On 5 June, the officers and soldiers joined in a *A solemn engagement* not to disband until their grievances were redressed. *A declaration or representation*, probably from the hand of Henry Ireton, Cromwell's son-in-law, was an immediate result. The Army had now emerged as a revolutionary threat to Parliament. Political thinking had moved a great distance from the rubrics of the catechisms: authority was no longer seen as inherent in a permanently fixed hierarchy of office but as depending upon the quality of acts in response to the will of God made manifest in providence.

### *10.6.1 The rank and file to the general officers*

Sirs,

We your soldiers, . . . have served under your commands with all readiness to free this our native land and nation from all tyranny and oppressions whatsoever – and that by virtue and power derived from this present Parliament, given not only to his excellency, Sir Thomas Fairfax . . . but likewise all the late Generals, his predecessors, under whom we . . . the whole soldiery have served both the State and you faithfully and diligently – by which means God hath been pleased to crown us with victory in dispersing our common enemies . . . We hoped to put an end to all tyrannies and oppressions, so that justice and equity according to the law of the land should have been done to the people, and that the meanest subject should fully enjoy his right, liberty, and proprieties in all things (which the Parliament hath made known to all the world in divers of their Declarations, to which they have often bound themselves to perform by their Oaths, Vows, Covenants and Protestations). Upon this ground of hope we have gone through all difficulties and dangers, that we might purchase to the people of this land, with ourselves, a plentiful crop and harvest of liberty and peace. But instead of it . . . we see that oppression is as great as ever, if not greater. . . .

Is it not better to die like men than to be enslaved and hanged like dogs? [This] must and will be yours and our portion, if not now looked into, even before our disbanding. . . . We have been quiet and peaceable in obeying all orders and commands; yet now we have a just cause to tell you if we be not relieved in these our grievances, we shall be forced to that which we pray God to divert. . . .

[The soldiers then demand that the honour of the Army be defended against scandals, that an Act of Indemnity for actions in war be passed, that widows and maimed soldiers be provided for, that present arrears of pay be paid and past arrears be audited for payment, that soldiers might not be impressed for service in Ireland, and 'that the liberty of the subject may be no longer enslaved, but that justice and judgement may be dealt to the meanest subject of this land, according to the law'.]

Now unless these our humble requests be by you, for us your soldiers and yourselves stood for to be granted, it had better we had never been born, or at least had never been in arms, but that we had by the sword been cut off from the misery we and you are like to undergo. So we rest, in hopes of your faithfulness.

### *10.6.2 The General and Officers to Parliament*

. . . Though, had we upon our first addresses for our undoubted rights and dues, found a free and candid reception with a just and reasonable consideration and a reasonable satisfaction (or at least a free answer therein), we should have been easily persuaded to have abated or foreborn much of our dues . . . yet since upon these former addresses we have found such hard dealing . . . we find no obliging reasons in the least to decline or recede from what's our due, but rather still to adhere unto our desires of full and equal satisfaction in all things mentioned . . . not only in behalf of ourselves and the Army, but also of the whole soldiery throughout the kingdom. . . .

Nor will it now, we hope, seem strange or unreasonable to rational and honest men who consider the consequence of our present case to their own and the kingdom's – as well as our future concernments in point of right, freedom, peace and safety – if . . . we shall, before disbanding, proceed in our own and the kingdom's behalf, to propound and plead for some provision for our and the kingdom's satisfaction and future security in relation to those things; especially considering that we were not a mere mercenary army, hired to serve any arbitrary power of a State, but called forth and conjured by the several Declarations of Parliament to the defence of our own and the people's just rights and liberties. . . . We took up arms in judgement and conscience to those ends, and have so continued them. [We] are resolved (according to your first, just, desires in your Declarations, and such principles as we have received from your frequent informations and our own common sense, concerning those our fundamental rights and liberties) to assert and vindicate the just power and rights of this kingdom in Parliament for those common ends premised, against all arbitrary power, violence and oppression, and against all particular parties or interests whatsoever – the said Declarations still directing us to the equitable sense of all laws and constitutions as dispensing with the very letter of the same and being supreme to it when the safety and preservation of all is concerned, and assuring us that all authority is fundamentally seated in the office, and but ministerially in the persons.

Neither do or will these our proceedings . . . amount to anything not warrantable before God and men, being thus far much short of the common proceedings in other nations. . . . Truly, such kingdoms as have according to both the law of nature and nations appeared in vindication and defence of their just rights and liberties have proceeded much higher (as our brethren of Scotland, who in the first beginning of these late differences associated in covenant from the very same grounds and principles, having no visible form, either of Parliament or King, to countenance them). We need not mention the State of the Netherlands, the Portugals, and others, all proceeding upon the same principles of right and freedom. And accordingly the Parliament hath declared it no resisting of magistracy to side with the just principles of nature and nations (that law upon which we have assisted you) . . . The soldiery may lawfully hold the hands of the General who will turn his cannon against the army on purpose to destroy them . . . And such were the proceedings of our ancestors of famous memory, to the purchasing of such rights and liberties as they have enjoyed through the price of their blood . . .

[Fairfax then declares that the following things ought to be done: Parliament ought to be purged of delinquents; good men ought to be allowed to rule there – those with 'conscience and religion in them'; regular, 'free' and 'equal' elections should be provided for so that the same men do not rule permanently in the Commons, the 'great and supreme power'; the present Parliament should be dissolved, and government settled for the future; the actions of military governors should be scrutinised, as should the use of monies obtained for war.]

## 10.7 GOD'S ARMY

From William Sedgewick, *A second view of the army remonstrance* (1648), 12–18, 33–35: Wing S 2389

William Sedgewick (1610?–69) was one of the chaplains of the New Model. It is tempting to make fun of him: he was known as 'doomsday Sedgewick' as a consequence of his having too-eagerly expected the Second Coming; and the King, whom he approached with one of his books, is said to have thought him to be in need of some sleep. Anti-royalist at first, by late 1648 he had begun to plead for charity towards the King and the Parliament in response to a *Remonstrance* of 20 November drawn up by the Army officers and presented to Parliament. The *Remonstrance* had demanded justice on the King and a dissolution of Parliament; and it proposed biennial Parliaments elected on 'equal' constituencies. Sedgewick told them in *Justice upon the army remonstrance*: 'You have back-slidden from a formal and carnal profession of the Kingdom of Christ living in God, to embrace the tail of this present world; to petty, beggarly, unbelieving, malicious projects for peace and safety. . . . You are not Saints yet.' His *Second view*, however, published not two weeks later, is kinder to the Army, and makes clear not only Sedgewick's own volatility in matters of political policy, but the surreal productiveness of populist–millenial thinking. As Hill says of popular heresy during the period, 'literally anything seemed possible' (1972). Sedgewick himself was to relapse into Muggletonian political quietism in the 1650s and was to conform as an Anglican in 1663; but Cromwell was to continue to have troubles with millenarian enthusiasts like him, as is made abundantly clear in a remarkable interview he had with John Rogers in 1655 (Abbott 1937–47, vol. III).

The kingdoms of the earth and the way of God's dealing with them in these last times are described in Nebuchadnezzar and his vision, *Daniel* iv. A kingdom is a great tree growing out of the earth unto a great strength and height, *reaching unto heaven, and the sight thereof unto the ends of the earth*. It grows out of the people and receives its life and nourishment from the lowest element, the inferior people, but arises up to such a height as touches heaven, i.e. comes near the heavenly glory, the kingdom of heaven or Christ. The tree hath *fair leaves and much fruit, meat for all*. It brings forth honour, order, peace, justice, love, riches: advantage to all. Kingdoms afford a universal benefit. *The beasts of the field have shadow under it, and the fowls of the heaven dwell in the boughs thereof, and all flesh feed of it*. All sorts of men receive protection from it. Those that labour and toil as beasts of the earth, they enjoy their wealth and safety under it; and those that fly in the air of wisdom [and] learning, they make their nests of honour and preferments in it; and all live upon it... But *behold a watcher, and an holy one came down from heaven... He cried aloud, and said thus, 'Hew down the tree, and cut off his branches, shake off his leaves, and scatter his fruit; let the beasts get away from under it, and the fowls from his branches'*. Here's harsh, cruel things from one who comes from heaven.... Cut down all government, dominion, King [and] Parliament, with all power and order. *Cut off the branches* of laws, offices, places. *Scatter the fruit*: let there be no safety, peace, getting of estates. *Let the beasts get from under it, and the fowls from the branches*: let the inhabitants be scattered; let wealth be removed; let honour and preferments cease....

The intent of God in this which is sure and decreed,... [is] required and shall be effected *that the living may know:* First, *that the most high ruleth in the kingdom of men*. God will make you know that himself... (not a minister or angel of his, not a vicegerent, not a civil magistrate only, but the high God, the highest glory of God) ruleth, not only over but in the kingdom of men. This, beastly, ignorant man knows not, but you must know it though you oppose it.... Secondly, *and giveth it [i.e. rule] to whomsoever he will*. He rules not in an abstracted sense without us, but gives it to whom he pleases... and in bestowing of it will not be bound to any person or family (as King) nor any society or company of men (as Parliament) nor to any form or custom of men, but when he pleaseth will pull down some and exalt others... And thirdly, *setteth over it the basest of men*: will not leave [over] till he set the bottom over the top, advanceth the basest, mean, common sort of men, men of basest account, of lowest, smallest worth, not renowned either for honour, riches, learning, wisdom or any other excellency, but set up men of base, ignoble birth, base spirits etc. over it. These three things hath the majesty of God written out clearly in these times....

Now it is exactly to be observed how secretly God passes out of one form into another, as from King to Parliament, and from Parliament to the Army (and not so secretly but his footsteps are seen visibly upon and in the actions of men, and he rides his journey upon their backs). This very much concerns the clearing of the Army's case and the scattering the mists that yet cover them and hinder them from seeing their own right, and others from discerning and acknowledging their power.... The rising of the Army is an act of God, who is the Lord of Hosts, and hath a peculiar prerogative in gathering them together, and delights much to show himself in this form. And the Parliament were but his instruments, God the main, in raising an army for his great designs. And therefore as soon as these are set up he begins to show forth his glory in them and to withdraw himself from the other, leaves Parliament to weakness, divisions, vanities [and] disgrace, and appears in the army in union, success, power [and] vigour. . . . The Parliament doing nothing suitable to their trust or worthy a Parliament, the Army discharge their place gallantly, faithfully and happily; so that we see the Parliament hath expowered itself and empowered the people, emptied and made void themselves of authority, and filled and formed the people with it . . . There is a transition of the glory of God from one to the other, and so a translation of dominion from the Parliament (the representative) to the body of the people themselves.

Power did arise from simple, poor man, had its original from the dust of the earth, common people, and receives its life and being from human nature in its simple state. There it was purest, unmixed [with] pride, cruelty [and] deceit. It was quietest and at rest without violence and disturbance, though in a mean and rude manner. And thence it rises into glory of kingdoms; into lordship, monarchy, and all such greatness. Now when it comes to the top and begins to corrupt (finds storms of wrath, malice and mischief in those heights) it naturally returns to its centre and retires, for its own safety and recover, to itself in the roots of the earth, the people. . . . [Bodies politic] at best . . . are the people dressed or set out with some outward honour, and they therefore must return to mingle themselves with the dust of *common men*. . . .

The people so raised and called up are the supreme power or superior to all others, even to them that begat them, the Parliament. The Parliament called the people (as is manifest in their declarations) to judge, saying, 'let the people judge'. They appeal[ed] to them and so they have subjected themselves to the people. And 'tis but reason they should judge. For the people themselves have in themselves the truest and purest light of judging (which is reason) and the most exact sense of their rights and of good and evil respecting their liberty and safety. And those principles in them of discerning men and things relating to the public weal or woe are more clear, more incorrupted than they are in men raised by them into place and office, especially when all high places are polluted by the Devil, and the minds of men grow worse by preferments and honours. . . . The Parliament itself is but one heap of self-seeking, they being generally biased, both on the one side and the other, with places, advantages, office, particular interests, and so not fit to be the judges of the public and common right. Therefore 'tis reason that God should call up the people, who though they be rude, despicable and unlearned, yet have a plain and honest sense in them of good and evil; and they are now set up to be judges of the affairs of the kingdom by God and by the Parliament (as his hand).

As they are the higher (being made judges and appealed unto) so they are the stronger, and more able to do justice and defend themselves than any instituted power. In all representatives there is something of weakness, being but figurative. They are indeed very elegant, beautiful and stately administrations of justice; but they have not that sufficiency and fundamental, stable strength that is in the people. And being but forms of government, we have found them (as in this Parliament) trifling about punctilios of honour, circumstances and points of privilege and prerogative, and not gone downright to the root of the matter. [This] lightness of spirit is not a proper remedy for the huge bulk of wickedness that hath gotten into the kingdom. . . . [Parliament] would be a whole age and more in purging out these evil humours in their dull, formal and customary way of proceeding, which is wholly unsatisfactory to the justice of God. . . . The people, thus authorised and empowered by the sword, and inflamed with wrath and zeal against their adversaries, have with much difficulty a long while contested with these evils and at last got the better of them which would have long ago . . . swallowed up the Parliament. And by this 'tis evident this of the people is the stronger power. . . .

If I give a man my sword I make him my lord and give him my life. So did Parliament in committing the sword to the people submitted themselves to them. . . . Now 'tis reason that those that give life should give laws too; and them upon whom we depend for our being, we must depend upon them likewise for our rule; so that the Parliament have made the Army the Lords Protector of themselves and of the right and interest of England. . . .

This Army are truly the people of England and have the nature and power of the whole in them. They are of popular stature: men of the common and ordinary rank of people, most of them of trades and husbandry (with a small mixture of the gentry) which are the body and strength of the kingdom and in whom the common interest most lies. They are the heart and life of the people: men in whom appear strong and lively affections for the public good, manifested in their great labours and hazarding their lives so often for the kingdom, by which they have merited the honour to be accounted the very breast and strength of England and to have in them the soul and life of the nation. . . . Being valiant for truth to step up upon this throne of judicature offered to them, they are unquestionably to be entitled the people of England. . . . This Army, in their general carriage towards the people, have by their tenderness of them, care of preserving them (though absolutely in their power) . . . showed that they have a public spirit and that the peace and good of the nation lives in them. And although they be not so absolute and perfect in this . . . yet they have generally . . . . so behaved themselves that the people everywhere have witnessed their great approbation of them. . . . So that they are rightly and truly *the people*: not in a gross heap, a heavy, dull, body, but in a selected, choice, way. They are the people in virtue, spirit and power, gathered up into heart and union, and so most able and fit for the work they have in hand (the people in gross being a monster, an unwieldly rude bulk of no use). . . . The clear understanding of this will be a great means to compose the dissaffections of the people to them. . . .

When he comes in his last and great glory he brings his hosts with him and comes as a General and *Lord of Hosts, thousands of thousands* attending upon him, and all his *saints and angels*. . . . In the providence of God in the world, God hath made great use of armies. . . . They have been the parents of all empires and kingdoms in the world. All the present commonwealths upon earth must own the sword to be their original and confess that from it they had their beginnings . . . Kingdoms come out of an army , so are [they] much cherished and upheld by the same (most kingdoms flourishing while their military virtues are kept bright and clear by use, and quickly languish[ing] when the sword is wholly laid aside, the presence of the sword keeping off destruction from them). As kingdoms are begot and nourished by armies, so do they again resolve into them as into their first principles. And when by strength of wickedness civil societies are disturbed, they naturally return to a military, as to their own father, for safety. . . . And therefore armies are not such hideous evils as some imagine, but are beautiful, glorious and exceeding profitable societies: not only scourges but saviours and protectors, they shall have motherly bowels as well as iron hands. . . .

The work that God hath now in hand is not an earthly, fixed, thing: but he is upon motion, marching us out of Egyptian darkness and bondage into a Canaan of rest and happiness. And therefore 'tis proper for him to gird up himself, to contract himself from a vast body of a kingdom into a narrower compass, into a few spirits in an active body such as an army is, loose and free from the clog of old forms and customs, to act lively his pleasure and to follow him into those new ways and paths of truth and liberty [down which] he shall lead them . . .

I have no more to say . . . *Behold the Lord hath proclaimed unto the end of the world; Say unto the Daughter of Sion, Behold thy salvation cometh; behold his reward is with him, and his work is before him; And they shall call them the holy people, the redeemed of the Lord. And thou shall be called, sought out a city, not forsaken.* 'Tis your salvation that is come. You shall see evil no more. Let all the world know it . . . He gives you a reward of all your pains and sufferings. He brings all good with him. You will need no supplies but what he will daily bring forth to you. . . . 'Tis now clear what he will do: reign over the nations in righteousness, set up an *everlasting kingdom* for the saints that shall never be destroyed. And all must own and confess you to be the holy people. . . . God hath sought you out, wandering in a wilderness and not knowing whither to go, and manifested you are not forsaken nor left to your own ways, wills or counsels, but taken into the nearest union with the power, wisdom and glory of God. Though for a little moment he left you, *with everlasting kindness he has gathered you*, and will not forsake you any more.

## 10.8 A NEW ISRAEL

From Gerrard Winstanley, *The new law of righteousness* (1649), 'To the twelve tribes of Israel', 2–9, 11–12, 20–2, 30, 34–41, 48–50, 61–2, 78–[80], 83: Wing W 3049. The tract is reprinted in Sabine (1941) and Hill (1973).

*The new law of righteousness* heralded the birth of the 'digger movement'. The poor are called to withdraw their labour from their landlords and their faith from the traditional instruments of oppression. They are to band together and dig the commons. Gerrard Winstanley (*fl.* 1643–53), a ruined clothier, led the most famous experiment in this regard [10.9]. But the movement for agrarian reform, set off by the anarchy of the war years, was by no means confined to his community at St George's Hill in Surrey (Hill 1972). Moderate and constitutionalist 'levellers' like Lilburne disowned these 'true levellers' and there was never any question of their success: Cromwell and Fairfax seem rather to have regarded Winstanley as light relief from more worrying tasks. The analogising scripturalism of Winstanley's *New law* allows him a freedom of thought unrestricted by the 'dead letter' of the Word. His mystic millenarianism frees him to cast a cool eye on the concrete, material details of class oppression, for the Spirit is present, and moving, in all flesh. The *New law* is a libertarian tract; but Winstanley was to turn to a more oppressive Utopianism in the succeeding months of 1649, growingly convinced of the degeneracy of human nature and of the need for 'true magistracy' (Petegorsky 1940; Davis 1976, 1981). That Marxist and socialist historians have been led to dwell on Winstanley's career is understandable; it is very difficult to give an account of his thought which sees him simply as talking of things of the spirit (though Mulligan *et al.* 1977 try) and his desire for radical social reform is manifest. Nevertheless, it is hard to see why, when the publishers of Pelican Books wished to represent the thought of the civil war period in their Political Classics series, they should have produced an edition of Winstanley's writings (however useful that edition is, Hill 1973). The reader will by now appreciate just how atypical of his times the man was.

To the twelve tribes of Israel, that are circumcised in heart and scattered throughout the nations of the earth:

Dear Brethren,

Though you have been, and yet are, the despised ones of the world, yet the blessing of the Most High (your King of Righteousness) is in you and shall spread forth of you to fill the earth... Though dark clouds of inward bondage and outward persecution have overspread you, yet you are the firmament in whom the Son of Righteousness will rise up, and from you will declare Himself to the whole creation. For you are Sion whom no man regards, out of whom salvation will come....

You are the Abrahamites in whom the blessing remains, that lives not now in the type [the pattern prefigured in the Old Testament], but enjoys the substance of circumcision. For he is not a Jew that is one outward, in the flesh. But he is a Jew that is one inward, whose circumcision is in the heart, whether he be born of the nation of the Jews extant in the world or whether he be born one of other nations in whom the blessing remains. It is Abraham's promised seed that makes a Jew; and these are they of whom it is said, *Salvation is of the Jews*....

This new Law of Righteousness and Peace which is rising up is David your King, which you have been seeking a long time, and now shall find Him coming a second time, in the personal appearance of His sons and daughters.... He will throw down the mountains of the flesh, fill up the low valleys of the spirit.... He will throw all the powers of the earth at your feet and Himself be your governor and teacher.

If anyone say 'the glory of Jerusalem is to be seen hereafter, after the body is laid in the dust', it matters not what they say. They speak their imagination, they know not what. I know that the glory of the Lord shall be seen and known within the creation of fire, water, earth and air . . . The swords and councils of the flesh shall not be seen in this work. The arm of the Lord only shall bring these mighty things to pass in the day of His power. And the hearts of men shall tremble and fail them with fear, to see the misery that is coming upon the world. For the glory and riches of men shall be brought low, and the Lord alone shall be exalted. Therefore all I say is this: though the world, even the seed of the flesh, despise you and call you reproachful names at their pleasure, yet wait patiently upon your King. He is coming. He is rising. The Son is up and His glory will fill the earth. . . . Then shall Jacob rejoice and Israel be glad. So I rest . . . a waiter for the consolation of Israel,

Gerrard Winstanley.

In the beginning of time the whole creation lived in man and man lived in his maker, the Spirit of Righteousness and Peace. For every creature walked evenly with man, and delighted in man, and would be ruled by him. There was no opposition between him and the beasts, fowls, fishes, or any creature in the earth; so that it is truly said the whole creation was in man . . . and walked even with him . . . And man lived in his maker, the Spirit, and delighted in no other. . . . But when man began to fall out of his maker and leave his joy and rest which he had in the Spirit of Righteousness, and sought contentment from creatures and outward objects, then he lost his dominion and the creatures fell out of him and became enemies and opposers of him. And then rise up mountains and valleys and hills and all unevenness in man's heart and in man's actions. And as the man is become selfish so all the beasts and creatures become selfish; and man and beast act like each other, by pushing with their horns of power and devouring one another to preserve self. . . . The covetousness, the subtlety, the cruelty, the pride, the envy, the devouring power that is in the flesh of man are the very distempers that are in such and such beasts and fowls. So that while man is ruled by such powers and declares no other actions but what is in the beast, he indeed goes in the shape of a man, but properly he is a beast . . .

And this now is the curse. Man is gone out of his maker to live upon objects. And the creatures are gone out of man to seek delight in pushing and devouring one another and the whole creation of fire and water, earth and air; and all besides made of these are put out of order through man's rejecting the Spirit to live upon objects. . . .

Experience shows us that every beast doth act in oppression and cruelty towards such creatures as he can master to his advantage. And thus doth the flesh of man which is king of the beasts . . . For this first Adam is such a selfish power that he seeks to compass all the creatures of the earth into his own covetous hands and make himself a lord and all the others his slaves. And though he gets lands, monies, honours, government into his hands, yet he gives the King of Righteousness but a company of fawning words of love and obedience . . . And so he becomes the chief rebel, the serpent, the Devil, the murderer, oppressing creation, setting himself above all in tyranny. And this power is the curse which the whole creation groans under, waiting for a restoration by Christ, the King of Law and Righteousness, who is the restorer of all things. . . .

This Adam appears first in every man and woman. But he sits down in the chair of magistracy in some above others. For though this climbing power of self-love be in all, yet it rises not to its height in all. But everyone that gets an authority into his hands tyrannises over others: as many husbands, parents, masters [and] magistrates . . . do carry themselves like oppressing lords over such as are under them, not knowing that their wives, children, servants [and] subjects are their fellow creatures and have equal privilege to share with them in the blessing of liberty. And this first Adam is to be seen and known in a two-fold sense. First, he is the wisdom and power of the flesh in every man . . . and he spreads himself within the creation, man, into divers branches: as into ignorance of the creator of all things, into covetousness after objects, into pride and envy, lifting himself above others, and seeking revenge upon all that crosses his selfish honours, and into hypocrisy, subtlety, lying imagination, self-love. From whence proceeds all unrighteous outward acting. Secondly, the first Adam is the wisdom and power of the flesh broke out and set down in the chair of rule and dominion in one part of mankind over another. And this is the beginner of particular interest, buying and selling the earth from one particular hand to another, saying, 'this is mine', upholding this particular propriety by a law of government of his own making, and thereby restraining other fellow-creatures from seeking nourishment from their mother earth (so though a man was bred up in a land yet he must not work for himself where he would sit down, but [for] such a one that had bought part of the land or came to it by inheritance of his deceased parents and called it his own land) . . . He that had no land was to work for those (for small wages) who called the land theirs. And thereby some are lifted up into the chair of tyranny and others trod under the footstool of misery, as if the earth were made for a few, not for all men. For truly the common people by their labours . . . have lifted up their landlords and others to rule in tyranny and oppression over them. And let all men say what they will, so long as such are rulers as call the land theirs, upholding this particular propriety of 'mine' and 'thine', the common people shall never have their liberty nor the land ever [be] free from troubles, oppressions and complainings, by reason whereof the creator of all things is continually provoked. . . . O thou proud, selfish, governing Adam in this land called England! Know that the cries of the poor, whom thou layeth heavy oppressions upon, is heard . . .

But when the earth becomes a common treasury as it was in the beginning . . . . a man shall have meat and drink and clothes by his labour in freedom. And what can be desired more in earth? Pride and envy likewise is killed thereby, for everyone shall look upon each other as equal in creation. . . . And so this Second Adam, Christ the Restorer, stops or dams up the runnings of those stinking waters of self-interest, and causes the waters of life and liberty to run plentifully in and through creation, making the earth a storehouse, and every man and woman to live in the Law of Righteousness and Peace as members of one household . . . As the man Christ Jesus swallowed up Moses, and so the Spirit dwelt bodily in the Lamb, . . . that same Spirit that filled every member of that one body [shall] in these last days be sent into the whole mankind, and every branch shall be a joint or member of the mystical body or several spreadings forth of the vine, being all filled with one spirit, Christ the Anointing, who fills all with Himself and so becomes alone King of Righteousness and Peace that rules in man.

And the powers of the flesh . . . shall be subdued under Him, and mankind made only subject to that one Spirit which shall dwell bodily in everyone as He dwelt bodily in the man Jesus Christ, who was the son of man (1 *Corinthians* xii. 13; *Acts* ii. 17, *Jeremiah* xxxi. 34) . . . So that upon the rising up of Christ in the sons and daughters, which is His second coming, the ministration of Christ in one single person is to be silent and draw back, and set the spreading power of righteousness and wisdom in the chair, of whose kingdom there shall be no end. So that as all things were gone out from the Spirit and were gone astray and corrupted, the Spirit in this great mystery of truth, being manifested in the flesh, burns up that dross out of creation and draws all things back again into Himself and declares Himself to be the alone wisdom and power and righteousness that rules, dwells, that governs and preserves both in, and over, the whole creation . . . Here we may see what the *dividing of time* (*Daniel* vii. 25) is, which is the last period in which the Beast is to reign . . . And this is no new gospel but the old one. It is the same report that the penmen of the scriptures gave for the everlasting gospel: *God with us or God manifest in the flesh*, the Father exalted above all. . . .

Assure yourselves this Adam is within every man and woman . . . Therefore when a man falls, let him not blame a man that died 6,000 years ago but blame himself, even the powers of his own flesh which leads him astray . . .

When every son and daughter shall be made comfortable to that one body of Jesus the Anointed, and the same power rules in them as in Him . . . the oppression shall cease and the rising up of this universal power shall destroy and subdue the selfish power. But that is not done by the hands of a few, or by unrighteous men that would pull the tyrannical government out of other men's hands and keep it in their own heart (as we feel that to be the burden of our age). But it is done by the universal spreading of the divine power, which is Christ in mankind making them all to act in one spirit and after one law of reason and equity. . . .

And surely, as the scriptures threaten misery to rich men, bidding them *howl* and *weep* . . . and the like, surely all those threatenings shall be materially fulfilled. For they shall be turned out of all, and their riches given to people that will bring forth a better fruit. And such as they have oppressed shall inherit the land. The rich man tells the poor that they offend reason's law if they take from the rich. I am sure it is a breach in that law in the rich to have plenty by them and yet will see their fellow creatures, men and women, to starve for want. Reason requires that every man should live upon the increase of the earth comfortably, though covetousness fights against reason's law. The rich doth lock up the treasures of the earth and hardens their hearts against the poor. The poor are those in whom the blessing lies, for they first *receive the gospel*, and their gifts of love and tenderness to preserve another shall be the condemnation of the rich . . . Selfish counsellors, selfish governors, selfish soldiers, shall never be honoured in settling this restoration. . . . Lordly proud flesh that hath got the government and saith the Spirit hath given it him. Indeed thou hast it for a time, not by right of blessing but by permission, that through thy unrighteousness thou mayest fall and never rise again, and that the righteous Jacob may arise, who hath been thy servant, and never fall again. And then the elder shall serve the younger.

I do not speak that any particular man may challenge and take their neighbour's goods by violence or robbery (I abhore it). . . . But everyone is to wait till the Lord Christ do spread Himself in the multiplicities of bodies, making them all of one heart and one mind, acting in righteousness one to another. It must be one power in all, making all give their consent to confirm that law of righteousness and reason (*Revelation* xi. 15) . . . And this universal power of a righteous law shall be so plainly writ in everyone's heart that none shall desire to have more than another or to be lord over other or to claim anything as his. This phrase 'mine and thine' shall be swallowed up in the law of righteous actions one to another; for they shall all live as brethren, everyone doing as they would be done by, and he that sees his brother in want and doth not help shall smart for his iniquity from the hand of the Lord . . . There shall be no need of lawyers, prisons, or engines of punishment one over another, for all shall walk and act righteously . . . But everyone shall put to their hands to till the earth and bring up cattle. And the blessing of the earth shall be common to all. When a man hath need of any corn or cattle, [he shall] take from the next storehouse he meets with (*Acts* iv. 32). There shall be no buying or selling, nor fairs or markets. But the whole earth shall be a common treasury for every man . . . When a man hath meat and drink and clothes he hath enough. And all shall cheerfully put to their hands to make these things that are needful, one helping another. There shall be none lords over others, but everyone shall be a lord of himself, subject to the Law of Righteousness, reason and equity, which shall dwell and rule in him . . .

('If it be thus', saith the scoffer, 'men's wives shall be common too? Or a man shall have as many wives as he please?' The Law of Righteousness says no. For when man was made, he was made male and female. One man and one woman conjoined together by the law of love makes the creation perfect in that particular: *Therefore a man shall forsake father and mother, and cleave only to his wife, for they twain are but one flesh* . . . And he or she that requires more wives or husbands than one, walks contrary to the law.) . . . .

As I was in a trance not long since . . . I heard these words: 'Eat bread together. Declare this all abroad.' Likewise I heard these words: 'Whosoever it is that labours in the earth for any person or persons that lift up themselves as lords and rulers over others, and doth not look upon themselves equal to others in the creation, the hand of the Lord shall be upon that labourer. I the Lord have spoke it and I will do it. Declare this all abroad.' . . . . The poor people by their labours in this time of the first Adam's government have made the buyers and sellers of land or rich men to become tyrants and oppressors over them. But in the time of Israel's restoration . . . none shall work for hire neither give any hire, but everyone shall work in love for another. . . . No man shall have any more land than he can labour himself or to have others labour with him in love . . . He that is now a possessor of lands and riches, and cannot labour, if he say to others, 'you are my fellow creatures and the Lord is now making the earth common amongst us. Therefore take my land and only let me eat bread with you', that man shall be preserved by the labour of others.

But if any man have land and neither can work nor will work, . . . the hand of the Lord shall fall upon him . . . He shall be made to work and eat with the sweat of his own brows, not of others, till he know himself to be a member, not a lord over, creation. And thus he shall be dealt with that hath lost the benefit of sonship . . . All the punishment that anyone shall receive for any unrighteous act, whereby he begins to bring the curse again upon creation, he shall only be made a Gibeonite to work in the earth (not a prison) and all eyes shall be upon him. And the greatest offence will be this: for any to endeavour to raise up some few to rule over others, and so set up a particular interest again, and to bring in buying and selling land again . . . Israel is not to imprison or torment any by death or smaller punishments but only to cause them to work and eat their own bread.

As the enclosures are called such a man's land and such a man's land, so the commons and heath are called the common people's. And let the world see who labours the earth in righteousness. And those to whom the Lord gives blessing, let them be the people that shall inherit the earth. . . . Was the earth made to preserve a few covetous, proud men to live at ease, and for them to bag and barn up the treasures of the earth from others, that they might beg or starve in a fruitful land? Or was it made to preserve all her children? Let reason, and the Prophets' and Apostles' writings be judge. The earth is the Lord's. It is not to be confined to particular interest. None can say their right is taken from them. For let the rich work alone by themselves and let the poor work together by themselves; the rich in their enclosures saying 'this is mine', the poor upon their commons saying 'this is ours'. The earth and the fruits are common, and who can be offended at the poor for doing this? . . . . Divide England into three parts. Scarce one part is manured, so that there is land enough to maintain all her children.

... Many die for want, or live under a heavy burden of poverty all their days. And this misery the poor people have brought upon themselves by lifting up particular interest by their labour.

There are yet three doors of hope for England to escape destroying plagues. First, let everyone leave off running after others for knowledge and comfort, and wait upon the Spirit, reason, till He break forth out of the clouds of your heart and manifest Himself to you (*Luke* xxiv. 49). This is to cast off the shadow of learning and to reject covetous, subtle, proud flesh that deceives all the world by their hearsay and traditional preaching of words, letters and syllables without the Spirit, and to make choice of the Lord, the true teacher of everyone in their own inward experience... Secondly, let everyone open his bags and barns that all may feed upon the crops of the earth... Leave off buying and selling of the land or of the fruits of the earth... and let the word of the Lord be acted amongst all. Work together; eat bread together. Thirdly, leave off dominion and lordship one over another, for the whole bulk of mankind are but one living earth. Leave off imprisoning, whipping and killing... Surely... particular propriety of 'mine' and 'thine' hath brought in all misery upon people? For first, it hath occasioned people to steal one from another. Secondly, it hath made laws to hang those that did steal. It tempts people to do an evil action, and kills them for doing of it....

And this let me tell you and you shall find it true. Go read all the books in your university that tell you what hath been formerly; and though you can make speeches of a day long from those readings, yet you shall have no peace.... Many a poor, despised man and woman... [hath] more sweet peace, more true experience of the Father, and walks more righteously in the creation, in spirit and in truth, than those that call themselves teachers and zealous professors. And why? Because these single-hearted ones are made to look into themselves, wherein they read the work of the whole creation and see that history seated within themselves. They see the mystery of righteousness... But those that are called preachers and great professors (that run a-heaving, seek for knowledge abroad in sermons in books, and universities, and buys it for money... and then delivers it out again for money, for £200 or £300 a year) [call] those men that speak from an inward testimony of what they have seen and heard... 'locusts', 'blasphemers' and whatnot, as the language of the pulpit runs. But the Lord will whip such traders out of the temple....

Therefore you dust of the earth that are trod underfoot, you poor people that makes both scholars and rich men your oppressors by your labour, take notice of your privilege. The Law of Righteousness is now declared... Therefore you selfish tithe-taking preachers and all others that preach for hire, with all covetous professors, take notice that you are the Judases that betrayed Christ. ...

I have now obeyed the command of the Spirit that bid me declare this all abroad. I have declared it and will declare it by word of mouth. I have now declared it by my pen. And when the Lord doth show me the place and the manner how He will have us that are called the common people to manure and work upon the common lands, I will then go forth and declare it in my action.

## 10.9 THE DIGGERS IN ACTION

From *The declaration and standard of the levellers of England delivered in a speech to . . . Fairfax* (1649): Wing E 3544

William Everard was another digger leader. The report below is taken from a contemporary newsbook. It speaks for itself.

Upon the 19th of this instant April 1649, the Council of State received information that one Mr [William] Everard, formerly of the Army who calls himself prophet, with others, came several days last week to St George's Hill in Surrey and began to dig, then to sowing the ground with parsnips, carrots and beans. Their number increases every day. They began with five and are now about fifty but they say they will shortly be above five thousand. They have prepared seed corn and intend to plough up the ground in Oatlands Park, Windsor Park and other places, and to level the pales etc. inviting all to come in, and promise them meat and drink and clothes, declaring to the people that they will shortly make them come up to the hills and work, and threaten the people that if they let their cattle come in amongst them, they will cut off their usurping heads and their four-footed legs. For

'Our thoughts are lofty, proud and full of ire,
We can be good or bad as times require.'

Upon the 20th of this instant, the said Mr Everard, and one [Gerrard] Winstanley, came to Whitehall to give his Excellency an account of their proceedings in digging up the ground on St George's Hill as aforesaid. Everard declared that he was of the race of the Jews and that all the liberties of the people were lost by the coming in of William the Conqueror, and that ever since, the people of God have lived under tyranny and oppression worse than that of our forefathers under the Egyptians.

But now the time of deliverance was at hand and God would bring His people out of this slavery and restore them their freedoms in the enjoying the fruits and benefits of the earth. And that there had lately appeared a vision to him which bade him, 'Arise, and dig and plow the earth, and receive the fruits thereof.' And that their intent is to restore the creation to its former condition, and that as God had promised to 'make the barren ground fruitful', so now what they did was to renew the ancient community of the enjoying the fruits of the earth, and to distribute the benefits thereof to the poor and needy, to feed the hungry and to clothe the naked. And that they intend not to meddle with any man's propriety, nor to break down any pales or enclosures, but only to meddle with what was common and untilled, and to make it fruitful for the use of man. But that the time would suddenly be that all men should willingly come in and give up their lands and estates, and willing to submit to this community; and for those which shall come in and work, they shall have meat, drink and clothes, which is all that is necessary for the life of man; and that for money there was not any need of it, nor of any clothes more than to cover their nakedness; and that they will not defend themselves by arms, but will submit unto authority and wait till the promised opportunity be offered, which they conceived to be near at hand; and that as their forefathers lived in tents so it would be suitable to their condition now to live in the same.

Here they say they are resolved to stand, and do account their forefathers' principles a perfect rule and standard for them to walk by.

It is observable that while Everard and Winstanley stood before the Lord General they stood with their hats on, and being demanded the reason, said he was 'but their fellow creature'. Being asked the meaning of that place: 'Give honour to whom honour is due', they seemed to be offended and said that their mouths should be stopped who gave them that offence.

*Part eleven*
# THE INDEPENDENTS' REVOLUTION

## 11.1 CROMWELL AND IRETON HESITATE AT PUTNEY

From C. H. Firth (Vol. I, 1891), I, 236–8, 268–9, 296–7, 300–8, 310–11. The modern edition of the Putney debates is A. S. P. Woodhouse (1951).

The union of soldiers and officers expressed in the *Solemn engagement* (headnote to [10.6]) was always a fragile one. The debates between agitators and officers at Putney church from 26 October to 1 November 1647 saw the disunity displayed. The agitators argued for an Agreement of the People which seemed to demand manhood suffrage; the officers plumped for a radical programme on which they were negotiating with the King. The debates are justly celebrated. Recorded in surprising detail by William Clarke, the Secretary of the Army, they demonstrate the puritan revolutionary mind at work. These extracts record the hesitations felt by Cromwell and Ireton – soon to be at once the destroyers of the 'levellers' and architects of the revolution of the independents – at the proposals that the King and Lords should be stripped of their power, and at what they alleged to be the leveller claim for universal suffrage for all males. Cromwell will be seen to be pointing out how the ends of political action are less important than the means, and dwelling on the danger of neglecting the 'ancient constitution'; Ireton speaks, like his father-in-law, of the dangers of reading more into providence than is there, and gives a remarkable analysis of the material basis of the old constitution – one perhaps conjured up less by a belief that the levellers actually intended the abolition of all property than in an attempt to embarrass them by accusing them of a policy quite unthinkable to any but the most extreme [10.8; 10.9]. For their part, the levellers were able to depict Ireton as backsliding from his own principles as set out in the many declarations of the army (e.g. [10.6.2]). Much of great interest has been written on and around these debates: Woodhouse (1951), Macpherson (1962), Thomas (1972), Davis (1974), Hampsher-Monk (1976), and Aylmer (1980) would make a good start for the student.

*Lieutenant-General Oliver Cromwell*: Truly this paper does contain in it very great alterations of the very government of the kingdom – alterations from that government that it hath been under, I believe I may almost say, ever since it was a nation . . . And what the consequences of such an alteration as this would be, if there were nothing else to be considered, wise and godly men ought to consider. . . . How do we know if whilst we are disputing these things, another company of men shall gather together and they shall put out a paper as plausible perhaps as this? . . . . And if so, what do you think the consequence of that would be? Would it not be confusion? Would it not be utter confusion? . . . . 'It is for your liberty; 'tis for your privilege; 'tis for your good.' (Pray God it prove so, whatsoever course we run.) But truly I think we are not only to consider what the consequences are if there were nothing else but this paper, but we are to consider the probability of the ways and means to accomplish [the things proposed in the Agreement]. . . . Truly, to anything that's good, there's no doubt on it, objections may be made and framed; but let every honest man consider whether or no there be not very real objections [to this] in point of difficulty. I know a man may answer all difficulties with faith, and faith will answer all difficulties really where it is; but we are very apt, all of us, to call that faith, that perhaps may be but carnal imagination, and carnal reasonings. Give me leave to say this. There will be very great mountains in the way of this, if this were the thing in present consideration; and therefore we ought to consider the consequences: and God hath given us our reason that we may do this. It is not enough to propose things that are good in the end; but suppose this model were an excellent model, and fit for England and the kingdom to receive, it is our duty as christians and men to consider consequences, and to consider the way. . . .

*Commissary-General Henry Ireton*: Let us take heed that we do not maintain this principle [that we are not bound so absolutely to personal obedience to any magistrates or personal authority, that if they work to our destruction we may not oppose them] [till it] leads to destruction. If the case were so visible as those cases the Army speaks of, of a General's turning the cannon against the army . . . there is no man but would agree with you. But when men will first put in those terms of destruction, they will imagine anything a destruction if there could be anything better; and so it is very easy and demonstrable that things are counted so abhorred and destructive [when] at the utmost a man [c]ould make it out by reason that men would be in a better condition if it be not done, than if it be done.

And though I cannot but subscribe to [it] that in such a visible way I may hold the hands of those that are in authority as I may the hands of a madman; but that no man shall think himself [bound] to acquiesce particularly and to suffer for quietness' sake, rather than to make a disturbance (or to raise a power if he can to make a disturbance) in the State – I do apprehend and appeal to all men whether there be not more folly or destructiveness in the spring of that principle than there can be in that other principle of holding passive obedience. . . . We have said [in the Army Declarations] we desire. . . . to have the constitution of the supreme authority of this kingdom reduced to that constitution which is due to the people of this kingdom, and, reducing the authority to this, we will submit to it. . . . The reducing of the supreme authority to that constitution by successive election, as near may be, we have insisted upon as an essential right of the kingdom; and no man can accuse the Army of disobedience, or holding forth a principle of disobedience, upon any other ground. . . .

[It is] not to me so much as the vainest or lightest thing you can imagine, whether there be a King in England or no, whether there be Lords in England or no. For whatever I find the work of God tending to I should desire quietly to submit to. If God saw it good to destroy not only King and Lords but all distinctions of degrees – nay if it go further, to destroy all property, that there's no such thing left, that there be nothing of civil constitution left in the kingdom – if I see the hand of God in it I hope I shall with quietness acquiesce, and submit to it, and not resist it. . . . I would not have [the Army, though] incur the scandal of neglecting engagements. . . . I would not have us give the world occasion to think that we are the disturbers of the peace of mankind. . . . [The debaters turn to the question of the franchise]

*Maximilian Petty*: We judge that all inhabitants that have not lost their birthright should have an equal voice in elections.

*Colonel Thomas Rainborough*: I desired that those that had engaged in [the *Agreement* might be included in the franchise]. For really I think that the poorest he that is in England hath a life to live as the greatest he; and therefore truly Sir, I think it's clear that every man that is to live under a government ought first by his own consent to put himself under that government; and I do think that the poorest man in England is not at all bound in a strict sense to that government that he hath not had a voice to put himself under. . . .

*Ireton*: . . . . Give me leave to tell you that if you make this the rule, I think you must fly for refuge to an absolute natural right, and you must deny all civil right; and I am sure it will come to that in the consequence. This, I perceive, is pressed as that which is so essential and due: the right of the people of this kingdom (and as they are the people of this kingdom distinct and divided from other people) and that we must for this right lay aside all other considerations [because] this is so just, this is so due, this is so right to them. And that those that they do thus choose must have such a power of binding all and loosing all according to those limitations – this is pressed as so due, and so just, as [it] is argued that it is an engagement paramount [to] all others; and you must for it lay aside all others; if you have engaged any otherwise, you must break [that engagement]. . . . For my part, I think it is no right at all. I think that no person hath a right to an interest or share in the disposing of the affairs of the kingdom, and in choosing those that shall determine what laws we shall be ruled by here – no person hath a right to this that hath not a permanent fixed interest in this kingdom. And *those* persons, together, are properly the represented of this kingdom, and consequently are [also] to make up the Representers of this Kingdom, who taken together do comprehend whatsoever is of real or permanent interest in the kingdom. . . . We talk of birthright. Truly [by] birthright there is thus much claim. Men may justly have by birthright – by their very being born in England – that we should not refuse them air and place and ground, and freedom of the highways and other things, to live among us – not any man that is born here, though by his birth there come nothing at all to him that is part of the permanent interest of this kingdom. . . . I am sure if we look upon that which is the utmost within m[en]'s view of what was originally the constitution of this kingdom, look upon that which is most radical and fundamental, and which if you take away there is no man hath any land, and goods, [or] any civil interest, that is this: that those that choose the Representers for the making of laws by which this State and kingdom are to be governed are the persons who, taken together, do comprehend the local interest of this kingdom; that is the persons in whom all the land lies, and those in corporations in whom all trading lies. This is the most fundamental constitution of this kingdom, which if you do not allow, you allow none at all. . . . I say this: that those that have the meanest local interest – that man that hath but forty shillings a year, he *hath* as great voice in the election of a Knight for the Shire as he that hath ten thousand a year or more. . . . But this [interest] still the constitution of this government hath had an eye to (and what other government hath not an eye to this?). It doth not relate to the interest of the kingdom if it do not lay the foundation of the power that's given to the Representers in those who have a permanent and a local interest in the kingdom and who, taken all together, do comprehend the whole [interest of the kingdom]. There is all the reason and justice that can be, if I will come to live in a kingdom, being a foreigner to it, or live in a kingdom having no permanent interest in it – if I will desire as a stranger or claim as one free-born here, the air, the free passage of the highways, the protection of the laws and all such things – if I will desire them . . . I must submit to those laws and those rules which those shall choose who, taken together, do comprehend the whole interest of the kingdom. . . .

*Rainborough*: . . . . I do think that the main cause why Almighty God gave men reason . . . was that they should make use of that reason, and that they should improve it for that end and purpose that God gave it them . . . I think there is nothing that God hath given a man that any else can take from him. Therefore I say that either it must be a law of God or the law of man that must prohibit the meanest man to have this benefit as well as the greatest. I do not find anything in the law of God that a lord shall choose twenty burgesses and a gentleman but two – or a poor man shall choose none. I find no such thing in the law of nature, nor in the law of nations. I *do* find that all Englishmen must be subject to English laws; and I do verily believe that there is no man but will say that the foundation of all law lies in the people; and if [it lie] in the people, I am to seek for this exemption [from obedience so long as I have not consented]. . . .

*Ireton*: . . . . What I said was to this effect: that if I saw the hand of God leading so far as to destroy King, and destroy Lords, and destroy property . . . I should acquiesce in it; and so did not care, if no King, no Lords, or no property, in comparison of the tender care that I have of the honour of God, and of the people of God, whose name is so much concerned in this Army. This I did deliver *so*, and not absolutely.

All the main thing that I speak for is because I would have an eye to property. I hope we do not come [to the debate here] to contend for victory; but let every man consider with himself that he do not go that way to take away all property. For here is the case of the most fundamental part of the constitution, which if you take away, you take away all by that. . . . Now those people [that have freeholds] and those that are freemen of corporations were looked upon by the former constitution to comprehend the permanent interest of the kingdom. For he that hath his livelihood by his trade, and by his freedom of trading in such a corporation which he cannot exercise in another, he is tied to that place, his livelihood depends upon it. And . . . that man hath an interest, hath a permanent interest there upon which he may live – and live a freeman, without dependence. These, constitutions of this kingdom hath looked at. Now I wish we may consider of what right *you* will challenge, that all the people should have a right to elections? Is it by right of nature? If you will hold forth that as your ground then I think you must deny all property too; and this is my reason. For thus: by that same right of nature, whatever it be that you pretend by which you can say one man hath an equal right of choosing him that shall govern him, by the same right of nature he hath an equal right in *any* goods he sees: meat, drink, clothes – to take and use them for his sustenance. He hath a freedom to the land, [to take] the ground, to exercise it, till it. He hath the [same] freedom to anything that anyone doth account himself to have a propriety in. . . . If this be allowed [because by right of nature] we are free, we are equal, one man must have as much voice as another, then show me what step or difference [there is] why by the same right of necessity to sustain nature [I may not claim property as well]? . . . . Since you cannot plead to it by anything but the law of nature, [for anything] but for the end of better being, and [since] that better being is not certain, and . . . more, destructive to another – if upon these grounds you do, paramount to all constitutions, uphold this law of nature – I would fain have any man show me their bounds, where you will end . . .

*Rainborough*: . . . . Sir, because I say a man pleads that every man hath a voice [by right of nature] that therefore it destroys [property by the same argument, is mistaken]: else why [hath] God made that law: 'Thou shalt not steal'? If I have no interest in the Kingdom I must suffer by all their laws, be they right or wrong. I am a poor man, therefore I must be pressed. . . .

*Ireton*: . . . . The answer [of Rainborough's] that had anything of matter in it . . . seemed to be that there is a law: 'Thou shalt not steal'. The same law says, 'Honour thy father and mother'; and that law doth likewise extend to all that are our governors in that place where we are in. So that by that there is a forbidding of breaking a civil law when we may live quietly under it, and a divine law. Again it is said indeed before, that there is no law (no divine law) that tells us that such a corporation must have the election of Burgesses, or such a Shire, and the like. And so, on the other side, if a man were to demonstrate his [right] to property by divine law, it would be very remote. Our property, as well as our right of sending Burgesses descends from other things. That divine law doth not determine particulars but generals in relation to man and man, and to property, and all things else; and we should be as far to seek if we should go to prove a property in [a thing] by divine law, as to prove that I have an interest in choosing Burgesses of the Parliament by divine law....

## 11.2 CROMWELL BROODS FURTHER ON PROVIDENCE

From Cromwell to William Lenthall, Speaker of the House of Commons, 20 August 1948; Cromwell to Colonel Robert Hammond, 25 November 1648. Extracted from Thomas Carlyle, (n.d), I, 213–14, 239–43. (The modern and authoritative edition of Cromwell's letters and speeches is Abbott 1937–47.)

Cromwell wrote these two letters, the one before, the other after, the Army leadership had come to the conclusion that Charles Stuart, 'that man of blood' (Crawford 1977) should be brought to justice. The first, to the Speaker of the Commons, expresses Cromwell's growing discontent with Parliament's still continuing to treat with him at Newark in the Isle of Wight even after he had fostered a new war; the second, to a near relation who was Governor of Carisbrooke Castle where Charles was a prisoner, shows the conviction of a mind almost made up. Cromwell writes from Army camps as God's instrument in victory. His role in the events leading to the decision as to the trial of the King is very unclear, and perhaps he designed it so.

What is clear is the activist conclusion he derives from a combination of providentialism with independent arguments on the right to resist for the 'safety of the people'. Resistance now suggests at least severe punishment for the transgressors. Cromwell has travelled a long way from Putney (Haller 1955; Hill 1970).

### *11.2.1 To Lenthall*

Thus you have a narrative of the particulars of the success which God hath given you [and] which I could hardly at this time have done, considering the multiplicity of business. But truly, when I was once engaged in it, I could hardly tell how to say less, there being so much of God in it; and I am not willing to say more, lest there should seem to be any of man. Only give me leave to add one word showing the disparity of forces on both sides, that you may see, and all the world acknowledge, the great hand of God in this business. The Scots army could not be less the 12,000 effective foot – well armed – and 5,000 horse; Langdale had not less than 2,500 foot and 1,500 horse: in all, 21,000. And truly very few of their foot but were as well armed if not better than yours, and at divers disputes did fight two or three hours before they would quit their ground. Yours were about 2,500 horse and dragoons of your old army, also about 1,600 Lancashire foot and about 500 Lancashire horse: in all about 8,600. You see by computation about 2,000 of the enemy slain, betwixt 8,000 and 9,000 prisoners, besides what are lurking in hedges and private places which the County daily bring in or destroy. Where Langdale and his broken forces are I know not; but they are exceedingly shattered.

Surely Sir, this is nothing but the hand of God; and wherever anything in this world is exalted or exalts itself, God will pull it down; for this is the day wherein He alone will be exalted. It is not fit for me to give advice, nor to say a word what use you should make of this, more than to pray you and all that acknowledge God, that they would exalt Him and not hate His people, who are as the apple of his eye, and from whom even Kings shall be reproved; and that you would take courage to do the work of the Lord in fulfilling the end of your magistry in seeking the peace and welfare of this land: that all who will live peaceably may have countenance from you, and they that are incapable and will not leave troubling the land may speedily be destroyed out of the land. And if you take courage in this, God will bless you and good men will stand by you; and God will have glory, and the land will have happiness by you, in spite of all your enemies. Which shall be the prayer of

Your most humble and faithful servant,

Oliver Cromwell

### *11.2.2 To Hammond*

Dear Robin,

.... Thou desirest to hear of my experiences. I can tell thee. I am such a one as thou didst formerly know, having a body of sin and death. But I thank God through Jesus Christ our Lord there is no condemnation, though much infirmity; and I wait for the redemption. And in this poor condition I obtain mercy and sweet consolation through the Spirit. . . . As to outward dispensations, if we may so call them: we have not been without our share of beholding some remarkable providences and appearances of the Lord. His presence hath been among us and by the light of His countenance we have prevailed. We are sure that the goodwill of Him who dwelt in the bush has shined upon us; and we can humbly say we know in whom we have believed; we can and will perfect what remaineth – and us also in doing what is well-pleasing in His eyesight. . . .

I find some trouble in your spirit. . . . You say: 'God hath appointed authorities among nations, to which active and passive obedience is to be yielded. This resides in England in the Parliament. Therefore active or passive resistance [to the will of Parliament is sinful].'

Authorities and powers are the ordinance of God. This or that species is of human institution, and limited, some with larger, others with stricter bands: each one according to its constitution. But I do not therefore think the authorities may do *anything* and yet such obedience be due. All agree that there are cases in which it is lawful to resist. . . . Indeed, dear Robin, not to multiply words, the query is whether ours be such a case? . . . .

To this I shall say nothing . . . but only desire thee to see what thou findest in thy own heart to two or three plain considerations. First, whether *salus populi* be a sound position? Secondly, whether in the way in hand [to continue treating with a guilty King], really, and before the Lord, this be provided for, or if the whole fruit of the war is not like to be frustrated and all most like to turn to what it was, and worse (and this contrary to the engagements [and] explicit covenants with those who ventured their lives upon those covenants and engagements) . . . .? Thirdly whether this Army be not a lawful power called by God to oppose and fight against the King upon some stated grounds, and being a power to such ends may not oppose one name of authority for those ends as well as another name – since it was not the outward authority summoning them by *its* power made the quarrel lawful, but [that] the quarrel was lawful in itself? . . . But truly, this kind of reasonings may be but fleshly, either with or against – only it is good to try what truth may be in them. And the Lord teach us.

My dear friend, let us look into providences; surely they mean somewhat. They hang so together; have been so constant, so clear, unclouded. Malice, sworn malice against God's people, now called 'Saints', to root out their name; and yet they, 'these poor Saints', getting arms, and therein blessed with defence, and more! I desire he that is for a principle of suffering [abused by authority without resistance] would not much slight this. I slight not him who is so minded; but let us beware lest fleshly reasoning see more safety in making use of this principle than in acting! Who acts, if he resolve not, through God, to be willing to part with all? Our hearts are very deceitful, on the right, and on the left.

What think you of providence disposing the hearts of so many of God's people this way, especially in this poor Army wherein the great God has vouchsafed to appear? . . . . We trust the same Lord who hath framed our minds in our actings is with us in this also. And all contrary to a natural tendency and to those comforts *our* heart[s] could wish to enjoy as well as others; and the difficulties probably to be encountered with; and the enemies – not a few, even all that is glorious in this world: appearance of united names, titles and authorities – all against us. And yet not terrified, we only desiring to fear our great God, that we do nothing against His will. . . .

This trouble I have been at because my soul loves thee and I would not have thee swerve or lose any glorious opportunity the Lord puts into thy hand. The Lord be thy counsellor. Dear Robin, I rest thine,

Oliver Cromwell

## 11.3 ON CONFUSIONS AND REVOLUTIONS

From Anthony Ascham, *A discourse: wherein is examined what is particularly lawful during the confusions and revolutions of government* (1648), 1–4, 14–17, 21–5, 36–7, 69–72, 87–8: Wing A 3919. There is a modern reprint (Rumble 1975) of the second edition of this work.

If Cromwell, as the second war progressed, became increasingly certain of the righteousness of his cause, Anthony Ascham (*c.* 1615–50) did not. 'Had Ascham not himself been of the conquering party, his theme would have appeared to have been begotten by despair upon the impossibility of resistance', Wallace notes (1968). He has been rightly depicted as a rational calculator in politics (Skinner 1965): nevertheless, aware as he was of the pointlessness of conducting a deontological politics based on law or scriptural injunction – and thus of the necessity of calculating how best to save one's skin – it cannot be said that he adopted that conclusion with any great sign of pleasure. He argues to have been forced to it by 'necessity', 'fortune' or 'providence' – he uses all these modes to depict the instability, unpredictability and alien force of things – and was more of a calculating victim than an optimistic Machiavellian like Francis Osborne or Marchamont Nedham. His *Discourse*, from which the extracts here are taken, was published in July 1648; he added more material to it, and in 1649 came out with a new edition, *Of the confusions and revolutions of governments*. The new edition defends the Commonwealth, but on no grounds additional to those he had already given: that submission ought to be granted to he who has possession of power. Ascham was sent as the Commonwealth's ambassador to Madrid. He was assassinated by royalists soon after his arrival. His few writings have been examined as demonstrations of unprincipled cowardice, 'loyalism', 'pessimistic' – and common – republicanism, and as constituting part of the 'ideological context' of the reception of Hobbes' political thought. The literature is assessed in Skinner (see headnote to [6.1]).

There can be only three considerations of the state of war: first, in its beginning; secondly, in its continuance; and thirdly, in its end. From these arise three questions: first, what may be the original and justifiable causes of men's forming a party in the beginning of a war; secondly, how far a man may lawfully submit to and obey opposite parties during the confusions of war actually formed and introduced; thirdly, what may be lawful for a man to submit to upon the issue of a war which may end to the advantage of him who by unjust force hath possessed himself of another's right. These two latter fall into the compass of this discourse. The first is a question apart, to which, though much may be said, yet I hold not the knowledge of it so necessary to those who are the *Achivi*,* and of the rank of the people to whom I now speak. These are the anvil on which all sorts of hammers discharge themselves. They seldom or never begin a war, but are all concerned in it after it is begun.... Many things will be proved lawful for men to do in the state and winding up of a war introduced by others which would not have been so for them in its beginning.... Our consciences more than our capacities should put us upon the search of these two capital difficulties, that so if occasion should be, we might the steadier stand those straits and blows of a fortune to which the human condition lies open in the revolution and confusion of governments.

Our forefathers, above one hundred years ago, were above twenty years in examining the second question and about four years in the third.... before twenty-four years of confusions and revolutions ended peaceably in the reign of Henry VII.... But neither then nor since hath it been declared unto us what in such cases is lawful to do in matter of right, every present power, whether established or struggling to be established, having this interest: that they

* *Achivi* literally means 'the Greeks'. But here Ascham is referring to a piece of Ciceronian wisdom made proverbial by Horace as *Quiquid delirant reges plecuntur Achiva*, the force of which was to suggest that whatever errors the great committed, it was the people who must suffer. The Greeks stand for those who suffer. Cicero, *Div*, i, 14; Horace, *Ep*, I, ii, 14.

who are *de facto* under their power, should not during that time presume to question their right, it being some kind of victory already gained to have gained the repute of a better cause. Many other questions hang upon these, which are all the difficulter because the subject of them, which is civil war, consists in confusion, in which the minds of men are floating and divided, according to the variety of successes and divisions which armies make in the places where they and their whole substance are fallen into their possession. And let men argue at as much ease as they please, yet it is certain that no man is of such a captivated allegiance, as by reason of it to engage himself to a party, believing upon the engagement he shall be certainly destroyed in it. There is nothing in the skin – as they say – which will not do its best to save it; and he must be a rare example who makes not his last resolution for his own life or subsistence (which is equivalent to life). And therefore the valiantest and most strictly obliged troops stick not to ask quarter when they cannot defend themselves any longer, and are justified for it, even by those for whom they swore to die. . . .

Our general rights surely are not yet all lost, though all the world be now trampled over and impropriated in particular possessions and rights. There yet remains some common right or natural community among men, even in impropriation, so that that which is necessary for any natural subsistence and [un]necessary to another belongs justly to me. . . . The will of those who first consented mutually to divide the earth into particular possessions was certainly such as receded as little as might be from natural equity. For written laws are even now as near as may be to be interpreted by that; and from hence it is that in extreme and deperate necessity the ancient right of using of things as though they had still remained in common is revived. 'Tis necessity which makes laws, and by consequence ought to be the interpreter of them after they are made. . . . When the sea breaks in upon a country we may dig in the next grounds to make a bank without staying for the owner's permission. In such cases of necessity human laws do not so much permit, as expound, their natural equity; and that which men give to those who are so innocently distressed, who borrow life only from the shadows of death . . . is not so properly a charity to them as a duty; and if he be a christian who gives, perhaps he doth more charity to himself than to the receiver. . . .

I may . . . descend now into the bottom of the question, and speak to the main parties, whether just or unjust, who by the variety of success may, one after another, command us and our estates, and in both reduce us to . . . extreme necessity: in which condition or confusion the question is what [it] is lawful for us to do. I find that most here seek to satisfy their scruples in searching first whether those parties have lawful power over us or no, that so finding the lawfulness of their right they may be easilier assured of the lawfulness of their own obedience, secondly, in examining the cause of their wars, whether it be justifiable or no – they supposing that if the cause be bad all effects which have any dependence on it must needs be so to. I conceive that these two considerations serve only to add to the perplexity of a man's conscience, and are not necessary at all for us to be informed of.

As for the point of right, it is a thing always doubtful and would be ever disputable in all kingdoms if those governors who are in possession should freely permit all men to examine their titles *ab origine*, and those large pretended rights which they exercise over the people. And though this party's title may be as good or a little better than that party's, yet a man in conscience may still doubt whether he have a *limpidium titulum*, a just title or clear right, especially in those things which are constituted by so various and equivocal a principle as the will of man is. Besides, most governors on purpose take away from us the means of discovering how they came by their rights, insomuch that though they may really have that right to which they pretend, yet through the ignorance we are in of what may be omitted in their history either through fear, flattery, negligence or ignorance, it is dangerous for us upon probable, human grounds only, to swear their infallible right. . . . And if the parties' rights be but one as good as another's, then his right is the best who hath possession, which generally is the strongest title that princes have. A whole kingdom may be laid waste before it can be infallibly informed concerning the parties' true rights which they require men to die for, and to avow by oath. As for prescription of long time, every man's conscience is not satisfied that that added to possession makes a true right. This we know: that it conduces much to the public quiet; but the canonists maintain against the civilians that prescription upon an unjust beginning and *ex titulo inhabili*, doth by its continuance increase and not diminish the injustice and faultiness of the act. For the lapse of time cannot change the morality of an act. . . .

As for the point of fact on which we would ground the matter of right or a justifiable cause (*viz.* that such or such things have been done or plotted or advised, therefore the other party may lawfully do this or that): that we know is without end, and ever is perplexed and difficult to have perfect intelligence of, especially such as a man may safely adventure his own life or take away another's upon it. Wherefore, if we may reasonably doubt of the point of right – which yet is a more clear and uniform thing – then we may be more reasonably perplexed in the story of fact, which depends on so many accidents, so various circumstance, both in its principal, the will, in its existence, and in evidence for the infallible knowledge of it.

From hence therefore I conclude that we may in this great case ease ourselves of this vast perplexity [of] examining whether or no the invading party have a just title or cause . . . or whether he have a juster title than he whom he opposes. But here I desire to be rightly understood; for I affirm this not as if knowledge of all this were not very convenient and much to be desired, but that, as it is almost impossible for us to have, so it is not necessary for us to search after. . . . These negatives show only what we need *not* ground our consciences on in order to a lawful obedience. But it must be a positive and a clear principle which we must ground on if we would be warranted of a just submission to the orders of one who commands us, perhaps unjustly; for it is a matter which concerns the misery of others who never did us wrong. . . . Because I state this question in a war already formed and actually introduced upon the people, therefore in answer to this positive demand, I as positively say: that for a justifiable obedience, it is best and enough for us to consider whether the invading party have us and the means of our subsistence in his possession or no. . . .

For . . . proof, I might aptly reflect on those arguments which were discussed [before], concerning the transcendent right which we naturally have in the preservation of ourselves and of those things without which we cannot be preserved, as also on the high privilege of extreme necessity – nature itself being more intent to the preservation of particular than of public bodies, which are made out of particulars, and as much as may be for the preservation of each singular – no man obliging himself to any particular society without the consideration of self-preservation, according to the right of the more general society of mankind. . . .

In government it ought to be most prudently cautioned that a society of state ravel not out into a dissolute multitude. For in confusion there is a rage which reason cannot reclaim and which must be left to calm and settle, as waves do after a tempest, both upon themselves and of themselves.

'Tis confusion rises most out of the reflection which particular men make on their particular rights and liberties which perhaps may lawfully belong to them but are not always convenient for them to have, no more than knives and daggers are for young children. (The liberty of one may well be the slavery of all) . . .

We think our service here very hard, being on every hand exposed to perpetual combats; and fain we would meliorate our condition by experimenting whatsoever presents itself first to our pressures. But in vain; for like men in fevers, we may change the sides of the bed but not our temper. The state of monarchy is of all the rest most excellent, especially when it represents God's dominion more in justice than in the singularity of the governor. But because there is no prince who is enabled with prudence and goodness any way so great and sovereign as is his power, therefore he cannot but commit great errors, and, standing on the people's shoulders, he makes them at last complain of his weight and of the loss of their liberty which is always their desired end. Aristocracy stands like a moderator betwixt the excesses of kingly and popular power; but this mixture oftentimes produces monsters. The bloodiest commotions that are, happen in this state – though esteemed most temperate – just as the greatest storms are found in the middle region of the air . . . No one part can be strengthened but by cutting the sinews of another . . . and impotency, representing at the same time both misery and scorn, takes life even in despair; and if it cannot be beholden to the relief of an enemy will make the public ruins of a kingdom its grave. Take away arms and liberty and every man is without interest and affection for his country; invade his goods and the fountain of a treasury is immediately dried, and he as soon made a beggar. And after these distresses, as Machiavelli saith, he will not lament so much the loss of his public parent as of his private patrimony. Democracy reduces all to equality, and favours the liberty of the people in everything. But withall, it obliges every man to hold his neighbours' hands; it is very short-sighted; permits everyone in the ship to pretend to the helm, yea in a tempest; through policy it is oft constrained to introduce all those desolations which ought to be feared only from envy. . . . Finally, if this supreme power fall into the hands of a heady and inconstant multitude, it is lodged in a great animal, which cannot be better than in chains.

This is the circle which we so painfully move in, without satisfying our desires; and no wonder, seeing nature in every part is sick and distempered and therefore can find rest in no posture. Human laws grow out of vices, which makes all governments carry with them the causes of their corruption and a complication of their infirmities; and for this reason they are ever destitute of virtue, proportional to the devotions of our crazy complexions. . . .

We should be exceeding happy, if in the midst of these embroilments we could know God's decree concerning the princes and governors which he would have reign over us as certainly as the ancients did by revelation and the prophets. Yet though we know not so much, this we know assuredly: that the great changes of government happen not by chance but by order of the most universal cause, which is the fountain of dominion. . . . *By me princes reign; for the governing powers which are, are of God*. God hath declared that he will chastise and change princes and governors; and though now we doubt of their families and persons, yet when we see changes and chastisements we may be sure they are by God's order – yea though the invading or succeeding governors be [evil] like Jehu, Nebuchadnezzar, or those who show us a severe though a secret part of God's justice. Wherefore it can be no less than sin in us or treason against God to swear we will ever obey any but this or that prince or State, or any but of such a family, or to think that none shall reign over us but such. For this depends on God's providence and justice, which sets the bounds to the duration of governors and governments. . . . We are bound to own princes so long as it pleases God to give them the power to command us; and when we see others possessed of their powers, we may then say that the King of Kings has changed our viceroys.

## 11.4 'RIGHT AND MIGHT WELL MET'

From [John Goodwin], *Right and might well met* (1648), 2–9, 12–17, 22–24, 27, 29, 31: Wing G 1200.

Goodwin (1594?–1665) was the minister of an independent congregation at St Stephen's in Coleman Street, and a prominent figure in London clerical politics (Liu 1973). In *Right and might well met* he defended Pride's Purge in much the terms to be adopted in the more aggressive defences of the trial of the King and the setting up of the Commonwealth. Haller (1955) rightly calls the tract one in which 'all Puritan theorising about sovereignty up to that moment led'. The reader will recognise traces of Parker's insistence that *salus populi* must be seen to in times of emergency, Palmer's too, that governments exist for a purpose which must be fulfilled, Burroughes's that no government is immune from dissolution if it does not fulfil that purpose, Cromwell's that providence points the way to the future, and Clarkson's, that 'the Saints' should rule. The doctrine of callings, originally a Protestant device by which the formal official hierarchies of church government might be challenged as inimical to the doing of His will through individuals chosen to express it, and evident in the Army's declarations of their call to see religion and justice maintained, is now used to justify a complete abandonment of the 'ancient ways of proceeding'. Milton was to add little in his *Tenure of Kings and magistrates* of 1649. The contrast with Ascham's defence of revolutionary politics could not be greater (Zagorin 1954).

Though some other things have been of late acted by the Army wherein many pretendingly complain of want of conscience and justice, yet I suppose they have done nothing either more obnoxious to the clamourous tongues and pens of their adversaries or more questionable in the judgements and consciences of their friends than that late garbling of the Parliament wherein they sifted out much of the dross and soil of that heap, intending to reduce this body.... to such members who had not manifestly turned head upon their trust, nor given the right hand of fellowship to that most barbarous, inhuman and bloody faction amongst us who for many years last past have with restless endeavours procured the deep trouble and attempted the absolute enslaving.... of the nation....

The firstborn of the strength of those who condemn the said act of the Army as unlawful lieth in this: that the actors had no sufficient authority to do what they did therein, but acted out of their sphere and so became transgressors of that law which commandeth every man to keep order and within the compass of his calling. To this I answer: (1) As our Saviour saith that the *Sabbath was made for man* (i.e. for the benefit of man) *and not man for the Sabbath* (*Mark* ii. 27) so certain it is that callings were made for men and not men for callings. Therefore.... if the law of callings at any time opposeth or lieth cross to the necessary conveniences of men, during the time of this opposition it suffereth a total eclipse of the binding power of it... Therefore unless it can be proved that the Army had no necessity lying upon them to garble the Parliament as they did, their going beyond their ordinary callings to do it will no ways impair the credit or legitimacy of the action. (2) Nor did they stretch themselves beyond the line of their callings to act therein as they did. Their calling and commission was to act in the capacity of soldiers for the peace, liberties and safety of the kingdom. What doth this import but a calling to prevent, or suppress by force, all such persons and designs whose faces were set to disturb or destroy them? Nor did their commissions, I presume, limit or conclude their judgments to any particular kind of enemies.... but all such, without exception, whom they upon competent grounds (. . . such as upon which, discreet men in ordinary cases are wont to frame acts of judgement and to proceed to action accordingly) should judge and conclude to be enemies. . . . Those Parliamentmen whom they have excluded from sitting in that House, having notoriously discovered themselves to be men [who were] friends and abettors of those who very lately were, and yet in part are, in arms against the peace and safety of the kingdom, in this consideration fall directly and clearly under their commission. And consequently, by warrant hereof, they have and had a calling to proceed against them as they did. (3) If the calling which the Parliament itself had to levy forces against the King and his party, to suppress them and their proceedings as destructive to the peace, liberties and safety of the kingdom was warrantable and good, then was the calling of the Army to act as they did in the business under debate warrantable and good also. . . .

The Parliament (or at least the Parliamentmen who did the thing) had no other calling to oppose the King and his by force, but only the general call of the major part of the people by which they were enabled to act in a parliamentary capacity (i.e. more effectually and upon more advantageous terms than singly, or out of such a capacity they could) for their good. By this call by the major part of the people they were enabled only in a general, implicit and indefinite manner to raise forces against the King and his complices for the safety and behoof of the kingdom. So that the particularity of the action was not warranted simply by the nature or tenure of their call, but by the regular and due proportion which it had to the accomplishing of the end for which they were chosen and called, *viz.* the people's good. From whence it follows that whether they had been in a parliamentary capacity or not, yet if they had been in a sufficient capacity of strength or power for the matter of execution, their call to do it, for substance had been the same, though not for form. . . . [Indeed] every member as well in a body politic as natural hath a sufficient call, nay an engagement lying by way of duty upon [him] to act at any time and in all cases according to its best and utmost capacity and ability for the preservation and benefit of the whole. . . .

Lawgivers, whilst they are sober and are in their right minds, may very probably make such laws for the ordering and restraint of persons distracted and mad, which in case they [themselves] afterwards become distracted, may and ought to be put in execution against themselves. . . . Secondly . . . *the punishment of evil doers*, and so the procurement of the public good, doth not lie by way of office or duty upon the chief magistrate only, but upon all subordinate magistrates also and officers whatsoever. This is evident from this passage in Peter: *Submit yourselves to every ordinance of man for the Lord's sake, whether it be to the King as supreme, or unto governours* (i.e. inferior magistrates or officers) *as to them that are sent by him for the punishment of evil doers, and for the praise of them that do well* (1 *Peter* ii. 13–14). So then the punishment of evil doers (and this simply, without all partiality or distinction of persons).... and likewise the protection and encouragement of those that do well, lying by way of office and duty upon all those who by the King or supreme officer are invested with any power of authority (though subordinate) evident it is, that whensoever a King or other supreme authority creates an inferior, they invest it with a legitimacy of magisterial power to punish themselves also in case they prove evil doers – yea and to act any other thing requisite for the praise or encouragement of the good.... Kings and magistrates of the highest.... are very capable also of forfeiting that dignity which is natural and essential to them as Kings, or supreme, and of rendering themselves obnoxious to those authorities and powers which, out of such cases are under them, but upon such miscarriages are above them....

The call of the Parliament we spake of, was from the persons of the people expressed by formality of words or other ordinary gestures testifying such a call from them. And this call they.... received from the people whilst as yet they (the people) were in no visible (at least in an imminent or present) danger of being swallowed up in slavery and tyranny. But the call of the Army to deny the opportunity of the House to those Members of Parliament whom they sequestered was from the strong importunities of the people's liberties, yea and of many of their lives.... Now the calls of the miseries and extremities of men for relief are more authorising, more urging, pressing and binding upon the consciences of men who have wherewithall to afford relief unto them than the formal requests or elections of men to places of trust or interest when the electors have no such present or pressing necessity upon them for the interposal of the elected on their behalf. The necessities of men call more effectually than the men themselves....

The common saying, that 'in case of extreme necessity all things are common' (Aquinas, 21e qu. 32 art. 6), extends to callings also. In cases of necessity all callings are common in order to the supply of the present necessity.... [And] when the pilot or master of a ship at sea be either so far overcome and distempered with drink or otherwise disabled.... so that he is incapable of acting the exigencies of his place, for the preservation of the ship.... anyone or more of the inferior mariners, having skill, may in order to the saving of the ship and of the lives of all that are in it, very lawfully assume and act according to the interest of the pilot or master and give orders and directions to those with them in the ship accordingly (who stand bound at the peril of their lives in this case to obey them). By such a comparison as this Master Prynne himself demonstrates how regular and lawful it is for Parliaments, yea, and for particular men... to assume that interest and power which the law appropriates to the office and vesteth only in the person of a King when the King steereth a course in manifest opposition to the peace and safety of the kingdom.... It is lawful for any man, even by violence, to wrest a sword out of the hand of a madman though it be never so legally his from whom it is wrested.... This is the very case in hand. The members of Parliament dishoused by the Army were strangely struck with a political frenzy (as Plato termeth it).

There is no client that hath entertained a lawyer or advocate to plead his cause but upon discovery, yea, or jealousy of prevarication and false-heartedness in his cause, may lawfully discharge him. There is the same liberty in a pupil or a person in his minority to dis-entrust his guardian (how lawfully soever chosen) upon suspicion of maladministration or unfaithfulness. And why should the like liberty be denied unto a people or nation for removing of such persons whom they have chosen for guardians to their estates and liberties from these places of trust, when they evidently discern a direct tendency in their proceeding to betray them, both in the one and the other, unto their enemies?....

Whether we place the lawfulness of a parliamentary judicature in respect of the King's delinquency either in their election by the people or in the conformity of this their election unto the laws of the land, certain it is that the Army were judges every whit as competent and lawful a constitution of *their* delinquencies in the same kind. For first: if we measure the lawfulness of parliamentary judicature by the call of the people thereunto, the Army... hath every whit as lawful a constitution to judge who are the enemies to the peace and safety of the kingdom as the Parliament itself hath. Nor doth it argue any illegality in their judgements about the Parliamentmen that they had not the explicit and express consent of the people therein or that they had no call by them to judge, no more than it proveth an illegality in many votes and ordinances of Parliament that were both made and published not only without the particular and express consent but even contrary to the mind and desires of the people, or at least, a major part of them. Besides it is a ridiculous thing to pretend a want of a call from the people against the lawfulness of such an act which is of that sovereign necessity for their benefit and good (which the actings of the Army were) especially at such a time when there is no possibility of obtaining or receiving a formal call from the people without running an eminent hazard of losing the opportunity for doing that excellent service unto them which the providence of God, in a peculiar juncture of circumstances, exhibits for the present unto us. Men's consents unto all acts manifestly tending to their relief are sufficiently expressed in their wants and necessities. . . . Physicians called to the care and cure of persons under distempers need not stand upon the contents of such patients, either subsequent or antecedent, about what they administer to them. . . .

Secondly: if we estimate the lawfulness of that judicature by the conformity of their elections thereunto to the laws of the land, the investiture of the Army into that judicature which they have exercised in the case in question [conforms] unto a law of far greater authority than any one, yea than *all* the laws of the land put together: I mean the law of nature, necessity and of love to their country and nation, which, being the law of God himself written into the fleshly tables of men's hearts, hath an authoritative jurisdiction over all human laws and constitutions whatsoever. [It hath] a prerogative right of power to over-rule them and to suspend their obliging influences in all cases appropriate to itself. Yea, many of the laws of God themselves think it no disparagement unto them to give place to their elder sister, the law of necessity, and to surrender their authority into her hand when she speaketh. So that whatsoever is necessary is somewhat more than lawful, more I mean in point of warrantableness. If then the Army stood bound by the law of nature and necessity to judge the Parliamentmen as they did, *viz.* as men worthy to be secluded from their fellows in parliamentary interest, this judicatory power was vested in them by a law of greater authority than the laws of the land; and consequently the legality or lawfulness of it was greater than of that in the Parliament, which derives its legality only from a conformity to the established laws of the land. Yea the truth is that the law of necessity, by which the Army were constituted judges of the parliamentary delinquents we speak of, cannot in propriety of speech be denied to be one of the laws of the land, being the law of nature and consequently the law of all lands and nations whatsoever, established in this and in all the rest by a better and more indubitable legislative authority than resides in any Parliament or community of men whatsoever . . .

They cannot . . . be said to 'assume' a power of judicature unto themselves who only judge either of persons or things in respect of themselves and with relation to what concerns themselves by way of a duty either to do or to forbear. The exercise of such a judging or judicative power as this is imposed by God by way of duty upon all men; and woe unto them who do not judge both persons and things in such a consideration as this. The neglect or non-exercise of that judging faculty or power which is planted in the souls and consciences of men by God, upon such terms and with reference to such ends as these, draweth along with it that sin which the wise man calleth the *despising of a man's ways* (*Prov.* xix. 16) and threateneth with death. *But he that despiseth his ways shall die*. . . . Every man is bound to consider, judge and determine what is meet and necessary for him to do either to, with, or against all other men (or at least to all such to whom he stands in any relation either spiritual, natural or civil). That judgement then which the Army passed in their own breasts and consciences upon those Parliamentmen . . . . whom they stood bound in duty as having the opportunity in their hand to do it to cut off as unsound members from their body, was nothing else but the issue, fruit and effect of that consideration of them and their ways . . . .

The reason why no human law can reasonably be judged to be of universal obligation (no, not according to the intention of the lawmakers themselves) is first, because the adequate end and scope of lawmakers in their laws is presumed to be the public and common benefit and good of the community of men who are to obey them. Now as Aquinas the schoolman well observeth, it 'often falls out that that which ordinarily and in most cases is much conducing to the common good, in some particular case would be most repugnant and destructive to it . . . . therefore in such cases wherein the observation of the law cannot but be of dangerous consequence, and prejudicial to the public, it is to be presumed that it was no part of the intention of the lawgivers that it should be observed or bind any man'. (12e qu. 96 art. 6). Secondly, 'it being out of the sphere of all earthly lawmakers to foresee or comprehend all particular cases that may possibly happen, they generally content themselves with framing such laws the keeping whereof ordinarily and in cases of a more frequent occurrence is conducing to public benefit and safety, not intending by any of these laws to obstruct or prejudice the public in any anomalous or unthought of case, but to leave persons of all interests and qualities at full liberty to provide for the public in such cases...' (Aquinas loc. cit.). Lastly.... it were not expedient (saith my author) for the commonwealth, that they should multiply laws to such a number as the particular stating and regulating of all such... cases would necessarily require. Confusion in laws ought to be avoided, which yet could not be avoided if particular and express provision should be made in them for the regulation of all persons of what different capacities or conditions soever, under all possible occurrences, in a due proportion to the common interest and benefit of men....

Those laws of God.... prohibiting such actions which are intrinsically and in their proper natures... contrary to the essential purity and holiness of God... must needs be of universal obligation in as much as no necessity whatsoever can be greater than, nor indeed equal to this: that a man refrains all such actions which are morally, essentially and intrinsically corrupting and defiling; whereas the civil or politic laws of men restrain only such actions, the forbearance whereof, as in ordinary cases it is commodious for the public interest, so in many others possibly incident, would be detrimentous and destructive to it. (In which respect all the necessity of obeying laws such as these may for the time not only be balanced but even swallowed up and quite abolished by a greater necessity of obeying them.) And, concerning such laws of God himself which we call 'typical' or 'ceremonial', because they restrain only such actions which are not intrinsically sinful or defiling, as not being in themselves repugnant to the holiness of God, but had the consideration of sin put upon them by a law in reference to a particular end.... God was graciously pleased and judged it meet to subject such laws as these to the pressing necessities of the outward man (or rather indeed, to those other laws of His by which He commanded relief for them)....

A... grand objection wherewith some encounter that action of the Army... is this: they therein (say these men) made themselves covenant-breakers and sinned against the solemn vow and oath which they.... sware unto God.... In the [*Solemn League and Covenant*] they promised and sware that they would 'endeavour with their estates and lives mutually to preserve the rights and privileges of Parliaments', whereas by that violent dismembering of the Parliament they brake, and trampled upon them. To this we answer.... that most certain it is that it is no right or privilege to vote or act in opposition to the good of the kingdom and those who have entrusted them. It is impossible that any thing which is sinful should be the right or privilege of any person or society of men under heaven. . . . When either the laws or people of the land speak of 'rights and privileges of Parliament', they, doubtless, do not take the word 'Parliament' in an equivocal and comprehensive sense, wherein it may be extended to anything which in any sense or consideration may be called a Parliament, but in an emphatical and restrained sense, *viz.* as it signifieth a political body, consistory or court of men, chosen by the people into parliamentary trust, faithfully prosecuting and discharging the import of the trust committed to them. If this property be wanting in them, they are but a Parliament so-called. . . . That which gives a kind of sacred inviolableness unto the rights and privileges of Parliament is that typical relation which they bear to the rights, privileges and liberties of the kingdom and commonwealth. Now types are always inferior to the things imported and represented by them, as servants are unto masters. . . . Lastly, suppose there had been no express clause in the Covenant joining the 'preservation of the liberties of the kingdom', as well as of 'the rights and privileges of Parliament', yet had the Army more than warrant sufficient to have stood up for the preservation of them as they did, and that without any breach of covenant. Men by the tenure of their very lives and beings, which they hold of the God of nature, their great creator, stand bound to the laws of nature, and that against all other obligations of bond whatsover. . . . Now there is no law of nature that speaks more plainly or distinctly than this: that the strong ought to stand by the weak in cases of extremity and danger imminent, especially when relief cannot reasonably be expected from other hands.

## 11.5 THE RUMP'S REVOLUTION

From *A declaration of the Parliament House of Commons . . . declaring that the people are under God* (1649): Wing E 2565. *Commons Journals*, VI, iii.

On 2 January 1649, the Commons sent up a proposed ordinance to the Lords which created a special court to try the King. At the Lords' refusal to join with them, the Commons passed a resolution that recorded their determination to do away with King and Lords, and gave their grounds for doing so. Unrepresentative as the purged Commons was – with fewer than sixty members it was operating on a quorum of forty – the declaration reads like a parody of leveller ideals. However that may be, the House of Lords was condemned on 6 February as 'useless and dangerous'; on the 7th, the office of kingship was also condemned, as 'unnecessary, burdensome, and dangerous to the liberty, safety, and public interest of the people of this nation.' In March both institutions were abolished by Act.

### *A resolution of 4 January 1649*

The Commons of England in Parliament assembled, do declare that the people are, under God, the original of all just power: And also declare that the Commons of England in Parliament assembled, being chosen by and representing the people, have the supreme power in this nation: And also declare that whatsoever is enacted or declared for law by the Commons in Parliament assembled hath the force of law: and all the people of this nation are concluded thereby, although the consent and concurrence of the King or House of Peers be not had thereto.

## 11.6 THE RUMP'S OFFICIAL DEFENCE

From *A declaration of the Parliament of England, expressing the grounds of their late proceedings* (1649): Wing E 1499; extracted from *OPH*, II, cols 1292–1304.

This declaration was published on 22 March 1649. The Commons ordered 2,000 copies printed for the use of their members in their localities, and it was ordered printed in Latin, French and Dutch. It is the Rump's official defence. The regime was on the defensive, and the declaration shows it in its combining the populist ideals of its more radical supporters with attempts to argue the legality of its cause and to reassure the doubtful about just how little had been lost in the revolution. The protectoral régimes were never to transcend their origins, tainted as they were with illegality.

The Parliament of England, elected by the people whom they represent, and by them trusted and authorised for the common good, having long contended against tyranny, and to procure the well-being of those whom they serve, and to remove oppression, arbitrary power, and all opposition to the peace and freedom of the nation, do humbly and thankfully acknowledge the blessing of almighty God upon their weak endeavours, and the hearty assistance of the well-affected in this work, whereby the enemies thereunto, both public and secret, are become unable for the present to hinder the perfecting thereof. And, to prevent their power to revive tyranny, injustice, war, and all our further evils, the Parliament have been necessitated to the late alterations in government and to a settlement which they judge most conducible to the honour of God and the good of the nation – the only end and duty of all their labours. And that this may appear the more clearly and generally, to the satisfaction of all who are concerned in it, they have thought fit to declare and publish the grounds of their proceedings.

They suppose it will not be denied that the first institution of the office of King in this nation was by agreement of the people, who chose one to that office for the protection and good of them who chose him, and for their better government, according to such laws as they did consent unto. And let those who have observed our stories recollect how very few have performed the trust of that office with righteousness, and due care of their subjects' good.... And in the whole line of them how far the late King hath exceeded all his predecessors in the destruction of those he was bound to preserve.... dissolution of Parliament in the second year of his reign... an unnatural forgetfulness to have the violent death of his father examined... the sad business of la Rochelle and the Isle of Rhé.... the Loans, unlawful imprisonments, and other oppression which produced that excellent law of the *Petition of Right*... the multitude of projects and monopolies established by him; his design and charge to bring in German horse to awe us into slavery... his grand project of Ship Money, to subject every man's estate to whatsoever proportion he pleased to impose upon them... the oppressions of the Council Table, Star Chamber, High Commission, Court Martial; of wardships, purveyances, knighthood, afforestations... the exact slavery forced upon those in Ireland, with the army of papists to maintain it... the long intermission of our Parliaments... the great mistake in first sending the Service Book into Scotland.... [and so on, through the atrocities leading up to and constituting the two civil wars].

Upon all these and many other unparalleled offences; upon his breach of faith, of oaths and protestations; upon the cry of the blood of Ireland and of England; upon the tears of widows and orphans, and childless parents, and millions of persons undone by him, let all the world of indifferent men judge whether the Parliament had not a sufficient cause to bring the King to justice.

But it was objected (and it was the late King's own assertion), 'That those in his high place are accountable for their actions to none but God, whose anointed they are.' From whence it must follow that all men of this land were only made for the sake of that one man, the King, for him to do with them what he pleased, as if they had been created for no other purpose but to satisfy his lusts and to be a sacrifice to the perverse will of a tyrant. This will not easily be believed to be so ordained by God who punisheth, but never establisheth, injustice and oppression, whom we find offended when the people demanded a King [1 *Samuel* viii. 7], but no expression of his displeasure at any time because they had no King. . . . For the phrase 'anointed', no learned divine will affirm it to be applicable to the Kings of England as to those of Judah and Israel, or more to a King than to every other magistrate or servant of God. . . .

Another objection was, 'That to bring a King to trial and capital punishment is without precedent.' So were the crimes of the late King; and certainly the children of Israel had no known law or precedent to punish the Benjamites for their odious abuse of the Levite's wife, yet God owned the action. [*Judges* xix–xx]. There want not precedents of some of his predecessors who have been deposed by Parliaments, but were afterwards, in darkness and in corners, basely murdered. This Parliament held it more agreeable to honour and justice to give the King a fair and open trial by above an hundred gentlemen in the most public place of justice. . . .

The objection is obvious, 'of injustice to disinherit those who have a right and title to the Crown'. Surely the elder right is the people's whom they claim to govern. If any right or title were in the eldest son, the same is forfeited by the father's act . . . even of offices of inheritance, which, being forfeited for breach of trust (a condition annexed to every office) none will deny but that the same excludeth the children as well as the officer. But here the elder sons levied war against the Parliament, and it cannot be alleged that the younger children were born to anything. But the same power which first erected a King and made him a public officer for the common good, finding him perverted to the public calamity, it may justly be admitted at the pleasure of those whose officer he is whether they will continue that officer any longer or change that government for a better, and instead of restoring tyranny, to resolve into a free state. Herein the Parliament received encouragement by their observation of the blessing of God upon other States. The Romans after their *regifugium*, for many hundred years together prospered far more than under any of their Kings or Emperors. The State of Venice hath flourished for 1300 years. How much do the commons in Switzerland and other free States exceed those who are not so in riches, freedom, peace, and all happiness? Our neighbours in the United Provinces, since their change of government have wonderfully increased in wealth, freedom, trade, and strength, both by sea and land. In commonwealths they find justice duly administered; the great ones not able to oppress the poorer, and the poor sufficiently provided for; the seeds of civil war and dissension, by particular ambition, claims of succession, and the like . . . wholly removed; and a just freedom of their consciences, persons and estates enjoyed by all sorts of men. . . .

But an objection is frequently made concerning the Declaration of the Houses of April 1646, 'for the governing the kingdom by King, Lords, and Commons', and other declarations, 'for making him a great and happy prince'. This was then fully their intent, being at that time confident that, the King's ill counsel once removed from him, he would have conformed himself to the desires of his people in Parliament and [that] the peers who remained with the Parliament would have been a great cause of his so doing. But finding after seven fruitless addresses made unto him that he yet both lived and died in the obstinate maintenance of his usurped tyranny, and refused to accept of what the Parliament had declared; [and that] the Lords were all obliged in regard of their own interest in peerage, whereby they assumed to themselves an exorbitant power of exemption from paying of their just debts and answering suits in law – besides an hereditary judicatory over the people tending to their slavery and oppression – the Commons were constrained to change their former resolutions. . . .

Another objection is, 'That these great matters ought, if at all, to be determined in a full House, and not when many Members of Parliament are by force excluded, and the privilege so highly broken that those who are permitted to sit in Parliament do but act under a force and upon their good behaviour.' To this it is answered that every Parliament ought to act upon their good behaviour, and few have acted but some kind of force hath at one time or other been upon them – and most of them under the force of tyrannical will and fear of ruin by displeasure thereof, some under the force of several factions or titles to the Crown. Yet the laws made, even by such Parliaments, have continued and been received and beneficial to succeeding ages. All which, and whatsoever hath been done by this Parliament since some of their Members deserted them and the late King raised forces against them . . . if this objection take place, are wholly vacated. For any breach of privilege: It will not be charged upon the remaining part . . . that they have not enjoyed the freedom of their own persons and votes, and are undoubtedly by the law of Parliaments far exceeding that number which makes a House authorised for the despatch of any business whatsoever; and that which is called a force upon them is some of their best friends, called and appointed by Parliament for their safety, and for the guard of them against their enemies. . . .

There remains yet this last and weighty objection to be fully answered, 'That the Courts of Justice, and the good old laws and customs of England (the badges of our freedom, the benefit whereof our ancestors enjoyed long before the Conquest, and spent much of their blood to have confirmed by the Great Charter of the Liberties and other excellent laws which have continued in all former changes, and, being duly executed, are the most just, free, and equal of any other laws in the world) will, by the present alteration of government, be taken away and lost to us and our posterities.' To this they hope some satisfaction is already given by the Shorter Declaration lately published; and by the real demonstrations to the contrary of this objection by the earnest care of this Parliament that the Courts of Justice at Westminster should be supplied the last term, and all the circuits of England this vacation, with learned and worthy judges: that the known laws of the land, and the administration of them, might appear to be continued. They are very sensible of the excellency and equality of the laws of England, being duly executed; of their great antiquity, even from before the time of the Norman slavery forced upon us; of the liberty and property and peace of the subject, so fully preserved by them; and (which falls out happily, and as an increase of God's mercy to us) of the clear consistency of them with the present government of a republic upon some easy alterations of the form only, leaving entire the substance – the name of King being used in them for form only, but no power of personal administration or judgement allowed to him in the smallest matter contended for. They know their own authority to be by the law, to which the people have assented; and besides their particular interests (which are not inconsiderable) they more intend the common interest of those whom they serve, and clearly understand the same not possible to be preserved without the laws and government of the nation – and that if those should be taken away, all industry must cease; all misery, blood and confusion would follow; and greater calamities, if possible, than fell upon us by the late King's government, would certainly involve all persons, under which they must inevitably perish. . . .

And they do expect from all true-hearted Englishmen, not only a forebearance of any public or secret plots or endeavour against the present settlement, and thereby to kindle new flames of war and misery among us, whereof themselves must have a share, but a cheerful concurrence and acting for the establishment of the great work now in hand, in such a way that the name of God may be honoured, the true protestant religion advanced, and the people of this land enjoy the blessings of peace, freedom and justice to them and their posterities.

# GUIDE TO FURTHER READING

## A. BIBLIOGRAPHICAL AIDS

### *The primary sources*

The best starting-point is Fortescue's (1908) catalogue of the Thomason Tracts in the British Library. Though Thomason's collection of tracts, 1640–60, does not list all the publications of the time, it does include a good proportion. Moreover, because Thomason dated each piece and Fortescue rendered the titles fully enough to give the student a good idea of what is in each, reading through the catalogue is an education in itself. Wing's (1945–51) catalogue has already been mentioned in the Foreword as listing publications from 1641 to 1700: Pollard and Redgrave's catalogue (1946) covers the period from 1475 to 1640. Almost all extant publications have been listed by them or in works supplementing them. Primary sources in particular areas will often be found to have been indicated in modern works listed in the Bibliography and References below, and in the headnotes to each document I have indicated useful starting-points. Royalist writings may be traced in particular in the works of Daly; royalist and parliamentarian in Allen (1938), Judson (1949) and Weston (1965); 'puritan' writings may be traced in Haller (1934, 1938, 1955): 'leveller' writing in the bibliographies in Frank (1955) and Gregg (1961); the publications of those still more radical are referred to in Morton (1970) and Hill (1972). A good guide to the burgeoning newspaper industry is Frank (1961): and there are specialist bibliographies of Cromwell (Abbott 1937–47), Milton (Wolfe, 1953–), and Hobbes (start with Skinner 1972b). Of course, printed documents are not the only evidence of the political thinking of the civil war period: a useful guide to other primary as well as secondary sources is Davies and Keeler (1970).

*Modern commentaries*

Richardson (1977) provides a brief history and catalogue of the historiography of the 'English revolution', and has a useful but short section on modern books about political thought. So do Davies and Keeler (1970). But to find lists of modern writings on the subject it is best to consult books on particular topics: Daly (1979b) on royalism, Weston (1965) on royalists and parliamentarians and Frank (1955) on levellers and related subjects are particularly useful. Lutaud's book on Winstanley (1976) has a fine bibliography which does not limit itself to writings on radicals: and it has the virtue of listing many continental works as well. Many anglophone periodicals regularly publish articles on civil war thought. Two catalogues are especially useful for keeping up with the subject, the *Humanities Index* (Pingree 1975) and the *Social Sciences Index* (Bloomfield 1975–). The *DNB* (Stephen and Lee 1908–9–), though ageing, is still the most valuable collection of biographies of individual writers.

## B. COLLECTIONS OF PRIMARY SOURCES

There are valuable collections of radical and libertarian writings in Abbott (1937–47), Aylmer (1975), Cohn (1962), Haller (1934), Haller and Davies (1944), Hill (1973), Sabine (1941), Wolfe (1941, 1944, 1953–) and Woodhouse (1951). But there is not much readily available on anything else. Some modern libraries will contain Rushworth's collections (1721–22) and the *OPH* (*Old Parliamentary History*). Both contain much of interest, Rushworth's on the politics of the New Model, the *OPH* on Parliament in particular. There are nineteenth-century collections of the works of bishops Bramhall (H., A. W. 1842–45) and Joseph Hall (Wynter, 1863) and of Hobbes (Molesworth, 1839–45): but modern editions of non-radicals are non-existent except Laslett's edition of Filmer (1949). Continental collections (Gabrielli, 1959; Lutaud, 1976; Recupero, 1971; Walter, 1963) reflect the same concentration of interest on the radical end of the spectrum. There is, however, much material usually incidentally included in collections made mainly in the service of political, constitutional, cultural and social history: in particular in Firth (1891–1901), Gardiner (1899), Hill and Dell (1949), Kenyon (1966), Lamont and Oldfield (1975), Rollins (1923), Stone (1965) and Prall (1968). In recent years 'the Rota', edited from the Departments of History and Politics at the University of Exeter has published seventeenth-century sources, and

University Microfilms International have completed microfilming the contents of the Thomason collection (British Library, 1978) and have embarked on microfilming the whole of the contents of the Wing catalogue. The results of their work have been usefully indexed (University Microfilms International 1981–82).

## C. STRATEGIES OF APPROACH

The edition of Milton's prose works put out by Yale (Milton, *Complete Prose Works*) is invaluable as providing in vols 1–3 (Wolfe, Sirluck, Hughes) a blow-by-blow account of the ideological battles of the civil war period. Zagorin's (1954) history is the only one which deals with the period as a whole, and is excellent on levellers, diggers and engagers, but is light on more conservative thinkers. Earlier political thinking is most usefully approached through Allen (1928a, 1938), Figgis (1896), Gooch (1898), Haller (1938), Hill (1965, 1974), Judson (1949), Morris (1953), Skinner (1978), Tuck (1979) and a Wormuth (1939). Particularly useful on later developments in England are Franklin (1978, and see his bibliography), Pocock (1975) and Weston (1965).

To my mind the most fruitful approach to the period has been that outlined (1971) and demonstrated in practice (1966, 1975) by Pocock and the younger historians Skinner and Dunn. Powerful practical alternatives have been provided by Strauss (1953), Macpherson (1962) and Hill (since the late 1930s). Criticisms of Pocock's method of isolating the 'languages' and 'traditions' of political thought and recording their persistence and transformations through time have been made in regard to the study of Utopian literature by Davis (1981), and there is a sizeable methodological literature refining, supplementing and criticising Pocock's approach more generally. Mulligan *et al.* (1979) and Schochet (1974) provide the best approach to this topic. As to the histories of the period, the best recent one is Ashton's (1978). It accurately represents the state of contemporary knowledge and interest, and provides an intelligent synthesis and commentary on it and the times. The beginning student would do well to supplement this with Tanner (1928), a useful constitutional history, which points out many of the landmarks that most impressed civil war debaters. Both these books will lead the student in the end to the great histories of Gardiner and Firth (which are not included in the Bibliography and References) and to the huge post-war output of British and American historians especially.

# BIBLIOGRAPHY AND REFERENCES


ABBOTT, WILBUR C. (1937–47) *The writings and speeches of Oliver Cromwell*, (4 vols). Repr. 1970

ALLEN, J. W. (1928a) *A history of political thought in the sixteenth century*. London; repr. 1960

— (1928b) 'Sir Robert Filmer', in Hearnshaw (1928)

— (1938) *English political thought 1603–1644*. London; repr. New York 1967: only vol. 1 published

APPLEBY, JOYCE O. (1978) *Economic thought and ideology in seventeenth-century England*. Princeton

ASHLEY, MAURICE (1947) *John Wildman, plotter and postmaster*. London

ASHTON, ROBERT (1978) *The English civil war: conservatism and revolution*. London

ASTON, TREVOR (ed.) (1965) *Crisis in Europe, 1560–1660: essays from 'Past and Present'*. London

AYLMER, G. E. (1968) 'England's spirit unfoulded', *Past and Present*, **40** (July 1968), 3–15, and in Webster (1974)

— (ed.) (1972) *The interregnum: the quest for a settlement 1646–1660*. London and Hamden Conn.

— (1973) *The state's servants*. London

— (1974) 'Gentlemen levellers?', *Past and Present*, **49** (1970), 120–5, and in Webster (1974)

— (1975) *The levellers in the English revolution*. London

— (1980) 'The meaning and definition of "property" in seventeenth-century England', *Past and Present* **86** (1980), 87–97

BARKER, ARTHUR (1942) *Milton and the puritan dilemma, 1641–60*. Toronto

BERENS, L. H. (1906) *The digger movement*. London; repr. 1961

BLOOMFIELD, JOSEPH (ed.) (1975–) *Social Sciences Index*. New York

BLUNT, J. H. (ed.) (1893) *The annotated Book of Common Prayer.* London

BOWLE, JOHN (1951) *Hobbes and his critics.* London

BOYCE, BENJAMEN (1969) *The polemical character.* New York

BRAILSFORD, H. N. (1961) *The levellers and the English revolution.* London

BRENNAN, TERESA and CAROLE PATEMAN (1980) '"Mere auxiliaries to the commonwealth": women and the origins of liberalism', *Political Studies*, **27**: 2 (1980), 183–200

British Library (1978) *The Thomason Tracts 1640–1661: an index to the microfilm collection* [*by University Microfilms International*] (2 parts: 1978, 1979)

BROWN, KEITH (ed.) (1965) *Hobbes studies.* Oxford

CAPP, BERNARD S. (1972) *The fifth monarchy men.* London

— (1974) 'Godly rule and English millenarianism', *Past and Present*, **52** (1971), 106–17, and in Webster (1974)

CARLYLE, THOMAS (ed.) (n.d.) *Oliver Cromwell's letters and speeches,* (3 vols). Nottingham

CHRISTIANSON, PAUL (1973) 'From expectation to militance: reformers and Babylon in the first two years of the Long Parliament', *Journal of Ecclesiastical History*, **24** (1973), 225–49

— (1978) *Reformers and Babylon. English apocalyptic thought from the reformation to the eve of the civil war.* Toronto

COHN, NORMAN (1962) *The pursuit of the millennium.* London; rev. edn. London and N.Y. 1967

— (1970) 'The ranters', *Encounter*, **34**: 4 (1970), 15–25

COLTMAN, IRENE (1972) *Public men and private causes.* London

*CI* (*Commons Journals*) (1742–) Great Britain, *The Journals of the House of Commons.* London

CORNFORTH, MAURICE (ed.) (1978) *Rebels and their causes: essays in honour of A. L. Morton.* London

CRANSTON, MAURICE, and R. S. PETERS (eds) (1972) *Hobbes and Rousseau.* N.Y.

CRAWFORD, PATRICIA (1977) 'Charles Stuart, that man of blood', *Journal of British Studies*, **16**: 2 (1977), 41–61

DALY, JAMES (1966) 'Could Charles I be trusted? The royalist case', *Journal of British Studies*, **6**: 1 (Nov. 1966), 23–44

— (1971) 'John Bramhall and the theoretical problems of royalist moderation', *Journal of British Studies*, **11**: 1 (1971), 26–44

— (1978) 'The idea of absolute monarchy in seventeenth-century England', *Historical Journal*, **21** (1978), 227–50

— (1979a) *Sir Robert Filmer and royalist political thought.* Toronto

— (1979b) 'Cosmic harmony and political thinking in early Stuart England', *Transactions of the American Philosophical Society*, **69**, Pt 7 Philadelphia

DAVIES, GODFREY and MARY FREAR KEELER (eds) (1970) *Bibliography of British history: Stuart period*, 1603–1714, (2nd edn). London

DAVIS, J. C. (1976) 'Gerrard Winstanley and the restoration of true magistacy', *Past and Present*, **70** (1976), 76–93

— (1973) 'The levellers and christianity', in Manning (1973)

— (1974) 'The levellers and democracy', in Webster (1974)

— (1981) *Utopia and the ideal society*. Cambridge U.P.

DICKINSON, H. T. (1976) 'The eighteenth-century debate on the sovereignty of Parliament' *Transactions of the Royal Historical Society*, 5 series, **56** (1976), 189–210

DUNN, JOHN (1969) *The political thought of John Locke*. Cambridge U.P.

ECCELSHALL, ROBERT (1978) *Order and reason in politics: theories of absolute and limited monarchy*. Hull and Oxford

FIGGIS, H. NEVILLE (1896) *The divine right of Kings*. London repr. New York 1965, E. R. Elton (ed.)

FINK, ZERA K. (1945) *The classical republicans*. Evanston, Ill.

FIRTH, C. H. (ed.) (1891–1901) *The Clarke papers*, (4 vols). Camden Soc., London

— (1902) *Cromwell's army*. Repr. 1962

FIRTH, KATHERINE R. (1979) *The British apocalyptic tradition*. Oxford U.P.

FISCH, HAROLD (1974) *Jerusalem and Albion; the Hebraic factor in seventeenth century literature*. New York

FORTESCUE, G. K. (ed.) (1908) *Catalogue of the pamphlets, books, newspapers and manuscripts relating to the civil war, the commonwealth, and restoration, collected by George Thomason, 1640–1661.*

FRANK, JOSEPH (1955) *The Levellers*. Cambridge Mass.

— (1961) *The beginnings of the English Newspaper, 1620–1660*. Cambridge Mass.

FRANKLIN, JULIAN (1978) *John Locke and the theory of sovereignty*. London

FUSSNER, F. SMITH (1962) *The historical revolution: English historical writing and thought 1580–1640*. London

GABRIELLI, VITTORIO (1959) *Puritanesimo e libertà* (Turino, 1956)

GARDINER, S. R. (ed.) (1899) *The constitutional documents of the Puritan revolution*. Oxford; repr. 1979

GENTLES, IAN (1978) 'London levellers in the English revolution:

the Chidleys and their circle', *Journal of Ecclesiastical History*, **29** (1978), 281–309.

GIBB, M. A. (1947) *John Lilburne the leveller*. London

GLEISSNER, RICHARD (1980) 'The levellers and natural law: the Putney debates of 1647', *Journal of British Studies*, **20**: 1 (1980), 74–89

GOLDSMITH, M. M. (1966) *Hobbes's science of politics*. London and New York.

— (1980) 'Hobbes's "mortal god": is there a fallacy in Hobbes's theory of sovereignty?', *History of Political Thought*, **1** (1980), 33–50

GOOCH, G. P. (1898) *English democratic ideas in the seventeenth century*. London; repr. New York 1959

— (1915) *Political thought in England: Bacon to Halifax*. London, New York, Toronto; repr. 1946.

GOUGH, J. W. (1931) The Agreements of the People, 1647–9', *History*, n.s. **15** (1931), 334–41

— (1955) *Fundamental law in English constitutional history*. Oxford

GREENLEAF, W. H. (1966a) *Order, empiricism and politics: two traditions of English political thought 1500–1700*. Oxford

— (1966b) 'Filmer's patriarchal history', *Historical Journal*, **9** (1966), 157–71.

GREGG, PAULINE (1961) *Freeborn John: a biography of John Lilburne*. London

GUNN, JOHN A. W. (1969) *Politics and the public interest in the seventeenth century*. London

H. A. W. (1842–45) *The works of the most reverend . . . John Bramhall*, (5 vols). Oxford. Published by J. H. Parker.

HALLER, WILLIAM (ed.) (1934) *Tracts on liberty in the puritan revolution*, (3 vols). New York; repr. 1962

— (1938) *The rise of puritanism*. New York; repr. London 1957.

— (1955) *Liberty and reformation in the puritan revolution*. London; repr. New York 1963

— (1963) *Foxe's Book of Martyrs and the elect nation*. London

HALLER, WILLIAM and GODFREY DAVIES (1944) *The leveller tracts*. New York; Gloucester Mass. 1964

HANSON, DANIEL W. (1970) *From kingdom to commonwealth*. Cambridge Mass

HAMPSHER-MONK, IAIN (1976) 'The political theory of the levellers: Putney, property and Professor Macpherson', *Political Studies*, **24** (1976), 397–422.

HAYES, T. WILSON (1979) *Winstanley the digger: a literary analysis*. Cambridge Mass

HEARNSHAW, F. J. C. (ed.) (1928) *The social and political ideas of some English thinkers of the Augustan age*. London

HEINEMANN, MARGOT (1978) 'Popular drama and leveller style – Richard Overton and John Harris', in Cornforth (1978), 69–92

HELD, VIRGINIA (1975) 'Justification, legal and moral', *Ethics* 86 (1975–6), 1–16.

HEXTER, J. H. (1941) *The reign of King Pym*. Cambridge Mass.

HILL, J. E. CHRISTOPHER (1958) *Puritanism and revolution*. London; repr. 1962

— (1964) *Society and puritanism in pre-revolutionary England*. London 1964; 2 edn, New York 1967

— (1965) *The intellectual origins of the English Revolution*. Oxford

— (1970) *God's Englishman: Oliver Cromwell and the English revolution*. London and New York

— (1971) *Antichrist in seventeenth century England*. London and New York

— (1972) *The world turned upside down: radical ideas during the English revolution*. London and New York

— (ed.) (1973) *Winstanley. The 'law of freedom' and other writings*. London

— (1974) *Change and continuity in seventeenth century England*. London

— (1975) 'The film *Winstanley*', Past and Present, **69** (1975), 132

— (1977) *Milton and the English revolution*. London

— (1978) *Puritans and revolutionaries: essays in seventeenth-century history presented to Christopher Hill*. Edited by Donald Pennington and Keith Thomas. Oxford

— and EDMUND DELL (eds) (1949) *The good old cause*. London; repr. 1969

HINTON, R. W. K. (1960) 'English constitutional theories from Sir John Fortescue to Sir John Eliot, *English Historical Review*, **75**, (1960), 410–25

— (1967) 'Husbands, fathers and conquerors', *Political Studies* **25** (1967), 291–300; **26** (1968), 55–67

HIRST, DEREK (1975) *The representative of the people*? Cambridge U.P.

HISCOCK, W. G. (comp.) (1956) *The Christ Church supplement to Wing's short title catalogue*. Oxford

HÖPFE, HARRO and MARTYN P. THOMPSON (1979) 'The history of contract as a motif in political thought', *American Historical Review* **81** (1979), 919 44

— (1975) *'John Pocock's new history of political thought'*, *European Studies Review*, **5** (1975), 193–206

HUGHES, MERRIT Y. (1962) *Complete prose works of John Milton*, Vol. 3, covering 1648–49. Yale U.P., New Haven Conn.

JAMES, MARGARET (1930) *Social problems and policy during the puritan revolution*. London

— (1941) 'The political importance of the tithes controversy in the English revolution, 1640–60', *History* (1942), 1–18

JONES, W. J. (1971) *Politics and the bench: the judges and the origins of the English civil war*. London

JORDON, W. K. (1932) *The development of religious toleration in England*, (4 vols). London 1932–40

— (1942) *Men of substance: a study of the thought of two English revolutionaries, Henry Parker and Henry Robinson*. Chicago

— (1959) *Philanthropy in England 1480–1660*. London and New York

JUDSON, MARGARET A. (1936) 'Henry Parker and the theory of parliamentary sovereignty', in *Essays in history and political theory in honour of Charles Howard McIlwain*. Cambridge, Mass

— (1949) *The crisis of the constitution: constitutional and political thought in England, 1603–1645*. New Brunswick

— (1969) *The political thought of Sir Henry Vane the Younger*. Philadelphia

JURETIC, GEORGE (1975) 'Digger no millenarian: the revolutionising of Gerrard Winstanley', *Journal of the History of Ideas*, **36** (1975), 263–80

KENYON, J. P. (1966) *The Stuart constitution 1603–1688*. Cambridge U.P.

KING, PRESTON (1974) *The Ideology of Order*. London

KING, PRESTON and B. C. PAREKH (eds) (1968) *Politics and experience*. Cambridge U.P.

KISHLANSKY, MARK A. (1979a) *The rise of the New Model Army*. Cambridge U.P.

— (1979b) 'The army and the levellers: the roads to Putney', *Historical Journal*, **22** (1979), 795–825

KLIGER, SAMUEL (1952) *The Goths in England*. Cambridge Mass.

LAMONT, WILLIAM M. (1963) *Marginal Prynne, 1640–1669*. London

— (1969) *Godly rule: politics and religion, 1603–1660*. London

— and SYBIL OLDFIELD (eds) (1975) *Politics, religion and literature in the seventeenth century*. London

LASLETT, PETER (ed.) (1949) *Sir Robert Filmer: Patriarcha and other political works*. Oxford

— (1960) *John Locke: Two treatises of government*. Cambridge; 2nd edn New York n.d., 1963 (Mentor edn.).

— (1964) 'Market society and political theory', *Historical Journal*, **7** (1964), 150–4

— (1965) *The world we have lost: English society before and after the coming of industry*. London

LATHAM, R. C. (1945) 'English revolutionary thought 1640–1660', *History*, **30** (1945), 38–59

LEITH, JOHN H. (1973) *Assembly at Westminster: reformed theology in the making*. Virginia, John Knox Press 1973

LEVACK, BRIAN P. (1973) *The civil lawyers in England 1603–1641* Oxford

LIU, TAI (1973) *Discord in Zion . . . 1640–1660*. The Hague

LUTAUD, OLIVIER (1976) *Winstanley: socialisme and christianisme sous Cromwell*. Paris

MACPHERSON, C. B. (1962) *The Political theory of possessive individualism*. Oxford

MANNING, BRIAN (ed.) (1973) *Politics, religion and the English civil war*. London 1973

— (1976) *The English people and the English revolution*. London 1976, 1978

MCILWAIN, CHARLES H. (1935) 'A forgotten worthy: Philip Hunton', *Politica*, **1** (1935), reprinted in his *Constitutionalism* (1937)

— (1937) *Constitutionalism and the changing world*. Cambridge

— (1940) *Constitutionalism ancient and modern*. Ithaca, N.Y.

MCNEILLY, F. S. (1968) *The anatomy of Leviathan*. New York

MENDLE, M. J. (1973) 'Politics and political thought of 1640–1642', in Russell (1973), 219–45

MILTON, complete prose works of, *see* Hughes (1962), Sirluck (1959), Wolfe (1953–)

MINZ, SAMUEL R. (1970) *The hunting of Leviathan*. Cambridge

Modern Language Association (1967) *A gallery of ghosts; books published between 1641–1700 not found in the* [*i.e. Wing's*] *short title catalogue*. New York

MOLESWORTH, WILLIAM (ed.) (1839–45) *The English works of Thomas Hobbes of Malmesbury*, (11 vols). London

MORRIS, CHRISTOPHER (1953) *Political thought in England: Tyndale to Hooker*. Oxford; repr. 1965

MORTON, A. L. (1966) *The matter of Britain*. London

— (1970) *The world of the ranters*. London; repr. 1979

— (ed.) (1975) *Freedom in arms: a selection of leveller writings*. London

MOSSE, G. L. (1950) *The struggle for sovereignty in England*. East Lansing; repr. New York 1968

MULLIGAN, LOTTE, JOHN K. GRAHAM and JUDITH RICHARDS (1977) 'Winstanley: a case for the man as he said he was', *Journal of Ecclesiastical History*, **28** (1977), 57–75

MULLIGAN, LOTTE, JUDITH RICHARDS and JOHN K. GRAHAM (1979) 'Intentions and conventions: a critique of Quentin Skinner's method for the study of the history of ideas', *Political Studies*, **27**: 1 (1979), 84–98

OAKESHOTT, MICHAEL (ed.) (1946) *'Leviathan' . . . by Thomas Hobbes*. Oxford

OAKLEY, FRANCIS (1962) 'On the road from Constance to 1688: the political thought of John Major and George Buchanan', *Journal of British Studies*, 2 (1962), 1–31

ORR, ROBERT (1967) *Reason and authority: the thought of William Chillingworth*. Oxford

*OPH* (The *Old Parliamentary History*), William Cobbett (ed.) (1751–62) *The parliamentary or constitutional history of England from the earliest times to the restoration of Charles II*, (24 vols). London

PALLISTER, ANNE (1971) *Magna Carta: the heritage of liberty*. Oxford

PETEGORSKY, DAVID W. (1940) *Left-wing democracy in the English civil war*. London

PINGREE, ELIZABETH A. (ed.) (1975) *Humanities Index*. New York

PLAMENATZ, JOHN P. (1963) *Man and society: a critical examination of some important social and political theories from Machiavelli to Marx*, (vol 1). London

POCOCK, J. G. A. (1957) *The ancient constitution and the feudal law: a study of English historical thought in the 17th century*. Cambridge; repr. Bath 1974

— (1965) 'Machiavelli, Harrington and English political ideologies', *William and Mary Quarterly*, 3rd series, **22** (1975), 549–83.

— (1966) "The onely politician", Machiavelli, Harrington and Felix Raab', *Historical Studies Australia and New Zealand* **16** (1966), 265–96

— (1968) 'Time, institutions and action: an essay on traditions and their understanding', in King and Parekh (1968, 209–37); and in Pocock (1971)

— (1970) 'James Harrington and the good old cause: a study of the ideological context of his writings', *Journal of British Studies*, **10** (1970), 30–48

— 1971) *Politics, language and time: essays on political thought and history*. New York

— (1973a) 'Political thought in the Cromwellian interregnum' in G. A. Wood and P. S. O'Connor (eds), *W. P. Morrell: a tribute*. Dunedin

— (1973b) *Obligation and authority in two English revolutions*. Wellington; W. E. Collins lecture

— (1971) *Politics, language and time: essays on political thought and history*. New York

— (1975) *The Machiavellian moment: Florentine political thought and the Atlantic tradition*. Princeton

— (ed.) (1977) *The political works of James Harrington*. Cambridge U.P.

— (1980) 'Authority and property: the question of liberal origins', in Barbara Malament (ed.), *After the reformation*. Univ. Pennsylvania Press

POLLARD, A. W. and G. R. REDGRAVE (eds) (1946) *A short title catalogue of books printed in England, Scotland and Ireland, and of English books abroad 1475–1640*. London; rev. edn 1976–

POLIZZOTTO, CAROLYN (1975) 'Liberty of conscience and the Whitehall debates of 1648–49', *Journal of Ecclesiastical History* **26** (1975), 69–82

PRALL, STUART E. (ed.) (1968) *The puritan revolution: a documentary history*. London and New York

RAAB, FELIX (1964) *The English face of Machiavelli: a changing interpretation, 1500–1700*. London

RECUPERO, A. (1971) *La rivoluzione borghese in Inghliterra, 1640–1660*. Milan

REUGER, ZOFIA (1964) 'Gerson, the conciliar movement and the right of resistance (1642–1644)', *Journal of the History of Ideas* **25** (1964), 467–86

RICHARDSON, ROGER C. (1977) *The debate on the English revolution*. London

ROBBINS, CAROLINE (1969) *Two English republican tracts*. Cambridge U.P.

ROBERTSON, D. B. (1951) *The religious foundations of leveller democracy*. New York

ROGERS, P. G. (1966) *The fifth monarchy men*. London

ROLLINS, HYDER E. (ed.) 1923 *Cavalier and puritan. Ballads and broadsides illustrating the period of the great rebellion*. New York

ROMMEN, HEINRICH A. (1945) *The state in catholic thought*. St Louis

RUMBLE, G. W. S. V. (ed.) (1975) *Anthony Ascham: Of the confusions and revolutions of governments (1649)*. New York

RUSHWORTH, JOHN (ed.) (1721–22), *Historical collections*, (8 vols). London

RUSSELL, CONRAD (1965) '*The theory of treason in the trial* of Strafford', *English Historical Review*, **80** (1965), 30–50

— (ed.) (1973) *The origins of the English civil war*. London

— (1979) *Parliaments and English politics 1621–1629*. Oxford; corrected repr. 1982

SABINE, GEORGE H. (1937) *A history of political theory*. London; rev. edn. 1951, etc.)

— (ed.) (1941) *The works of Gerrard Winstanley*. New York; repr. 1965

SALMON, J. H. M. (1959) *The French religious wars in English political thought*. Oxford

SANDERSON, JOHN (1974) '*Serpent-salve*, 1643: the royalism of John Bramhall', *Journal of Ecclesiastical History*, **25** (1974) 1–14

SCHENK, W. (1948) *The concern for social justice in the puritan revolution*. London

SCHOCHET, GORDON G. (1969) 'Patriarchalism, politics and mass attitudes in Stuart England', *Historical Journal*, **12** (1969), 413–41

— (1974) 'Quentin Skinner's method', *Political Theory*, **2**: 3 (1974), 261–16

— (1975) *Patriarchalism in political thought*. New York

SCHWOERER, LOIS G. (1971) 'The fittest subject for a King's quarrel: an essay on the militia controversy 1641–42', *Journal of British Studies*, **11**: 1 (1971), 45–76

— (1974) *No standing armies! The anti-army ideology in seventeenth century England*. Baltimore and London

SHARP, ANDREW (1974) 'Edward Waterhouse's view of social change in seventeenth century England', *Past and Present*, **62** (1974), 27–46

SHKLAR, JUDITH (1964) *Legalism*. Cambridge, Mass.

SIRLUCK, ERNEST (ed.) (1959) *Complete prose works of John Milton*, vol. 2, covering 1643–48. Yale U.P., New Haven, Conn

SKINNER, QUENTIN (1965) 'History and ideology in the English revolution', *Historical Journal*, **8** (1965), 151–78

— (1966) 'The ideological context of Hobbes's political thought', *Historical Journal*, **9** (1966), 286–317

— (1972a) 'The context of Hobbes's theory of political obligation', in Cranston and Peters (1972)

— (1972b) 'Conquest and consent: Thomas Hobbes and the engagement controversy', in Aylmer (1972)

— (1978) *The foundations of modern political thought*, (2 vols). Cambridge U.P.

SNOW, VERNON (1962) 'The concept of revolution in seventeenth-century England', *Historical Journal*, **5** (1962), 1967–74

SOLT, LEO (1959) *Saints in arms*. Stanford

STEPHEN, LESLIE, and SIDNEY LEE (eds) (1908–9–) *The Dictionary of National Biography* (*DNB*), (21 vols and supplements). London

STONE, LAWRENCE (ed.) (1965) *Social change and revolution in England 1540–1640*. London

STRAKA, GERALD M. (1972) 'Revolutionary ideology in Stuart England', in P. J. Korshin (ed.), *Studies in change and revolution*. Menston, Yorks

STRAUSS, LEO (1936) *The political philosophy of Hobbes*. Chicago; repr. 1963

— (1953) *Natural right and history*. Chicago 1953, 1957

TANNER, J. R. (1928) *English constitutional conflicts of the seventeenth century, 1603–1689*. Cambridge U.P.; repr. 1957

THOMAS, KEITH V. (1958) 'Women in the civil war sects', *Past and Present*, **13** (1958) in Aston (1965)

— (1969) 'Another digger broadside', *Past and Present*, **42** (1969), 57–68; and in Webster (1974)

— (1971) *Religion and the rise of magic*. London

— (1972) 'The levellers and the franchise', in Aylmer (1972, 57–78)

THOMPSON, CHRISTOPHER (1980) 'Maximilian Petty and the Putney debate on the franchise', *Past and Present*, **88** (1980), 63–69.

THOMPSON, FAITH (1948) *Magna Carta, its role in the making of the English constitution, 1300–1629*. Oxford

TOLMIE, M. (1977) *The triumph of the saints*. Cambridge U.P.

TOON, PETER (ed.) (1970) *Puritans, the millennium and the future of Israel*. Cambridge

TORRANCE, T. J. (1959) *The school of faith*. Edinburgh

TREVOR-ROPER, H. R. (1956) 'The fast sermons in the Long Parliament' in his *Religion, the reformation and social change*. London; repr. 1967

TUCK, RICHARD (1974) '*Power* and *authority* in seventeenth century England', *Historical Journal*, **17** (1974), 43–61

— (1979) *Natural rights theories: their origin and development*. Cambridge U.P.

TULLY, JAMES (1980) *A discourse on property: John Locke and his adversaries*. Cambridge U.P.

TYACKE, NICHOLAS (1973) 'Puritanism, arminianism and counter-revolution', in Russell (1973, 119–43)

UNDERDOWN, DAVID (1971) *Pride's purge*. Oxford

UNIVERSITY MICROFILMS INTERNATIONAL (1981–82) *Accessing early English books 1471–1700*), (4 vols). Ann Arbor, Michigan

VEALL, D. (1970) *The popular movement for law reform 1640–1660.* London

VILE, M. J. C. (1967) *Constitutionalism and the separation of powers.* Oxford

WALLACE, JOHN M. (1964) 'The engagement controversy, 1649–52: an annotated list of pamphlets', *Bulletin of the New York Public Library*, **68** (1964), 384–405

— (1968) *Destiny his choice: the loyalism of Andrew Marvell.* Cambridge

— (1980) 'The date of Sir Robert Filmer's *Patriarcha*', *Historical Journal*, **23** (1980), 155–65

WALTER, GERARD (1963) *La révolution anglaise, 1641–1660.* Paris

WALZER, MICHAEL (1965) *The revolution of the saints.* New York 1965; repr. London 1966

WEBSTER, CHARLES (1974) *The intellectual revolution of the seventeenth century.* London

— (1975) *The great instauration: science, medicine and reform 1626–1660.* London

WEDGEWOOD, C. VERONICA (1964) *The trial of Charles I.* London; paperback edn 1974

WESTON, CORINNE COMSTOCK (1960) 'The theory of mixed monarchy under Charles I and after', *English Historical Review*, **75** (1960), 426–43

— (1965) *English constitutional theory and the House of Lords.* New York

— (1970) 'Concepts of estates in Stuart political thought', in *Representative institutions in theory and practice: presented to the International Commission for the History of Parliamentary Representative and Parliamentary Institutions.* Brussels, **39**, 87–130

— (1980) 'The authorship of the *Freeholders Grand Inquest*', *English Historical Review*, **95** (1980), 74–98

WHITTAKER W. J. (ed.) (1895) *The mirror of justices.* London

WIENER, JONATHAN M. (1974) 'Quentin Skinner's Hobbes', *Political* Theory, 2: 3 (1974), 251–60

WILSON, JOHN F. (1969) *Pulpit in parliament. Puritanism during the English civil wars.* Princeton

WING, DONALD G. (ed.) (1945–51) *A short title catalogue of books printed in England, Scotland, Ireland, Wales, and British America and of English books printed in other countries, 1641–1700.* New York, 2nd edn, 1971–1. Cf. Hiscock (1956); Modern Language Association (1967)

WOLFE, DON M. (1941) *Milton in the puritan revolution.* New York 1941; repr. London 1963

— (1944) *Leveller manifestos of the puritan revolution*. London 1944; repr. 1963

— (ed.) (1953) *Complete prose works of John Milton*, vol. 1, covering 1642–44. Yale U.P., New Haven Conn.

— (gen. ed.) (1953–74) *Complete prose works of John Milton*, (7 vols). Yale U.P., New Haven Conn. Repr. with rev. edn. vol. 7, London 1980

WOODHOUSE, A. S. P. (ed.) (1951) *Puritanism and liberty, being the army debates*, 1647–9. Chicago 1951; repr. London 1974

WORDEN, BLAIR (1974) *The Rump Parliament 1648–1653*. Cambridge U.P.

WORMALD, B. H. G. *Clarendon: politics, historiography and religion*, 1640–1660. Cambridge 1951; repr. 1964

WORMUTH, FRANCIS D. (1939) *The royal prerogative, 1603–1649*. Ithaca and London

— (1949) *The origins of modern constitutionalism*. New York

WYNTER, P. (ed.) (1863) *The works of Joseph Hall*, (10 vols). Oxford

ZAGORIN, PEREZ (1954) *A history of political thought in the English revolution*. London 1954, 1965